From an Ontological Poir

NOT A SOMETHING BUT NOT A NOTHING
EITHER

From an Ontological Point of View

JOHN HEIL

Clarendon Press · Oxford

OXFORD

UNIVERSITY PRESS

Great Clarendon Street, Oxford OX2 6DP

Oxford University Press is a department of the University of Oxford.
It furthers the University's objective of excellence in research, scholarship,
and education by publishing worldwide in

Oxford New York

Auckland Cape Town Dar es Salaam Hong Kong Karachi
Kuala Lumpur Madrid Melbourne Mexico City Nairobi
New Delhi Shanghai Taipei Toronto

With offices in

Argentina Austria Brazil Chile Czech Republic France Greece
Guatemala Hungary Italy Japan Poland Portugal Singapore
South Korea Switzerland Thailand Turkey Ukraine Vietnam

Oxford is a registered trade mark of Oxford University Press
in the UK and in certain other countries

Published in the United States
by Oxford University Press Inc., New York

First published 2003
First Published in paperback 2005

British Library Cataloguing in Publication Data

Data available

Library of Congress Cataloging in Publication Data

Data available

Typeset by SNP Best-set Typesetter Ltd., Hong Kong
Printed in Great Britain
on acid-free paper by
Biddles Ltd., King's Lynn, Norfolk

ISBN 978-0-19-925974-8
ISBN 978-0-19-928698-0 (Pbk.)

For Charlie Martin
The philosopher's philosopher

Preface

Philosophy today is often described as a profession. Philosophers have specialized interests and address one another in specialized journals. On the whole, what we do in philosophy is of little interest to anyone without a Ph.D. in the subject. Indeed, subdisciplines within philosophy are often intellectually isolated from one another. The same could be said for most academic specialities. Historians, literary theorists, anthropologists, and musicologists pursue topics the significance of which would elude outsiders. What distinguishes philosophy is the extent to which philosophical problems are anchored directly in concerns of non-philosophers. Philosophical questions arise in every domain of human endeavour. The issues have a kind of universality that resists their being turned over to specialists who could be expected to announce results after conducting the appropriate investigations.

The professionalization of philosophy, together with a depressed academic job market, has led to the interesting idea that success in philosophy should be measured by appropriate professional standards. In practice, this has too often meant that cleverness and technical savvy trump depth. Positions and ideas are dismissed or left unconsidered because they are not *comme il faut*. Journals are filled with papers exhibiting an impressive level of professional competence, but little in the way of insight, originality, or abiding interest. Non-mainstream, even wildly non-mainstream, conclusions are allowed, even encouraged, provided they come with appropriate technical credentials.

I am speaking here of broad trends. Many philosophers have resisted the tides of fashion and continue to produce interesting and important work. My impression is that a disproportionate number of these philosophers are, by birth, training, or philosophical inclination, Australian. The present book was written during a memorable year as a visitor in the Monash University Department of Philosophy, surrounded by philosophers exemplifying the paradigmatic Australian trait: ontological seriousness. You are ontologically serious if you are guided by the thought that the ontological implications of philosophical claims are paramount. The attitude most naturally expresses itself in an allegiance to a truth-maker principle: when an assertion about the world is true, something about the world makes it true.

Such an attitude could be contrasted to the idea that, in pursuing philosophical questions, we must start with language and work our way outwards. My belief is that this attitude is responsible for the sterile nature of much contemporary analytical philosophy. If you start with language and try to work your way outwards, you will never get outside language. In that case, descriptions of the world, or 'stories', go proxy for the world. Perhaps there is something about the Australian continent that discourages this kind of 'hands-off' philosophizing.

I have tried to satisfy my Australian friends and colleagues by discussing a range of ontological issues without resorting to technical results. In so doing, I believe I have produced a book that will be more widely accessible than many books concerned with fundamental questions in metaphysics and the philosophy of mind. Some readers will be unhappy with this strategy. In refusing to address issues in a comfortably familiar technical vocabulary, I have left the discussion with an unacceptable degree of haziness. I am not convinced, however, that much of what I discuss would benefit from a technical overlay. In this I follow Aristotle's dictum that not every subject matter admits of an equal degree of theoretical precision.

The most interesting ideas advanced here have their roots in the work of C. B. Martin, much of which remains unpublished. I regard Martin as a major figure in twentieth-century philosophy. The influence of his ideas has been felt chiefly through his personal influence on a number of better-known figures. My hope in publishing this volume is that I can make Martin's views more available to a wider audience. I hasten to add that much of what I have to say is not attributable, directly or indirectly, to Martin, but is the result of his influence on the way I have come to think about philosophy. Indeed, I am confident that my construal of themes close to Martin's heart would fail to meet with his wholehearted approval.

I owe enormous philosophical debts to many people in addition to Martin. These include, especially, David Armstrong, John Bigelow, Jaegwon Kim, E. J. Lowe, Brian McLaughlin, David Robb, J. J. C. Smart, Peter Unger, and participants in my 1996 NEH Seminar on Metaphysics of Mind: Leonard Clapp, Randolph Clarke, Anthony Dardis, James Garson, Heather Gert, Muhammad Ali Khalidi, David

Pitt, Eric Saidel, Stephen Schwartz, Nigel Thomas, Amie Thomasson, Michael Watkins, and Jessica Wilson. I have profited from discussions with my colleagues, Ulrich Meyer and Brendan O'Sullivan. Many of the ideas taken up here have figured in conversations and correspondence with Edward Averill, Dorit Bar-On, Simon Blackburn, John Carroll, Monima Chadha, Brian Ellis, John Fox, Ian Gold, Toby Handfield, Alan Hazen, John F. Heil, Jr., Lloyd Humberstone, Alan Musgrave, Cynthia Macdonald, Michaelis Michael, Daniel Nolan, Josh Parsons, Laurie Paul, Denis Robinson, William Webster, and Dean Zimmerman. I am grateful, as well, to audiences at the Australian National University, Canterbury University, La Trobe University, Melbourne University, Monash University, the University of New South Wales, the University of Otago, the University of Queensland, Sydney University, and the University of Tasmania. Special thanks are due to the Hagan clan for providing a delightful environment at Ocean Isle for the revision of portions of the text. No words could express my debt to Harrison Hagan Heil.

Portions of Chapters 2–6 are taken from 'Levels of Reality and the Reality of Levels', *Ratio*, 16 (2003) 169–70; a version of Chapter 7 appears as 'Truth Making and Entailment', *Logique et analyse*, (2000), 231–42; parts of Chapters 8–11 are borrowed from 'Properties and Powers', in Dean Zimmerman (ed.), *Oxford Studies in Metaphysics* (Oxford: Oxford University Press, 2003). I am grateful to the editors for permission to use this material here.

John Heil

Melbourne
July 2002

Contents

ONTOLOGY

APPLICATIONS

CHAPTER I
Introduction

1.1 The Inescapability of Ontology

The twentieth century was not kind to metaphysics. In the English-speaking world, metaphysics was deflated by neo-Kantians, logical positivists, logical empiricists, as well as by philosophers who regarded the study of ordinary language as a fitting replacement for traditional philosophical pursuits. Elsewhere, philosophers promoting phenomenology, hermeneutics, and existentialist and deconstructionist creeds showed themselves equally disdainful of tradition. Metaphysical talk was replaced by talk about metaphysical talk; concern with conceptual schemes and patterns of ontological commitment supplanted concern with ontology. Presumably, we have something like direct access to ways we think and talk about the world. The world itself remains at arm's length, a subject for study by the empirical sciences. Metaphysics as traditionally conceived seems to pit philosophers against scientists in a way that is bound to favour the scientists and make the philosophers look ridiculous.

Attempts to keep philosophy aloof from metaphysics are largely self-defeating. Whether we approve or not, the world has an ontology. Theorists and theories of the world are themselves parts of the world.[1] This homely complication is too often forgotten or ignored by those who regard the world as a construct. If the world is theory dependent, what of theories themselves? Do these stand alone, or does their existence depend in some fashion on other theories ('theories all the way down')? Whatever the story turns out to be it will include an ontology measurable against competing ontologies.

I shall have more to say on this topic in subsequent chapters. For the

---

[1] Hilary Putnam (1981: p. xi) puts this nicely: 'the mind and world jointly make up the mind and world.' I prefer not to draw Putnam's difficult anti-realist conclusions from this observation.

present I want only to note the inescapability of ontology. We can suppress or repress ontological impulses. In so doing, however, we merely postpone the inevitable. Honest philosophy requires what the Australians call ontological seriousness. In the chapters that follow I endeavour to provide central ingredients of a fundamental ontology. I believe that what I have to say fits well with what we have learned or might learn from the empirical sciences and—importantly, in my judgement—with ordinary canons of plausibility. My defence of the conclusions I draw, however, will be indirect. The test of the overall view is not its derivability from uncontroversial truisms, but its power: the extent to which it enables us to make sense of issues we should otherwise find perplexing.

Wherever possible I have avoided technical terminology. Much current philosophy strikes me as technically astute but philosophically barren. The deep issues should be addressable in ways that are intelligible to non-philosophers willing to think hard about them. A technical vocabulary can be liberating, but it can be constraining as well, channelling thoughts along familiar paths. Occasionally this can lead to the dismissal out of hand of alternatives that could otherwise appear attractive. Philosophers, of all people, should be open-minded, especially in domains where there is little or no settled agreement. If over-reliance on a technical framework produces philosophical blind spots, we should be willing to forgo, or at least re-examine, the framework once we hit an impasse.

1.2 Consciousness

Such an impasse currently exists in the philosophy of mind. Many philosophers (and many non-philosophers) are convinced that the Problem of Consciousness is the last Big Problem. Physics (we are told) has all but provided a complete account of the material world. Consciousness, in contrast, is said to remain an utter mystery. To be sure, some theorists have attempted to deflate the mystery, but the overwhelming sentiment is that the deflators have missed the point. The dispute has the earmarks of classical philosophical disputes. Not only is there disagreement over particular answers, but there is little agreement over what the appropriate questions are. One possibility is that we are floundering because we lack an adequate conceptualization of the territory. Without this, our questions remain out of focus; we are in no position to recognize correct answers even if we had them, or to distinguish truths from pretenders.

An adequate conceptualization of the world and our place in it is founded, not on the analysis of concepts, but on an adequate ontology. Ontology is not an analytical enterprise. Earlier I noted that in engaging in ontological investigation we are endeavouring to make sense of issues we should otherwise find perplexing. The issues in question arise in the sciences, in the humanities, and in everyday life. To this extent they include an ineliminable empirical element. My belief is that, if we get the ontology right, these issues will take care of themselves in this sense: the remaining questions will be largely empirical hence susceptible to techniques we standardly deploy in answering empirical questions.

In pursuing ontological themes it is tempting to imagine that there is not a single, correct ontology, but many. Given one ontology, we can see how certain issues could be handled; given an alternative ontology, the same issues might be dealt with, perhaps more elegantly. It is true, certainly, that ontologies differ in these ways. I cannot, however, bring myself to believe that there is no correct ontology, only diverse ways of carving up ontological space. One impediment to a conception of this kind is that it is hard to make ontological sense of it. What is the ontology of ontology? In any case, I shall proceed on the assumption that our goal should be to get at the ontological truths. This may require triangulation rather than anything resembling direct comparison of theory and world. In that regard, however, ontological theories are no different from theories generally.

1.3 Conceivability and Possibility

Some philosophers are attracted to the idea that what is conceivable is possible. One proponent of this thesis, David Chalmers, deploys it as the linchpin of an elaborate defence of a kind of mind–body dualism (D. Chalmers 1996). Chalmers argues from the conceivability of 'zombies' (creatures physically indiscernible from ordinary human beings, but altogether bereft of conscious experiences) to the conclusion that mental properties are 'higher-level' properties, distinct from, although dependent on, their lower-level physical 'realizers'. These higher-level mental properties 'arise from' suitably organized physical systems owing to contingent laws of nature. These laws are 'basic' in the sense that they are independent of fundamental physical laws: laws governing consciousness are not derivable from laws governing physical processes. Chalmers sees this kind of nomological independence as grounding the possibility of worlds like ours physically, but lacking consciousness. These are the zombie worlds.

If conceivability implies possibility, the question must be: what is conceivable? Is it conceivable that water is not H_2O? It is conceivable that our chemistry is mistaken, so it is at least epistemically conceivable that water is not H_2O. It does not follow from this that water's being H_2O is a contingent matter. What of the zombies? Doubtless zombies are epistemically conceivable: we seem able to imagine zombies. This, however, is consistent with zombies being flatly impossible. For us to move from the conceivability of zombies to the possibility of zombies, and from there to mind–body dualism, we should have to be certain that the conceivability in question is not merely epistemic conceivability. This, I think, is less straightforward than it is sometimes thought to be.

A triangle's having more than three angles is not conceivable. Triangles, of necessity, have three angles: only a three-sided figure could count as a triangle. When it comes to zombies, however, matters are less clear. The conceivability of zombies depends on a range of substantive, but largely unacknowledged, *ontological* theses. Chalmers holds that, in the actual world, functional similarity guarantees qualitative similarity. Your conscious experiences arise from your functional organization. That functional organization is grounded in your physical make-up. We could swap out components of that make-up—replacing neurons with silicon chips, for instance—but, so long as your functional organization remains intact, the character of your conscious experience would remain unaffected. Imagine now subtracting the laws that tie consciousness to functional organization. If Chalmers is right, this would leave the physical world unaffected.

The possibility envisioned by Chalmers depends on a particular conception of properties: objects' qualities (including conscious qualities) can vary independently of their causal powers (or, as I prefer, their dispositionalities). This, in fact, is merely one of a number of substantive ontological theses required for the conceivability of zombies. Others include the idea that laws could vary independently of the properties and the notion that the world comprises 'levels of being'. If these theses are false, the conceivability of zombies is cast into doubt. If you find the zombie possibility hard to swallow, you might be moved to reject one or more of these supporting theses.

I shall discuss these matters in detail presently. My aim here is simply to point to the ineliminability of metaphysics, and, in particular, ontology, from serious discussion of issues in the philosophy of mind.

1.4 The Picture Theory

Although my focus is on fundamental questions in ontology, I have a good deal to say about the relation language, or thought, or representation bears to the world. My contention is that metaphysics as it has been conceived at least since Kant has been influenced by an implicit adherence to a Picture Theory of representation. I leave it to others to decide the extent to which the Picture Theory I describe resembles Wittgenstein's famous doctrine (Wittgenstein 1922/1961).

I do not contend that many philosophers nowadays explicitly endorse the Picture Theory; its acceptance is largely implicit. This makes the theory's influence both more subtle and more difficult to defuse than it might be otherwise. In large measure, learning to be an 'analytic philosopher' today is a matter of inculcating tenets of the Picture Theory. It was not always thus, although, given the inevitable practice of reformulating the views of historical figures in a more contemporary and congenial idiom, this can fail to be obvious. Whatever its standing among philosophers, I believe the Picture Theory is manifestly incorrect. I suspect, as well, that many philosophers would accept this verdict while continuing to practise in ways that belie their rejection of the theory's tenets.

My conviction that the Picture Theory is ill considered does not stem from my being in possession of a better, more plausible account of the connection words (or concepts, or thoughts, or representations generally) bear to the world. I have no such account, nor do I know of any. It is easier to recognize that a theory is defective than to advance a more promising alternative. Most readers will agree with my assessment: the Picture Theory is hopeless. Readers will diverge, however, in the extent to which they agree with my further claim that this theory has been, and remains, widely influential. Suppose I am wrong about that. In that case, my diagnosis of where we have gone off the rails ontologically will be misconceived. The ontological theses I defend, however, could still be correct. Indeed I believe these theses stand quite on their own. But this is to get ahead of myself.

What exactly is the Picture Theory? As I conceive of it, the Picture Theory is not a single, unified doctrine, but a family of loosely related doctrines. The core idea is that the character of reality can be 'read off' our linguistic representations of reality—or our suitably regimented linguistic representations of reality. A corollary of the Picture Theory is the idea that to every meaningful predicate there corresponds a property. If, like me, you think that properties (if they exist) must be mind independent, if, that is, you are ontologically serious about properties, you will find unappealing the idea that we can discover the properties by scrutinizing features of our language. This is so, I shall argue, even for those predicates concerning which we are avowed 'realists'.

The Picture Theory encompasses the idea that elements of the way we represent the world linguistically 'line up' with elements of the world. Few theorists would think this is so for the ways we ordinarily speak about the world. But consider the language of basic physics. Here it looks as though we have something close to what we need: a name corresponding to every kind of object ('electron', 'quark', 'lepton'), and a predicate corresponding to every property ('mass n', 'spin up', 'negative charge').

What about our more relaxed talk about the world? Consider, for instance, the assertion that Gus is in pain (and suppose this assertion is true). It is at this point that the apparatus of the Picture Theory asserts itself. We want to be 'realists' about pain. That is, we want to say that Gus *really is* in pain, that our ascription of pain to Gus is *literally true*. An adherent of the Picture Theory will want this to imply that corresponding to the pain predicate is some property (or state) of Gus. The very same predicate applies to others, of course, to creatures belonging to very different species, and it would apply to non-actual, merely possible creatures: Alpha Centaurians, for instance. It seems unlikely, however, that all of these creatures share a unique physical property in virtue of which the pain predicate applies truly to them. What follows? Perhaps this: either it is false that Gus is in pain (the pain predicate lacks application) or the property answering to 'is in pain' is something other than a physical property.

Many readers will recognize this style of argument, and many will be ready with a response: the pain property is a 'higher-level' property, a property possessed by actual or possible creatures in virtue of their possession of some lower-level (presumably physical) property. This lower-level property is the 'realizer' of the property of being in pain.

This is a version of the well-known argument for 'multiple realizability'. I shall have more to say about the argument in subsequent chapters. For the moment I mean only to call attention to one facet of it. We want to be realists about pain. We are invited to move from the fact that the pain predicate fails to correspond to a unique physical property to the conclusion that either (1) there are no pains—there is no pain property—or (2) the property of being in pain is a higher-level property. This line of reasoning appears persuasive, I think, because we have inculcated the Picture Theory. We expect to find a property corresponding to every predicate we take to apply literally and truly to the world. If no physical property fills the bill, we posit a tailor-made higher-level property. This is a property somehow dependent on, but distinct from, lower-level 'realizing' properties.

1.5 Levels of Being

Once set on this course, we quickly generate hierarchies of properties. We discover that most of the predicates we routinely use to describe the world fail to line up with distinct basic-level physical properties or collections of these. We conclude that the predicates in question must designate higher-level properties. Now we have arrived at a hierarchical conception of the world, one founded on the inspiration that there are levels of reality. Higher levels depend on, but are not reducible to, lower levels.

My contention is that the idea that there are levels of reality is an artefact spawned by blind allegiance to the Picture Theory. The Picture Theory gives us a model for the relation words bear to the world. Some

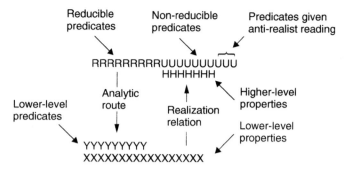

Figure 1.1. The levels conception

of what we say aligns with the basic facts. Other things we say are analysable in terms that correspond to items at the basic level. When this is so, we have an analytic route to the basic level. When it is not so—when, in other words, reduction fails—we are faced with a choice. We can go anti-realist: we can decide that the words in question apply to nothing at all, that they are 'projections' of our attitudes, or that we do not use the words with the intention of asserting truths (but only to express attitudes). When anti-realism seems unattractive or unworkable, we can accept that the disputed words do indeed line up with features of the world: higher-level features.

The levels conception as mandated by the Picture Theory is illustrated in Figure 1.1. *X*s represent reality at the basic level; *Y*s are predicates that line up with items at this basic level. *R*s and *U*s represent what could be called higher-level predicates. Some of these higher-level predicates, the *R*s, are analysable in terms of the *Y*-predicates. When this occurs, we establish that the *R*s are (or are really, or are nothing but) the *Y*s. The remaining higher-level predicates, the *U*s, are those that resist reduction. Some of the *U*s line up with higher-level properties, the *H*s, while some apply to nothing at all. The model is oversimplified in at least one way. In actual practice, we should discover many levels of predicates, and so many levels of properties.

I shall argue that the higher-level items, the *H*s, are a product of the Picture Theory operating hand in hand with a familiar conception of philosophical analysis. In abandoning the Picture Theory—as I urge—we abandon the need for levels of reality. In leaving behind levels, we leave behind myriad philosophical puzzles. These, if I am right, are puzzles of our own making.

In turning away from the Picture Theory, we turn our backs on the idea that ontology can be settled by analysis. Clarifying the nature of items picked out by our concepts is not a matter of analysing those concepts until we are in a position to read off the items' nature from the analytic outcome. What is the alternative? We must, I think, take seriously the idea of truth making. When a claim about the world is true, something about the world makes it true.

Imagine that you want to uncover the ontology of statues. (Why would you care? You might care because, having read countless philosophers on the topic, you are unsure of the relation a statue of Zeus bears to the lump of bronze that makes it up.) You might begin by asking whether talk of statues could be analysed into talk of material out of which statues are made. Alternatively, you might ask what the truth-makers might be for assertions of the form, 'This is a statue.' The history of philosophical analysis provides little reason to think that in this case, and in most other philosophically interesting cases, we could hope to find an analytic route from concept to truth-maker.

1.6 Propositions

One reason the Picture Theory has remained viable is the casualness with which philosophers introduce talk of propositions into discussions of truth making. 'Electrons have a negative charge' is true in virtue of electrons being negatively charged. What is this 'in virtue of' relation? Many philosophers contend that it is entailment: true assertions are entailed by their truth-makers. Entailment, however, holds between representations. Electrons being negatively charged, like the electrons themselves, entails nothing. Recognizing this, philosophers who regard truth making as entailment typically reformulate their thesis: the proposition that electrons are negatively charged entails the truth of assertions that electrons are negatively charged.

Thus deployed, propositions are patently representational entities, items having definite truth values. But what are propositions? In this context, propositions function as intermediaries standing between the world and statements or assertions about the world. As such, propositions are posited entities, at once linguistic (they are true or false) and non-linguistic (they are language independent, though 'expressible' by sentences in a given language). When pressed, philosophers will describe propositions as states of affairs or sets of possible worlds. But wait! Neither sets of possible worlds nor states of affairs—electrons being negatively charged, for instance—have truth values.

The ease with which we run together talk of propositions and talk of the world, or ways the world is, is just another facet of our commitment to the Picture Theory. This commitment encourages us to substitute descriptions for what is described in thoughts about what answers to concepts we rely on in describing the world and our place in it. The relation propositions bear to reality is so intimate that the propositions replace the reality in our thinking. When we do the ontology of propositions, we ignore their representational character and identify them with the reality they represent. In other moods, we invoke propositions as truth-bearers. It is easy to doubt that a single kind of entity could fulfil both these functions. In abandoning the Picture Theory, we leave behind one traditional motive for postulating propositions.

1.7   Ontology

Most of what follows concerns topics in basic ontology. Unsurprisingly, given what I have said already, I begin with a discussion of levels of reality, the idea that the world comprises layers of being. After spelling out what I take to be implied by such a view and discussing its liabilities, I argue that it results from giving innocuous talk of levels of description or explanation an unwarranted ontological reading. This I attribute to an implicit commitment to the Picture Theory. My recommendation is that we abandon the notion that reality is hierarchical. We can accept levels of organization, levels of complexity, levels of description, and levels of explanation, without commitment to levels of reality in the sense embraced by many self-proclaimed anti-reductionist philosophers today. The upshot is a conception of the world and our representations of it that is ontologically, but not analytically, reductive.

Today, reductionist theses have an unsavoury reputation. This I think is due largely to a conviction—encouraged by the Picture Theory—that reduction implies that talk of the reduced items (statues, for instance, or persons) could be translated into (and so replaced by) talk of the atoms and the void (or whatever we regard as occupying the lower levels). This is taken to imply that all there is are the atoms and the void. In rejecting the Picture Theory, I reject both these implications. Truth-makers for claims about statues or people could turn out to be configurations of the atoms in the void. This, however, while providing what might be thought of as the deep story about statues and people, falls well short of establishing that there are no statues or people.

In discussing these matters, I address the role of philosophical analysis and the notion of truth making. I argue that the widely held view that truth making is to be understood as entailment is misguided in principle and potentially misleading. Again, I detect the influence of the Picture Theory, which encourages us to conflate descriptions of the world and the world.

A clear view of these issues is important if we hope to obtain a sensible notion of what realism requires. Realism is too often characterized in ways that commit realists to unattractive doctrines. (The idea that there are levels of reality is just one such doctrine.) I prefer to associate realism with mind independence. You are a realist about a given domain—material objects, say, or numbers, or minds—if you regard that domain as mind independent: the domain is what it is quite independently of how we take it to be. Are minds mind independent? Well, minds are what they are independently of how we take them to be.

With these background issues settled, I move to a discussion of objects and properties. Properties, I contend, are ways objects are; objects are property-bearers. Properties—or, at any rate, intrinsic properties of concrete objects—contribute in distinctive ways to the powers or dispositionalities of their possessors. Although powers or dispositions are powers or dispositions *for* particular kinds of manifestation (with particular kinds of reciprocal disposition partner), they are not relations. An object's powers or dispositionalities are intrinsic features of that object.

Some philosophers who accept a view of this kind regard properties as pure powers, pure dispositionalities. I prefer to think of properties as simultaneously dispositional and qualitative. Properties contribute in distinctive ways to the dispositionalities and to the qualities of their possessors. This might be put by saying that a property is a quality and is a power. The power and the quality are not 'aspects' of the property, but the selfsame property differently regarded. This means that it is flatly impossible to prize apart powers and qualities. In the idiom of possible worlds, any world qualitatively indistinguishable from the actual world is dispositionally indistinguishable from the actual world; and any world dispositionally indistinguishable is qualitatively indistinguishable as well.

Properties—ways particular objects are—are modes, not universals. I prefer 'mode' to the more familiar 'trope'. Philosophers identifying themselves as trope theorists have, by and large, accepted some form of the 'bundle theory' of objects: an object is a bundle of compresent tropes. I believe it is important to distinguish objects from ways objects are and a mistake to regard objects as somehow made up of their properties. Properties are ways particular objects are, not parts of objects. The traditional term 'mode' captures the idea nicely. A mode is a particularized way an object is, not an ingredient or component of an object.

Modes are 'particularized ways', not universals. I argue that the fascination philosophers have with universals is misplaced. Universals are either Platonic entities residing 'outside' space and time or entities existing *in rebus*, wholly present in each of their instances. Universals have seemed attractive because they promise a simple solution to the 'one-over-many' problem: distinct objects can be 'the same' in particular respects. An apple, a billiard ball, and a rose are all red. A proponent of universals can say that these objects share a constituent: each 'instantiates redness'. If universals are Platonic entities, instantiation is a deeply mysterious relation. If universals are *in rebus*, then a universal is wholly present in each of its distinct instances. What this could mean is hard to say.

If you accept that properties are particular ways objects are, you will want to allow that these ways can be perfectly or imperfectly similar. An apple, a billiard ball, and a rose possess similar colours. The apple's redness is similar to, but distinct from, the redness of this billiard ball and the redness of that rose. The objects possess the same colour in the sense that two bankers might wear the same tie to work, drive the same car, or collect the same salary: although numerically distinct, the ties, cars, and salaries are similar, perhaps exactly similar. My contention is that similarity among modes can do the job universals are conventionally postulated to do. If, as I believe, proponents of universals are obliged to posit brute imperfect similarities among universals (to accommodate certain cases of imperfect similarity), then the putative advantage of universals over modes evaporates.

Properties are ways—ways objects are. But what are objects? I have said that objects are not bundles of properties. Ways cannot be combined to yield something that is those ways. It might be thought that, in distinguishing objects (or substances) from properties, I commit myself to the existence of mysterious entities: 'bare particulars', property-less substrata to which we add properties to produce ordinary objects. The envisaged consequence depends on a conception of objects and properties that I reject, a conception according to which objects and properties are components of a compound entity joined together by a kind of metaphysical superglue. Once we move beyond this conception we can recognize an object—this beetroot, for instance—as something that is various ways: red, spherical, pungent. The beetroot *is* the object.

Finally, I extend earlier claims about the relation of predicates and properties to substantial terms ('sortals') and substances, arguing that philosophical puzzles arising over coinciding or overlapping objects (statues and lumps of bronze, for instance) depend on assumptions of a kind countenanced by the Picture Theory. Rejecting the Picture Theory makes it possible for us to be realists about statues, lumps of bronze, and most ordinary objects, without thereby having to suppose that the world is made up of large numbers of overlapping or spatially coincident entities.

1.8 Applications

The remaining chapters address familiar topics—substantial identity, colour, intentionality, and consciousness—given the ontology sketched earlier. Ordinary objects are apparently coloured, but what are colours? Following Locke, I sketch a broadly dispositional account of colour that, if successful, reconciles ordinary colour experiences with pronouncements of colour scientists bent on sorting out the physical basis of colour in objects, in light radiation, and in the brain. The ontology of properties defended previously comes into play.

The final three chapters take up central themes in the philosophy of mind—intentionality, consciousness, and the possibility of 'zombies'—in the light of this ontology. Dispositionality provides a grounding for intentionality, the of-ness, or for-ness exhibited by many states of mind. The nature of properties as simultaneously dispositional and qualitative is, I argue, the key to understanding the place of consciousness in the material world. Properties of conscious experiences, the so-called *qualia*, are not dangling appendages to material states and processes but intrinsic ingredients of those states and processes.

Although in addressing such topics I make use of an ontology that stands or falls on its own, an important yardstick of that ontology's merit lies in its applications. Earlier I spoke of the power of an ontological theory. I understand power to be a measure of the capacity of the theory to resolve a wide range of problems in a natural way. On that measure, I believe the ontology sketched here stacks up well.

The time has come to stop looking ahead to where all this might lead and to start getting there. Before venturing forth, however, let me officially acknowledge my debt (registered in the preface and at various places in the pages that follow) to C. B. Martin, whose ideas underlie so much of what I have to say here.

ONTOLOGY

CHAPTER 2

Levels of Reality

2.1 The Levels Picture

Nowadays it is a commonplace that our world comprises levels of reality. In philosophy this idea is encountered in metaphysics, philosophy of science, and most especially in philosophy of mind. Talk of levels, of course, is by no means confined to philosophers. Biologists, psychologists, anthropologists, historians, journalists, and holistic healers routinely appeal to higher- and lower-level phenomena in discussions of a variety of topics. Reality, it is widely presumed, is hierarchical. Although items occupying higher levels are thought to be in some fashion dependent on lower-level items (you could not remove the lower levels without thereby eliminating the higher levels), what exists at a higher level cannot in general be 'reduced to' what exists at a lower level. Higher-level phenomena are in this regard taken to be *autonomous* with respect to phenomena at lower levels. The denial of autonomy amounts to crass scientistic reductionism.[1]

It is not hard to find examples of appeals to levels in the philosophical literature. Consider John Searle's depiction of the relation states of mind bear to neurological states as in a case of intentional action: 'At the microlevel [. . .] we have a sequence of neuron firings which causes a series of physiological changes. At the microlevel the intention in action is caused by and realized in the neural processes, and the bodily movement is caused by and realized in the resultant physiological processes' (Searle 1983: 270). Searle illustrates what he has in mind with a diagram (Figure 2.1). Consciousness, Searle believes, is an 'ontologically irreducible', 'causally emergent property of the behavior of neurons' (Searle 1992: 116).

---

[1] John Dupré (1993) and Nancy Cartwright (1999) excoriate reductionists, but much of what I have to say here is consistent with the thrust of Dupré's 'promiscuous realism' and Cartwright's 'dappled world'.

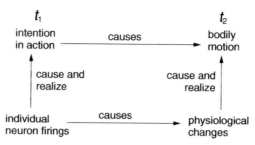

Figure 2.1. Searle's model

John Post sketches a similar picture. In a ringing defence of 'nonreductive physicalism', Post writes: 'Not all properties of a thing need be reducible or equivalent to physical properties, and many of them seem not to be. In particular, many of the properties in virtue of which we are human beings seem to be irreducible to physical properties or even to complex combinations of physical properties' (Post 1991: 98). Post envisions a world consisting of a hierarchy of properties and entities. Each level in this hierarchy is dependent on, but ontologically distinct from, items at lower levels. Post's preferred inter-level relation is a form of supervenience.[2]

This idea is made explicit by Jeffrey Poland:

It should be understood that the primacy of physics in ontological matters does not mean that everything is an element of a strictly physical ontology [. . .] physicalism [. . .] allows for non-physical objects, properties, and relations. The primacy of the physical ontology is that it grounds a structure that contains everything, not that it includes everything. [. . .] With regard to ontological matters, physicalism should not be equated with the identity theory in any of its forms. [. . .] I prefer the idea of a hierarchically structured system of objects grounded in a physical basis by a relation of *realization* to the idea that all objects are token identical to physical objects.   (Poland 1994: 18)

With characteristic vividness, Jerry Fodor imagines God creating the world. God calls together all his smartest angels. To one he assigns the task of working out laws of meteorology, to another the job of devising laws of geology, a third is dispatched to make up laws of psychology, and so for every domain of the special sciences. To the smartest

---

[2] Appeals to levels and appeals to supervenience seem made for one another. For a sceptical look at recent philosophical appeals to supervenience, see Kim (1990); Horgan (1993); Heil (1998a).

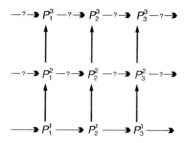

$$-?\to P_1^3 -?\to P_2^3 -?\to P_3^3 -?\to$$

$$-?\to P_1^2 -?\to P_2^2 -?\to P_3^2 -?\to$$

$$\longrightarrow P_1^1 \longrightarrow P_2^1 \longrightarrow P_3^1 \longrightarrow$$

Figure 2.2. Intra- and inter-level relations

angel God assigns the task of working out the laws of basic physics. 'But', God enjoins, 'don't get in the way of those other angels!'[3]

2.2 Horizontal and Vertical Laws

What all these authors have in common is a conception of reality as hierarchically organized. Higher-level objects and properties depend on, but are distinct from, objects and properties populating lower levels. The dependence relation, on most accounts, is governed by fundamental laws of nature. In creating the world, God creates objects, endows these with properties, then creates laws governing relations among objects. These relations hold in virtue of objects' properties. Some laws will be 'horizontal', governing the behaviour of objects on a given level. These are the familiar laws of physics, chemistry, and the special sciences. Other laws will be 'vertical', governing inter-level relations. These laws anchor higher-level objects and properties in lower-level circumstances.

In Figure 2.2, Ps represent properties (or objects, or states, or events), horizontal arrows represent causal relations, and vertical arrows stand for vertical dependence relations. (The reason for question marks will become evident in §2.3.) The lowest-level items might or might not represent an absolute lowest level. Perhaps there is no lowest level.[4]

---

[3] Used by permission. For a less colourful but more detailed examination of the point, see Fodor (1997).

[4] This, at any rate, is an abstract possibility. I confess ignorance as to how it is supposed to work given the dependence of higher levels on those below them: something, it seems, must ground the superstructure. Perhaps this is just a residual foundationalist prejudice. Perhaps vertical dependence relations are analogous to causal relations. Causal chains extending infinitely into the past seem possible. Still, if you think that higher-level causal relations (depicted in Figure 2.2 by arrows with question marks) depend on lower-level causal relations, it is not clear that these could fail to bottom out. If the only unattinuated causal relations are those at the basic level, there had better be a basic level.

Similarly, there might or might not be a highest level. Proponents of levels conceptions could differ on such matters.

2.3 Apparent Difficulties

One apparent difficulty for views of this kind is that it is hard to see how entities residing at higher levels are supposed to have an impact on reality. Suppose that a Volvo is a higher-level entity. It is natural to think that, when a Volvo strikes a pedestrian, it brings about a certain physical effect on the pedestrian. But note: we can account for the effects in such cases by remaining at the basic physical level. What matters causally is the Volvo's having a particular constitution and momentum, not its being a Volvo. The physical world is evidently 'causally closed': we take physics to uncover exceptionless laws governing our world's fundamental constituents. This suggests that, whenever a physical event occurs, it has a wholly physical explanation. We are obliged to assume that any effects the Volvo has are traceable to effects of its fundamental physical constituents. Any effects the Volvo might have 'over and above' the effects of these basic things must be grounded in its basic-level effects. This means that, if we regard a Volvo as a higher-level entity with its own independent reality, something distinct from its constituents (arranged in particular ways and variously connected to other things), we render it mysterious how Volvos could *do* anything at all.

You might regard this as too quick: perhaps higher-level entities could have effects on other higher-level entities, leaving the atoms to take care of themselves. The trouble with this suggestion is that it is unclear how a given higher-level entity could bring about a particular higher-level effect *except* by inducing some lower-level effect. Thus, if Volvos and human beings are higher-level entities, it is hard to see how a Volvo could have an effect on a human being except by having an effect on the fundamental entities making up that human being. This brings us back to the idea that the physical world is causally closed. The behaviour of the basic constituents is wholly determined by fundamental physical laws.

Thoughts of this kind leave a proponent of the view that reality is layered with two options. First, an advocate of levels might repudiate closure. Maybe our conviction that laws governing the basic entities are fundamental is just the expression of a narrow-minded reduction-ist impulse. Perhaps higher-level goings-on could have lower-level effects, effects that could not be accounted for by reference to lower-level mechanisms alone. A second option is to embrace *epiphenomenal-ism*. Causal work is confined to basic-level entities that ground those at higher levels. The apparent efficacy of higher-level items is illusory or a pretence we put up with for the sake of convenience.[5] For many of us, however, both the rejection of closure and appeals to epiphenome-nalism are decidedly unpromising options.

2.4 Looking Ahead

In the three chapters that follow, I endeavour to plumb the source of the thought that we must choose from among three equally off-putting options: (1) a commitment to higher-level entities (and an attendant commitment to epiphenomenalism or to the abandonment of closure), (2) reductionism, (3) eliminativism. I do not promise a solu-tion to deep philosophical questions, but at most a redistribution of the questions in a way that might come as close as we can reasonably hope to come to progress in this domain.

My contention is that the perceived need for levels of reality stems from surprising sources. These include a commitment to what I call the Picture Theory of language and a related commitment to a certain conception of philosophical analysis. I believe you could reject my diagnosis, however, without thereby rejecting the more fundamental contention that there are no levels of reality.

---

[5] This option can be given a more positive spin by replacing talk of causation with talk of explanation. A strong form of this view is defended by Lynne Rudder Baker, who argues that explanation talk is prior to causal talk; causal concepts can be understood only by reference to explanation (see Baker 1993). See also Burge (1993).

CHAPTER 3
Predicates and Properties

The decisive movement in the conjuring trick has been made, and
it was the very one that we thought quite innocent.

(Wittgenstein 1953/1968: §308)

3.1 Philosophical Puzzles

Wittgenstein held that philosophical conundrums are self-imposed.
Puzzles that attract philosophers' attention arise, not, as in the case of
scientific puzzles, from the nature of things, but from ways of thinking
and talking that can warp our understanding. Wittgenstein's remedy
was deflationary: if we attend carefully to the ordinary use of language,
we shall find that philosophical puzzles dissolve and with them the
need for distinctive philosophical theories.

Most philosophers nowadays think Wittgenstein overstated his case.
Yes, there is misdirection in philosophy; but this does not mean that
philosophers inevitably pursue difficulties spawned by their own theories, theories that are themselves responses to linguistic confusion.
Genuine philosophical problems remain untouched by careful attention to ordinary language.

In our haste to distance ourselves from 'ordinary language philosophy', we philosophers risk losing sight of Wittgenstein's broader point:
philosophical theorizing carries with it dangers of a special kind.
Philosophical theories, unlike empirical theories, are on the whole
unconstrained by experience. In consequence, the extent to which a
philosophical theory colours our thinking about particular issues is
often difficult to detect. Indeed, a theory may blend into the background in a way that makes it all but invisible. Lodged there, a theory

can exert influences that disguise themselves as deliverances of experience, common sense, or science.

3.2 Making the Picture Theory Explicit

I suspect that a certain conception of language works in just this way on our thoughts about the nature of the material world and the place of minds in that world.[1] The conception in its most general form is that language pictures reality in roughly the sense that we can 'read off' features of reality from our ways of speaking about it. For convenience, I designate this conception of language the Picture Theory. I leave open the relation what I am calling the Picture Theory bears to the theory of the same name advanced by Wittgenstein in the *Tractatus* (Wittgenstein 1921/1961).

Few philosophers would be willing to endorse the Picture Theory explicitly. This is not my contention, however. Rather, I think, we philosophers are trained to find it natural to reason in ways that implicitly invoke the Picture Theory for domains concerning which we are declared *realists*. Are you a realist about value? You are if you take normative predicates to designate authentic properties possessed by objects. The comparison class here includes predicates used 'non-descriptively' (to express attitudes, for instance) and those putatively designating properties that happen not to exist. On this conception, a realist about value must suppose that normative predicates designate genuine properties (or, a possibility I shall discuss in more detail presently, are analysable into predicates that themselves designate genuine properties).

I invoke the example of value realism merely to illustrate how natural it is to express questions about realism as to a given domain in terms of a commitment to predicates in that domain designating or expressing genuine properties. Paul Boghossian, in explicating 'non-factualist' accounts of a predicate, '*P*', suggests that what such conceptions have in common is

(1) The claim that the predicate '*P*' does not denote a property

and (hence)

---

[1] I shall speak of language and the world, although the conception I have in mind encompasses representation generally and the world. Not all representation is linguistic representation.

(2) the claim that the overall (atomic) declarative sentence in which it appears does not express a truth condition.[2]

Extending the idea, we can ask: are you a realist about states of mind, or colour, or consciousness? You are, it would seem, only if you think that possessing a particular state of mind, or being red, or feeling pain is a matter of something's possessing a genuine property answering to the predicate in question. These properties will be shared by every object to which the predicate applies.

In this context, reference to 'genuine properties' is just a way of marking off full-blooded properties from Humean 'projected' properties, or 'Cambridge properties', or other sorts of imagined property the possession of which apparently makes no difference to their possessors. Hume spoke of the mind's capacity for 'gilding and staining' the experienced world. Thus, Hume argued, although we seem to observe manifestations of power and causal connections, these are at bottom 'projections' of our own expectations onto what we do experience: entirely 'loose and separate' objects and events.[3] A child sees a dark shape across the garden as fearful. The shape is just a shape (an oddly pruned bush), but the child's experience of it is coloured by the child's state of mind. In this just way we all colour our experiences by assorted expectations and prejudices.

Talk of genuine properties typically includes as well an invocation of the idea of a connection between properties and powers or dispositions: genuine properties contribute in distinctive ways to the dispositionalities of objects possessing them.[4] What an object does or might do depends on its properties.[5] A billiard ball rolls because it is spherical; it depresses a scale because it has a certain mass; it would make a particular sound if you tapped it with a pencil because it is solid.

Does every predicate (or every significant predicate) designate a property? Some philosophers think so. According to Jerry Fodor, for instance, a particle has the property *being an H-particle* just in case it is a

---

[2] See Boghossian (1990: 161). Cf. Principle (Φ) below.

[3] This is the Hume of philosophical lore. For a different appraisal of Hume, see Strawson (1989).

[4] See Ch. 8. This is close to what Graham Oddie (1982) dubs 'the Eleatic Principle', and Jaegwon Kim calls 'Alexander's Dictum', see Kim (1993a: 202).

[5] Does this imply that so-called relational properties—being close to the surface of the Earth, for instance—are not genuine? Perhaps. Relational predicates hold of objects by virtue of relations involving those objects. This does not imply that there are properties corresponding to (that is, designated by) those predicates. I develop this point, albeit indirectly, below.

particle and a coin tossed by Fodor has landed heads (Fodor 1988: 33). This way of looking at properties counts any predicate that applies, or would apply, truly to an object as designating a property: the property of the object in virtue of which it satisfies the predicate in question.

Such an approach threatens the idea that properties differentially affect the causal powers of their possessors. Perhaps we could distinguish 'causally operative' properties from the rest by reference to laws: a predicate designates a causally operative property just in case the predicate figures in the statement of a law. If, like Fodor, you have a relaxed view of the laws, you could in this way accommodate a wide range of properties. *Being an H-particle* is unlikely to count as a causally operative property, but *being a belief that this is an H-particle* might. Your possessing this belief could figure in a causal explanation of why you behave as you do on a particular occasion. Let us call predicates that figure, or could figure, in the statement of causal generalizations projectable predicates.[6]

Nowadays philosophers worry that, if beliefs are properties, they are 'relational properties' (they are possessed by agents partly in virtue of relations those agents bear to their surroundings). It is hard to see how a relational property could affect the dispositionalities of its possessor.[7] The worry becomes acute when the non-relational component of the property could be shared by intrinsically indiscernible agents. These are lessons we are supposed to have learned from imaginative visits to Twin Earth.

Here we notice a tension between the conviction that genuine properties—properties answering to projectable predicates—ought to have 'causal relevance', and the conviction that many properties satisfying projectable predicates—mental properties, for instance—lack causal relevance owing to their (apparently) relational character. One option is to eschew causal talk and focus instead on explanation (see Baker 1993; Burge 1993). We recognize, for instance, that appeals to

---

[6] I mean to include, among the causal generalizations, lawlike generalizations. These are used to support claims concerning, not only how things stand, but how things *would* stand given appropriate conditions. Talk of projectable predicates originates with Goodman. See his (1965: ch. 4). Do not confuse a predicate's being projectable with the Humean notion of projection, which applies to properties observers 'project' onto' objects.

[7] Philosophers with such worries have been influenced by Hilary Putnam, Tyler Burge, Lynne Rudder Baker, and other proponents of 'externalism' (or 'anti-individualism'). See e.g. Putnam (1975a); Burge (1979); Baker (1987); Wilson (1995); and Ch. 18 below.

states of mind—even 'broad' states of mind—are explanatory and that they support counterfactuals. Your wanting a pickled egg, together with your belief that there are pickled eggs in the jar, straightforwardly explains your reaching for the jar. Further, and most significantly, had you not wanted a pickled egg, or had you not believed there were pickled eggs in the jar, you would not have reached for the jar. Perhaps, so the thinking goes, this is as close as we can come to attaching causal relevance to mental properties. The option, it would seem, is to deny that mental properties are causally relevant to action or, more dramatically, to deny that mental predicates designate properties. The latter option is standardly taken as an expression of defeat, an implicit endorsement of a form of eliminativism (or perhaps 'fictionalism') that is itself a kind of nihilism about the mental.

3.3 Principle (Φ)

All of this is, I suggest, off the mark. The difficulty stems from the acceptance of a Picture Theory of language, and, most especially, a corollary of the Picture Theory, a correspondence principle of the form

(Φ) When a predicate applies truly to an object, it does so in virtue of designating a property possessed by that object and by every object to which the predicate truly applies (or would apply).[8]

Principle (Φ) captures the idea that when a predicate applies truly to an object it does so in virtue of the object's properties. Consider a red billiard ball. The predicate 'is spherical' applies to the billiard ball in virtue of its shape (but not its colour); and the predicate 'is red' applies to the ball in virtue of its colour (but not its shape).

Principle (Φ) goes beyond this homely observation, however. According to Principle (Φ), whenever a predicate applies truly to an object, it does so by virtue of designating a property possessed by that object *and* possessed by any other object to which the predicate applies or would apply. It is easy to doubt that very many predicates satisfy this requirement.

---

[8] See Heil (1999). Compare (Φ) to the principle advanced in Boghossian (1990), quoted above, §3.2.

Take the predicate 'is red'. Does this predicate designate a property? If you think so, this may be because you believe that 'is red' applies truly to various objects and you accept (Φ). Philosophers and philosophically inclined colour scientists aside, most of us agree that 'is red' applies truly to objects. In that regard we are realists about red. But it is not easy to think of a property that (*a*) all red things share and (*b*) in virtue of which they satisfy the predicate 'is red'.[9]

In this context, properties must be taken seriously. If objects share a property, those objects have something—some one thing—in common (if properties are universals); or they must be precisely similar in some way (if properties are tropes—or, as I prefer, modes—and talk of 'sharing' or 'having the same' property is grounded in collections of precisely similar modes).[10] As it happens, however, objects can be red without—in any obvious sense—sharing a property in virtue of which they could be said to be red. A tomato, a pillar box, and a head of hair can all be red. We say that they are different *shades* of red. Perhaps a property corresponds to each of these shades of red. Then the predicate 'is red' truly applies to tomatoes, pillar boxes, and redheads, and it applies to these things in virtue of their possessing certain properties, but it does not apply to each of them in virtue of their possessing the *very same* property. Tomatoes, pillar boxes, and redheads possess similar-but-not-precisely-similar properties. And this evidently is enough for the predicate 'is red' to apply to them.

3.4 From Predicates to Properties to Levels of Being

Earlier I suggested that distinct properties (or, if properties are modes, properties belonging to diverse collections of precisely similar properties) might be thought to make distinctive contributions to the dispositionalities of objects possessing them. We can extend this principle to

[9] Clause (*b*) is important. Red things could share many properties. But, unless these properties constrain the application of the predicate 'is red', unless red objects are red in virtue of possessing one or more of these properties, we need not imagine that 'is red' designates a property.

[10] By 'mode' I mean something close to what other philosophers mean by 'trope'. I shall have more to say about the ontology of properties in subsequent chapters. Nothing I offer in this chapter, however, depends on the position developed there. Thus, I prefer to remain neutral for the time being on the question whether properties are universals or modes; see Chs. 11–13.

cases of less-than-perfect similarity. By virtue of possessing similar-but-not-precisely-similar properties, red objects possess similar-but-not-precisely-similar 'causal powers' or dispositionalities, and so behave (colourwise) in similar-but-not-precisely-similar ways. It is not surprising, then, that we see red objects as similar and find it natural to group them under a single predicate. So it is with most of the predicates we deploy: these predicates apply to objects by virtue of properties possessed by those objects, but few designate properties shared by every object to which they truly apply.

Failure to take seriously this simple point has led philosophers, especially philosophers of mind (the author included), into difficulties that are otherwise avoidable. Imagine that you are attracted to functionalism. You recognize that many very different kinds of creature can experience pain. You note, however, that the range of creatures that might experience pain lack anything approaching physiological uniformity. More particularly, they seem to share no physical property in virtue of which it is true that they are experiencing pain. This tells against 'type identity', the idea that the property of being in pain could be identified with some physical property: pain is 'multiply realizable'. To say that pain is multiply realizable is to say that the property of being in pain is possessed by sentient creatures in virtue of those creatures' possession of some other property, its 'realizer'. The realizing property could vary across individuals or species. If being in pain is a property, it is a 'higher-level' property.

In describing the property of being in pain as a 'higher-level' property, functionalists are not supposing that being in pain is a property of a property. Functionalists do not regard pains as properties of physical properties that realize them; pains are properties of sentient creatures, the very same entities that possess pains' physical realizers. In regarding pains as higher-level properties, functionalists imagine that the property of being in pain is one possessed by a sentient creature by virtue of that creature's possession of some distinct lower-level realizing property. Nor is the property of being in pain unique in this respect. According to functionalists, in so far as mental properties are functional properties, mental properties must be higher-level, multiply realizable properties.

If you find this line of reasoning congenial, you will discover higher-level properties everywhere. Take causal powers or dispositions, in par-

ticular take being fragile: a disposition to shatter when struck by a sufficiently massive solid object. Although many different kinds of object
are fragile, it appears unlikely that they share a single physical property
in virtue of which they are fragile. Rather, fragility is multiply realizable: being fragile is a higher-level property possessed by objects in
virtue of their possession of some lower-level realizing property. In this
way we arrive at what has come to be the default conception of
dispositional properties as grounded in non-dispositional, 'categorical'
properties (see Prior et al. 1982).

Now a whole vista opens before us. We can begin to see most properties we encounter in science and in everyday life as higher-level,
multiply realizable properties. Reflect on something's being red. To a
first approximation, objects are red by virtue of being some determinate shade of red. Clearly, being red cannot be reduced to any of these
determinate shades. Being red is a property possessed by objects in
virtue of their possession of any of a range of lower-level properties.
This vindicates the idea encompassed by our correspondence principle (Φ): the predicate 'is red' picks out a property possessed by objects
to which it truly applies and by any other object to which it applies or
might apply. The property in question is a higher-level property.

Now we have the makings of a conception of reality as comprising
a hierarchy of levels. If being red is a higher-level property possessed by
an object by virtue of that object's being some determinate shade of
red—crimson, say—then surely the object's being crimson is *itself* a
higher-level, multiply realizable property; and properties realizing this
property are themselves higher-level properties relative to *their* realizers. The upshot is a layered conception of reality, a conception of reality
as incorporating irreducible, 'downwardly' dependent levels of being.

Think of Fodor's angels in §2.1 as constructing different ontological
levels in something like the way construction crews might erect different floors of a new skyscraper. The special sciences are occupied by
objects, properties, and goings-on at higher levels. The levels are hierarchically arranged. Higher levels asymmetrically depend on lower
levels. But no level is less real or less important in the scheme of things
than any other. The structure as a whole rests on its foundations. Even
so, as Fodor puts it, the angel responsible for planning and constructing
the foundations needs to keep out of the way of those occupied with
planning and constructing higher-level projects.

The picture is one many theorists find attractive, even compelling. It moves us beyond tired reductionist sentiments, and makes room for a host of very different kinds of approach to the task of understanding our world. At the same time, however, a conception of reality as hierarchical brings with it a host of difficulties. When we come to look at the ontology of levels, the picture loses some of its lustre. In the next chapter, I shall say something about the less savoury aspects of a commitment to levels. Eventually, I shall defend a conception of the world that dispenses with levels, but not, I contend, with truths that levels enthusiasts tell us we need. Along the way, I shall say more about the role of the Picture Theory in motivating the conviction that reality is hierarchical.[11]

---

[11] As will become clear, I have no objection to the idea that reality is hierarchical in the sense that some things have other things as parts. Levels of organization, however, are not levels of reality in the stronger sense at issue here.

CHAPTER 4
Difficulties for the Levels Conception

4.1 Anti-Reduction

A conception of reality as comprising levels of being is at first liberating. In countenancing levels, we thumb our noses at narrow positivist and reductionist doctrines that threaten to reduce the special sciences (and indeed any domain of human knowledge) to some crabby, all-encompassing superphysics. Reduction of this kind appears wildly impractical. How, for instance, could we hope to re-express truths about the global political consequences of a decline in the GNP of Eastern Europe in terms of interactions among fundamental particles? Even if such a reduction were possible, however, it would be self-defeating. Important higher-level patterns and relations are invisible to physics.[1] The result is self-defeating and dehumanizing; we deprive ourselves of perspectives essential to an understanding of our place in the world. To many philosophers, reductionism seems not merely wrong but socially, even morally, benighted.

The anti-reductionists have a point. The question is, what follows? If we find anti-reductionist sentiments appealing, must we assent to the doctrine that reality is hierarchical? I believe that the widespread impression that anti-reductionism and levels of reality go hand in glove is a result of an unstated commitment to the Picture Theory. We have seen already how this might work. Predicates we regard as holding true of objects, most especially projectable predicates (those capable of figuring in counterfactual supporting lawlike generalizations), are taken to name properties shared by every object to which they truly apply.

[1] These and related points are forcefully endorsed by Dupré (1993), by Fodor (1997), and by Cartwright (1999).

This leads quickly to a proliferation of properties related hierarchically. In abandoning the correspondence principle (Φ), an important corollary of the Picture Theory, we leave behind the thought that respectable predicates necessarily correspond to properties. Before delving into more difficult matters, however, it might be useful to reflect on a few of the liabilities of a commitment to levels of reality.

4.2 Causal Relevance

Consider the problem of the 'causal relevance' of higher-level properties.[2] Suppose for a moment that mental properties are higher-level properties realized in the nervous systems of sentient creatures. How could such properties affect the behaviour of creatures possessing them? The potential causal contribution of any higher-level property would seem to be pre-empted by its lower-level realizing property. Suppose you are in pain by virtue of being in neurological state N. When you head for the medicine cabinet to find aspirin, are you driven by the feeling of pain, or by N, its neurological realizer? If you are inclined to see the feeling of pain as somehow getting into the act, how is this accomplished if not via N?

This worry about the causal relevance of mental properties extends smoothly to higher-level properties generally. If you like to think of the special sciences as occupied with higher-level properties and events, then you will need some accounting of how these properties and events could make a causal difference in our world.

In this regard, it might be thought that the causal relevance of higher-level properties could be secured to the extent that such properties figure in causal laws. (This is Fodor's position as I read him; see Fodor 1997.) The laws in question are neither reducible to nor derivable from the laws of physics or chemistry (recall Fodor's angels in §2.1). The latter laws are strict or exceptionless.[3] Laws governing higher-level occurrences, in contrast, are 'hedged' *ceteris paribus* laws.

---

[2] My focus here will be on putatively higher-level mental properties, but the discussion carries over to higher-level properties generally. My debt here to Jaegwon Kim will be obvious to anyone familiar with Kim's work.

[3] The notion that fundamental physical laws are 'strict, exceptionless' is borrowed from Davidson (1970). Such laws could be deterministic or probabilistic: a strict probabilistic law is not a law that admits 'exceptions'.

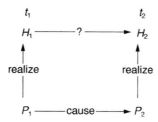

Figure 4.1. Higher-level causation

What is unclear, however, is how we are to understand causal relations encompassed by such laws. Are these distinct from lower-level
causal sequences on which they apparently depend? Perhaps higher-
level occurrences causally influence only other higher-level occurrences. But how is this supposed to work? Suppose H_1 and H_2 are
higher-level properties possessed by some object, o, over successive
intervals; and suppose you are inclined to think that o's being H_1 causes
o to be H_2. Suppose, further, that H_1 is realized in o, by P_1 (some
complex physical property), that H_2 is realized by P_2, and that o's being
P_1 is the cause of o's being P_2 (see Figure 4.1; and compare Figure 2.1).
Then it would seem that o's being H_2 is embarrassingly overdetermined: H_2 is on the scene because P_2 is at hand; *and* H_2 is present
because H_1 is. Maybe o's being H_1 brings about o's being H_2, not
directly, but by making it the case that o is P_2. But now o's being P_2 is
evidently overdetermined. Worse, perhaps, we are envisioning 'causation from above,' an apparent violation of the autonomy of the physical realm.[4]

You may care little for the principle that the physical realm is
autonomous. This idea, however, is implicit in appeals to the layered
view of reality. Earlier I invoked a distinction between strict laws governing the basic constituents of our world and 'hedged' *ceteris paribus*
laws thought to govern higher-level goings-on.[5] Part of the motivation
for this distinction lies in a conviction that we evidently regard the
actions of the basic items as wholly determined by basic laws.

[4] All this will be familiar to readers acquainted with recent work by Jaegwon Kim; see Kim (1993a). For
a different view of the territory, see Thomasson (1998).

[5] Davidson (1970) holds basic laws—perhaps any laws—to be exceptionless en route to a defence of
'anomalous monism'. Many of Davidson's critics, including Fodor, argue that higher-level laws could back
causal generalizations without being exceptionless. This is not an issue concerning which I care to take
sides. I embark on a very different approach to causation in subsequent chapters.

Consider, in contrast, higher-level causal explanations of intelligent action. A proponent of levels might regard something of the following form as a plausible higher-level psychological law:

(L) If an agent, *a*, prefers *F* to any alternative and believes *F* is obtainable by doing *A*, then *a* will do *A*, *ceteris paribus*.

We need a *ceteris paribus* rider here because, even assuming that (L) is well supported, any higher-level system is subject to lower-level disruption: *a* might, immediately prior to forming an intention to *A*, be struck by a swerving Volvo and so not undertake to *A*. This possibility (and of course endless others) is not encompassed within a psychological theory of the sort likely to include (L).

When you move to the basic entities—the electrons and quarks—matters are different. Laws governing such entities leave no room for outside disruption. At the basic level, there *is* no 'outside'. The moral, it would seem, is that any purported solution to the problem of the causal relevance of higher-level properties that abandons the idea that basic-level causal transactions are autonomous is a cure worse than the disease.

4.3 Causation and Laws

The foregoing discussion has taken for granted an intimate relation between causation and laws. The idea is that, when a particular event—your head's throbbing now—causes another event—your seeking out aspirin—the events in question are instances of a general law. The notion that every causal sequence is backed by a law, like the idea that causation is a relation among particular events, forms a part of philosophy's Humean heritage.

What are laws? For Hume, a law is simply a true, presumably exceptionless, generalization. If your head's throbbing (call this event *c*) causes you to seek aspirin (event *e*), then these particular events are instances of a general law of the form:

(L′) Whenever a *c*-type event occurs, an *e*-type event follows.

Of course, where headaches and aspirin seekings are concerned, there is little prospect that anything like (L′) could be true; there will be endless 'exceptions'. One possibility is that, at the fundamental level, we could, with sufficient ingenuity, locate exceptionless laws, then derive higher-level laws from these in a way that makes them exceptionless by making allowance for complicating factors. Such factors might be built into the circumstances surrounding an event's occurrence:

(L″) Whenever a c-type event occurs in circumstances C, an e-type event follows.

This might involve a 'reduction': a derivation of higher-level laws from those at a lower level, where reduction is understood as derivability: the higher-level laws are logically inferable from lower-level laws.[6]

The reductionist programme dispenses with levels of reality. Ultimately, there is but a single level describable in logically reducible ways. Talk of statues, or people, or pains is shorthand for talk of arrangements of fundamental entities. A complete description of the basic level, one that includes laws governing basic-level phenomena, should imply every other true description (see Jackson 1998; Chalmers and Jackson 2001).

This is the model attacked by anti-reductionists like Fodor. Not only has there been little progress in reducing the special sciences to 'more basic' sciences; there is little prospect that such reduction could succeed, even in principle, and no reason to think that the envisioned reduction would be in any way desirable. The special sciences, on this view, are autonomous; laws of the special sciences stand in no need of reductive grounding. This fits comfortably with the hierarchical conception of reality. Entities at each level are governed by laws tailor-made for those entities. These laws will be irreducibly 'hedged'. In this regard they will be unlike laws at more basic levels. Nevertheless, if causation is a matter of events falling under laws, this should be enough to ensure causal relations among higher-level entities and the causal relevance of higher-level properties.

I have already (§4.2) suggested that this conception of causality ultimately fits uncomfortably with the idea that higher-level entities and properties depend on lower-level entities and properties. If items at the lower levels suffice for items at the higher levels, then it is hard to see how higher-level causation is supposed to work. Recall Figure 4.1. A

---

[6] A canonical statement of this model can be found in Ernest Nagel (1961).

higher-level item, H_2, causally explained by another higher-level item, H_1, seems wholly accounted for by the presence of P_2, its lower-level 'ground'.

Not everyone would agree. I offer the point, however, not as a definitive refutation of the notion of higher-level causation, but as a potential source of embarrassment. My aim is to advance a view that accommodates what seems right about appeals to levels without the attendant ontological baggage. To that end, I shall sketch an alternative conception of laws as grounded in powers or dispositions possessed by objects. In the meantime it is worth noting that the Humean conception of laws figuring in the foregoing discussion is at odds with a conception nowadays associated with D. M. Armstrong.[7] On this view, laws are not a special kind of true generalization, but contingent features of the world: *second-order universals*. I shall postpone discussion of universals and laws (see Chapters 8–14). For the moment, let me merely note that the invocation of universals here provides no particular help with the problem of causal relevance.

4.4 Further Difficulties

The levels conception leads to puzzles about the causal relevance of higher-level items. Philosophers have offered ingenious solutions to the puzzle, but I think it fair to say that no solution advanced to date has won widespread support. A second category of puzzle concerns the nature of inter-level relations. Higher-level items are taken to be distinct from, but depend in some way on, lower-level items. Sometimes the relation is expressed by means of a supervenience principle. Suppose that As are higher-level properties taken to depend on lower-level realizing B-properties. (As might be mental properties, Bs physical properties.) Although the As and Bs are distinct (the As cannot be reduced to the Bs), As 'depend on and are determined by' Bs. Think of A and B, not as designating properties, but as representing property families (the mental properties and the physical properties, for instance). We can then formulate a supervenience principle:

---

[7] The conception of laws in question is often identified as the Dretske–Tooley–Armstrong conception in honour of its originators, who, as far as I know, arrived at their positions independently. See Dretske (1977); Tooley (1977); Armstrong (1978, 1983).

(S) Necessarily, if anything, x, has α in A, then there is a property, β, in B, and, necessarily, if any x has β, x has α.[8]

Principle (S) is meant to capture the idea that higher-level A-differences depend on B-differences at a lower level; the B-level state of the world determines the world's A-level state. However, (S) is silent on the nature of the envisaged dependence–determination relation. Supervenience, as characterized in (S), is a purely modal notion. In this regard supervenience resembles counterfactual dependence. Suppose it is true that, had you struck the match you are now holding, it would have ignited. This truth, like counterfactual truths generally, requires grounding. One possibility is that the truth of the claim about the match is grounded in dispositions (or 'causal powers') of the match, the surface on which it is struck, and the surrounding atmosphere. Similarly, if (S) holds, the question remains *why* (S) holds. To see the difficulty, note that (S) might be true if As *were* Bs, if As were wholly made up of Bs, if As were caused by Bs, or if As and Bs both had a common cause. None of these relations appears to be what a levels theorist has in mind, however. Higher-level items are not identifiable with, or made up of, or (Searle aside; see Figure. 2.1) caused by lower-level items. Rather higher-level items have lower-level *realizers*.

If (S) holds in virtue of a realizing relation, it is fair to ask what this relation is. It is not enough to point to (S). Our worry concerns, not (S), but (S)'s grounding: the truth-maker for (S). Perhaps (S) holds in virtue of laws of nature. Laws of nature ensure that As and Bs covary appropriately. Thus, for instance, it is a law of nature that whenever β occurs, α occurs as well. Again, however, this does little to pin down the realizing relation. So described, it is consistent with As causally depending on Bs or As and Bs causally depending on Cs. We have yet to uncover a substantive conception of dependence across *levels*.

A proponent of the levels view might, at this point, appeal to a *sui generis* notion of nomological dependence. A 'vertical' law of nature ties higher-level items to those at lower levels.[9] The nature of this tie is not

---

[8] My formulation of (S) expresses 'strong supervenience' (see Kim 1984). Readers familiar with the voluminous literature on supervenience will be aware that there are alternatives. Nothing I have to say here depends on any particular formulation of supervenience, however. For more on supervenience: see Heil (1992 ch. 3); 1998a; Horgan (1993); Kim (1993b).

[9] This is David Chalmers's view (1996) of the relation conscious qualities bear to physical states; see Ch. 20 below.

further explicable. A view of this kind has its own embarrassments, however. Suppose being in pain is multiply realized in a heterogeneous (and perhaps open-ended) collection of actual and possible physical states. Suppose this is so for mental properties generally. We will need a fundamental law of nature associating each mental property with a wildly heterogeneous collection of (actual and possible) physical properties. The envisaged laws are quite unlike fundamental laws of nature thus far countenanced in the natural sciences. I shall have more to say on the subject in Chapter 20. Meanwhile, let it be noted that, so long as the realizing relation thought to underlie (S) remains elusive, conceptions of levels of reality face potential embarrassment.

4.5 The Burden of Proof

Anti-reductionist philosophers sometimes suggest that concerns about inter-level connections are mere philosophical quibbles. Why should philosophers imagine that they are in a position to challenge the legitimacy of the higher-level sciences (the so-called special sciences), or higher-level social and political institutions? The idea that these must be tied somehow to physics is merely the expression of a kind of philosophical hubris that went out of fashion in the eighteenth century. Even if we find the nature of inter-level relations puzzling, we are in no position to challenge their existence. Non-locality in quantum physics is deeply puzzling, but philosophers have not rushed to challenge its legitimacy. The philosophical job, if there is one, is to work out an account of the relation. If no account is available, then the appropriate attitude should be one of modest acceptance. Explanation must, after all, stop somewhere.

The view just expressed presupposes precisely what is at issue. The question is not whether the special sciences are legitimate or whether putative higher-level items—planets, trees, people, social and political institutions—'really exist'. The question is whether our acceptance of such things requires a commitment to levels of being. My suggestion is that hierarchical conceptions of reality mis-construe the demands of realism. It is these conceptions, not their subject matter (the special sciences, for instance), that a rejection of levels calls into question. One symptom of trouble here is the difficulty of making independent sense of relations among levels. If the account I shall provide is correct, it will be easy to see why this is so. The argument proceeds, not by criticizing at the outset central tenets of the levels conception, but by offering an alternative account of the phenomena to which proponents of levels so often appeal. One virtue of the alternative account is that it does not appeal to a *sui generis* relation among levels of being.

We can, I think, do better than posit levels of being in comprehending the nature of the world around us and our place in that world. This, at any rate, is what I shall endeavour to establish now.

CHAPTER 5

Abandoning the Levels Conception: First Steps

5.1 Projectability and Similarity

In their enthusiasm to find a place for higher-level entities, proponents of levels of being risk rendering the favoured entities epiphenomenal. If you are attracted to the idea that properties are distinguished by the contribution they make to the powers or dispositionalities of their possessors, inert properties will lack appeal (see Chapter 8).

One response to this concern is to identify higher-level properties with—possibly open-ended—disjunctions of lower-level properties.[1] A difficulty for such a view is that it makes a hash of projectability. Consider a candidate higher-level mental property, being in pain, picked out by the predicate 'is in pain'. Suppose the property is identifiable with an open-ended disjunction of lower-level properties. It is not easy to see how such a view could accommodate applications of the predicate 'is in pain' to new cases. A purely disjunctive characterization of pain amounts to little more than a list.

If, as I recommend, we reject the idea that higher-level predicates like 'is in pain' must designate properties shared by objects to which they are applicable, we can avail ourselves of an appealingly simple account of projectability. Such a predicate applies to a range of *similar* cases. What unifies this list? Less-than-perfect similarity.[2] Because objects possessing less-than-perfectly similar properties commonly behave in similar (though less-than-perfectly similar) ways, we can

---

[1] A disjunction of properties, not a 'disjunctive property'. I regard 'disjunctive property' as an oxymoron.

[2] The pertinent similarity dimension here includes a strong dispositional component. In this we have the core of what is right about functionalism.

account for the character of familiar lawlike generalizations as these operate in the special sciences and in everyday life.

In *Mind in a Physical World* (1998), Jaegwon Kim dissects functionalism in a way that meshes nicely with what I have said here. Kim restricts his account to functional properties—or, as I would put it, to predicates amenable to a functional analysis. Such an analysis, Kim argues, provides an effective technique for associating the predicates in question with diverse physical properties (properties taken by functionalists to be realizers of functional properties). I believe Kim is making exactly the right kind of move, but that the lesson can, and should, be extended to any predicate, functional or otherwise, taken to designate a higher-level property.[3] The felt need for higher-level properties diminishes once we abandon a correspondence principle of the sort mandated by the Picture Theory. In relinquishing this theory, we relinquish as well a commitment to levels of being. Functionalism, the focus of Kim's discussion, is merely one high-profile target.

5.2 The Fruits of Analysis

What I have been calling a Picture Theory of language is, I believe, responsible for a tendency among philosophers to argue in a particular way. My suspicion is that we philosophers divide temperamentally into mutually exclusive and exhaustive groups in our attitudes towards this tendency. Let me illustrate the temperaments I have in mind by way of two moderately tendentious examples.

Motion. I have spoken of properties being possessed by objects. But what is an object? Some philosophers believe objects are bundles of properties. I prefer to think of objects as substances (see Chapter 15). What is a substance? Roughly, a substance is an object considered as a bearer of properties; a property is an object considered as being a particular way. You may not like this formulation, but bear with me and assume a substance–property ontology for the sake of illustration.

It would seem distinctly possible that there is but a single substance:

[3] Another possibility: every higher-level predicate *is* a functional predicate.

space–time or some all-encompassing quantum field.[4] Suppose we had reason to think this. In that case, ordinary objects—substances in the familiar sense—would be regions of space–time or the quantum field. These regions would themselves possess properties. Change would involve a given region's losing certain properties and acquiring others. The model here is a television screen. Jesse Helms appearing on your television screen is not a piece of the screen. Jesse is constituted by a pattern of illuminated pixels. When Jesse blushes, pixels in a certain region of the screen take on a reddish hue. When Jesse waves his arm, no piece of the screen moves. Instead, patterns of illumination are redistributed over stationary collections of pixels. What if reality were like this. Let us ask: *does anything really move?*

Consider two kinds of response to this question.

(A) No, nothing moves; motion is illusory.
(B) Yes, objects move; motion turns out not to be what we might have thought it was.

Response (A) begins with the concept of motion understood in a particular way (roughly: motion requires the existence of 'continuants' capable of persisting over time and occupying successive regions of space during successive intervals). Response (B) takes it that motion is like *this*: it is, for instance, what occurs when Mark McGwire trots around the bases after blasting a homer. If McGwire's trotting is at bottom a matter of properties altering their distribution over regions of space–time (or regions of the quantum field), this is the deep story about motion.

Agency. A second, rather more contentious, example of the kind of dispute I have in mind centres on the notion of agency.[5] Compatibilist accounts of free action have a long philosophical history, but many philosophers regard compatibilism as misguided in principle. Arguments on both sides are familiar. In the current context, however, I am less interested in the arguments than in attitudes those arguments betray.

Compatibilists take the concept of agency to encompass a spectrum of paradigm cases. If it is pointed out that the cases in question appar-

[4] See e.g. Plato's *Theatetus* 49–53; Locke (1706).
[5] By 'agency' in what follows I mean free agency: agency in the fullest sense.

ently allow for the possibility that what we ordinarily regard as free actions could, on closer examination, turn out to be wholly causally determined, a compatibilist is likely to shrug: this shows only that, in spite of what we might have thought, free action is at home in a deterministic world.

Incompatibilists, in contrast, are likely to begin with a set of requirements extracted a priori from the concept of agency. These imply that an action is free only when it is robustly spontaneous. Spontaneity, however, requires at a minimum an uncaused cause; it might require an uncaused *causer*. Anything less, the incompatibilist reasons, falls short of authentic agency. Faced with the response that we are unlikely to be in a position to reconcile agency in this sense with the idea that agents are, at bottom, physical beings—or at the very least that agents' actions have manifestly physical effects—an incompatibilist is likely to shrug. This is what agency—*genuine* agency—requires; if human beings fail to satisfy the pertinent conditions, then human beings fail to be genuine agents: agency is an illusion.[6]

5.3 The Picture Theory at Work

I do not know how to adjudicate such disputes. My suspicion, however, is that they turn on opposing perspectives on the relation our concepts bear to the world. It is possible to discern the hand of the Picture Theory at work here taking the form of an emphasis on reductive analytical techniques. If you cannot define (or analyse) the concept of a person, or a table, or a promise into 'lower-level' physical terms, either persons, tables, and promises must be something *more* than physical entities and their interactions, or such things must fail to exist. The idea that we must choose between these options may, however, be founded on a misconstrual of the nature of our concepts and their conditions of application.

You do not have to be an ardent Wittgensteinian to suppose that the concepts we use have evolved to satisfy a variety of purposes. The concept expressed by the predicate 'is red', for instance, seems

---

[6] A more daring incompatibilist might argue that (1) we have strong pragmatic grounds to accept the existence of genuine agency; (2) these grounds defeat competing empirical evidence to the contrary.

tailor-made for picking out a range of objects that are, in a particular way, less-than-perfectly similar to one another. The concept applies to objects by virtue of properties possessed by those objects, presumably an extremely complex and diverse class of physical properties. There is, I gather, no prospect of defining or analysing redness in terms of these physical properties. This is due, in some measure, to the fact that the properties in question are salient—to us—partly owing to the nature of our perceptual system.[7] Were we built differently, were we made of different materials, the diverse collection of properties that satisfy our concept of redness could well fail to stand out. In that case we should have no use for the concept.

I have used the predicate 'is red' as a stalking horse. This might raise suspicions in some quarters. The general point I want to make does not depend on the example, however. I could have used 'is rectangular', or 'is smooth', or 'is wise', or 'is toxic'. Precisely the same lessons apply. It is close to a truism that many of the concepts we use hold of objects by virtue of properties possessed by those objects; but this does not imply either that, if you are a realist with respect to a given concept (if you think that instances of the concept really do exist), you must assume that it picks out a single property shared by every object that satisfies it—Principle (Φ)—or that, failing a correspondence between the concept and a unique property, it must be possible to analyse the concept into concepts that correspond to a class of properties, any one of which suffices for the application of the concept. This is not how our concepts work.[8]

What is the truth, then? Many of the concepts we use, and the predicates we deploy to express these concepts, encompass a range of similar properties or a range of objects with similar properties, ranges salient to us. Concepts do not 'carve up' the world. The world already contains endless divisions, most of which we remain oblivious to or ignore. Some of these divisions, however, are salient, or come to be salient once we begin enquiring systematically. These are the divisions reflected in our concepts and in words we use to express those concepts. (I say more about similarity in Chapter 14.)

---

[7] Thus the anthropocentric component of our colour concepts; see Averill (1985). I discuss colour in more detail in Ch. 17 below.

[8] Perhaps this *is* how concepts of a fundamental physics work. My interest here is in ordinary concepts and those that occupy philosophers who like to invoke levels of being.

5.4 Higher-Level Causation

What follows from all this? Recall Figure 4.1, a schematic depiction of a causal relation involving putatively higher-level properties. Imagine now that the items identified in the figure as higher-level properties, H_1 and H_2, are taken instead to be higher-level *predicates*. The truth-makers for H_1 and H_2 (or, better, 'H_1' and 'H_2') are P_1 and P_2, respectively. That is 'H_1' and 'H_2' hold of a particular object at a particular time in virtue of that object's possession of P_1 and P_2. What of an apparent instance of higher-level causation: H_1's causing H_2? Here, the truth-maker for 'H_1 causes H_2' is just P_1's causing P_2. It is true, by my lights, to say that H_1 causes H_2. But this truth holds, not in virtue of some higher-level causal sequence, it holds by virtue of P_1's causing P_2, a ground-level sequence.[9]

To flesh this out with an example, imagine that P_1 and P_2 are complex neurological properties of your brain, that H_1 is your wanting a pickled egg and believing that there is a pickled egg in the jar, and H_2 is your forming an intention to open the jar. In what sense do your belief and desire cause your intention? The causal work is apparently done by neurological states: in this instance, your brain's possessing P_1 and P_2. This would seem to make your belief and desire, not to mention your intention, epiphenomenal.

Your belief, desire, and intention could be epiphenomenal, however, only if they existed apart from your neurological condition, which they do not. This is not an identity theory. There is no prospect of reducing talk of beliefs, desires, or intentions to neurological talk. Nor is 'type identity' in the cards. Nevertheless, the truth-makers for mental predicates ('is a belief', 'is a desire', 'is an intention', for instance) include a range of dispositionally similar neurological conditions. On this occasion, it is true in virtue of your being in state P_1 that you have these beliefs and desires, and it is true, by virtue of your being in P_2, that you have this intention. It is true, as well, that your belief and desire caused you to form the intention, true in virtue of P_1's causing P_2.

We can accommodate what might be called higher-level causation, then, so long as this is not construed as a relation involving higher-level

---

[9] John Carroll asks: does this imply that H_1 causes P_2? You could say this, perhaps, but it is apt to create confusion. In general, it is conversationally awkward to mix higher- and lower-level predicates in this way.

properties. Higher-level causal claims are grounded in causal occurrences involving the truth-makers for higher-level predicates. You will think this makes higher-level items—beliefs and desires, for instance—epiphenomenal only if you imagine that realism about beliefs and desires requires that these subsist 'over and above' their 'lower-level' truth-makers. If, as I have argued, this is a mistake, we can make sense of our unselfconscious deployment of higher-level predicates in the identification of causes and effects and in the formulation of causal generalizations of the sort familiar in everyday life and in the special sciences.

5.5 Kinds

Thus far I have more or less ignored a distinction of considerable traditional significance. Consider the predications

(*a*) 'is a horse'
(*b*) 'is red'

Terms of the former kind, substantival or sortal terms, purport to designate kinds of individual object. Predicates of the latter sort, characterizing predicates, are used to characterize individuals. In the usual case, sortal terms are thought to pick out countable objects with determinate identity and persistence conditions. If α is a horse and β is a horse, there is some specifiable fact of the matter as to whether α and β are one and the same horse or distinct horses. Further, when horses are present in the paddock, there is some fact as to *how many* horses are present in the paddock.[10]

The application of characterizing predicates like 'is red', in contrast, appears to involve neither identity conditions nor countability. The redness of this ball is no doubt distinct from the redness of the surface on which the ball rests, but the identity of the two instances of redness cannot be separated from the identity of their possessors. We can count the instances only by counting the objects.

---

[10] E. J. Lowe (1998: ch. 3) notes that some individuals—parts of a homogeneous stuff, for instance—possess definite identity conditions but are uncountable, and some—electrons in superposition—are countable but apparently lack determinate identity conditions. For simplicity I ignore these possibilities here.

The argument in the preceding sections was intended to capture the idea that characterizing predicates can truly and literally apply to objects even though those objects do not share a property in virtue of which the predicates apply. It is in virtue of objects' properties that the predicates apply, but significant predicates need not pick out a unique property common to all objects to which they apply (and to no others). How, if at all, does this kind of argument extend to sortals?

One possibility is that the distinction among kinds of predicate does not reflect a distinction in reality. Thus, 'is a horse' might be thought to function, as 'is red' does, by applying to objects by virtue of those objects' possessing appropriate properties, those required for an object to count as a horse. This need not be taken to imply that 'is a horse' designates a single property possessed by every horse and by nothing else. Like 'is red', 'is a horse', while not designating a unique property, being a horse, might hold of objects by virtue of those objects' possessing any of a range of imperfectly similar complex properties. If this is right, then the argument bearing on characterizing predicates general-izes smoothly to substantival terms.

A view of this kind is controversial, however. Many philosophers believe that semantic differences between sortal and characterizing expressions mirror real differences in the world.[11] Thus, 'is a horse' is satisfied, not by properties possessed by particular objects, but by sub-stances of particular *kinds*.[12]

The point can be illustrated by appeal to a familiar example. Think of a statue and the lump of bronze of which it is composed. One pos-sibility is that 'is a statue' is, in reality, a characterizing predicate. For something—this lump of bronze—to be a statue is for it to possess a certain property: being statue shaped. Against this is the idea that statues have distinctive identity conditions that oblige us to distinguish sharply between lumps of bronze and statues made up of these lumps.[13]

---

[11] See Lowe (1989, 1998); Ellis (2001).

[12] If you believe in universals, then you might take predicates like 'is a horse' to pick out kind universals (as distinct from characterizing universals).

[13] One line of reasoning to this conclusion involves an application of Leibniz's Law and an appeal to 'modal properties'. If α and β differ in their properties, then α cannot be identical with β. The statue and the lump of bronze have different 'modal properties,' however: on the one hand, the lump of bronze could be moulded into an entirely different shape, but in so doing, the statue would cease exist; on the other hand, bits of the bronze making up the statue could be replaced and the statue, but not the lump, survive. The idea here is that, although a statue and a lump of bronze could coincide spatially (and even temporally if the lump's existence coincides with that of the statue), they cannot be identified. See Ch. 16.

Suppose this were so for sortal terms generally. What follows? Here is one possibility: if you are a realist about statues (or horses), then you must suppose that 'is a statue' ('is a horse') applies to objects distinct from portions of matter that make up statues (horses). These might be higher-level objects, distinct from but spatially coincident with the portions of matter that make them up. Reductionism affords another option. You are a reductionist about statues, for instance, if you think that talk about statues could be analysed into talk about lumps of bronze: statues just *are* statue-shaped lumps of matter.[14] Given the incommensurabilty of identity conditions for statues and lumps of bronze, however, the prospects for analytical reduction appear bleak. This brings us to a third possibility: eliminativism. Eliminativists hold that there are no statues but at most statue-shaped lumps of bronze.

The moral of our reflections on characterizing predicates like 'is red' was that the conviction that these options exhaust those available to us arises from a tacit acceptance of the Picture Theory. Just as the idea that, if 'is red' holds of an object, it must designate a property possessed by that object and shared by every red object, so the idea that, if 'is a statue' holds of an object, it must designate an instance of a distinctive kind of substance that is either identifiable with or distinct from whatever makes it up. In leaving the Picture Theory behind, we open up another possibility: talk of statues, although not analytically reducible to talk of lumps of bronze, nevertheless truly applies to particular lumps in virtue of those lumps' possession of certain properties (and perhaps in virtue of the causal histories of those lumps). Statues exist: 'is a statue' holds truly and literally of certain objects, and it holds in virtue of properties possessed by those objects (and perhaps relations in which those objects figure). This is not an eliminativist thesis, let alone a version of reductionism or relativism, but an attempt to tell the deep story about statues.

I shall have more to say about such cases in Chapter 16. Meanwhile, I should like to indicate a provisional moral (one that fits neatly with earlier observations on characterizing predicates): realism about statues, human beings, and horses—the idea that 'is a statue', 'is a human being', 'is a horse' are literally and truly applicable to particular

---

[14] An analytical route could be semantic or conceptual in accord with traditional analytical techniques or something weaker: a specification of necessary and sufficient conditions for the application of a higher-level expression in exclusively lower-level terms.

objects—need not require either that statues are higher-level entities or that talk of statues be linked analytically to truth-makers for such talk.

5.6 Life without Levels

Words serve many purposes. Among these purposes are the marking of salient similarities and differences we find around us. We do not 'carve up' the world in the sense of manufacturing divisions where none previously existed, but we do commemorate boundaries that, for us, stand out. Which boundaries are salient depends on the world and, importantly, on features of us: our nature, and our interests. These features are not static. They can shift and evolve as our interests shift and evolve. The philosophical mistake is to imagine that sameness of word implies sameness of worldly correspondent. This is rarely so. Concepts, and words used to express these, are in most cases satisfied by endless *similar* things; and similarity grades off imperceptibly into dissimilarity.

Once we appreciate this, we are faced with a choice. We can deny that our words apply literally to the world: there are no human beings, tables, trees, stones, galaxies. Or we can turn away from a conception of language that drives this impulse and admit that there are tables, trees, stones, and galaxies, but resist the idea that these are what some philosophers say they must be. On the view I am recommending, we grant that there are tables, for instance (we are realists about tables), but not that being a table must be a matter of there being entities, either identical with collections of particles that make them up or something 'over and above' those collections, answering to the sortal predicate 'is a table'.[15] Similarly, we can be realists about colours—we can accept that objects really are red, for instance—without imagining that there is some one property, being red, possessed by every red object and in virtue of which these satisfy the predicate 'is red'.

Where does all this leave the notion of levels of reality? Here is one possibility. Reality has but one level—or, if the idea that reality has one level encourages the idea that it might have more, there are no levels of reality. We do not need levels to be realists about states of mind, trees,

---

[15] See §16.9. The position I am endorsing here is close to Locke's—as I read Locke.

statues, and people. We do not need a commitment to ontological levels to accommodate irreducible, projectable predicates definitive of everyday domains and those of the special sciences. We may find it occasionally useful to speak of levels of description or explanation, but these must not be confused with levels of being or promote the image of a layered world. I have a suspicion that this is all non-philosophers have in mind when they appeal to levels. The philosophical emendation abetted by the Picture Theory has rendered difficult problems in the philosophy of mind and elsewhere *more* difficult. Philosophy is hard enough as it is.

CHAPTER 6
Philosophical Analysis

6.1 The Analytical Project

Philosophers, and only philosophers, believe that it is possible to discover deep truths about the world purely by the analysis of concepts. No doubt the concepts we deploy are unlikely to have survived unless they were largely apt: they mark significant divisions in our world. What is not obvious is that this implies anything like the analytical principle (A):

(A) (Where Gs are presumed to be uncontroversial items—those posited by the physical sciences, for instance—and Fs are putatively higher-level items) if talk of Fs cannot be analysed, paraphrased, wholly decomposed into talk of Gs, either Fs are distinct from Gs or there are no Fs.[1]

We cannot analyse, paraphrase, or decompose talk of statues into talk of collections of particles, so statues must either be something distinct from the particles or non-existent. The idea is illustrated in Figure 6.1.

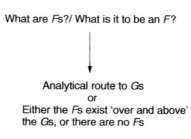

What are Fs?/ What is it to be an F?

Analytical route to Gs
or
Either the Fs exist 'over and above'
the Gs, or there are no Fs

Figure 6.1. The analytical problem

---

[1] Or Fs exist only as 'fictions', an option I shall not consider here.

Figure 6.2. Berkeleyan analysis

The thought encompassed by (A) has a long history. Pretend for a moment that Berkeley was right: although we can be confident that minds and their contents exist, we have reason to doubt the existence of mind-independent material objects. We can take the sting out of this discovery by showing that everything we might want to say about material objects can be analysed into talk of states of mind: ideas or 'sense data' (Figure 6.2). Analysis seems to reveal the real nature of material objects as being purely mental.

All this could be put more generally. Imagine that we are impressed by a particular domain of entities—Berkeleyan ideas, for instance, or material objects, or items posited by basic physics, or points in space–time. These are the Gs. Relative to entities in this favoured realm, entities in some other domain, the Fs, come to be contested. The contested domain might include, as in the example above, material objects generally; or it might be the domain of ordinary middle-sized material objects; or it might be the domain of numbers or sets. We can ask whether entities in the contested domain, the Fs, are reducible to entities in the favoured domain, the Gs, where reduction is understood as an analytical procedure: a process yielding, perhaps, what Katherine Elgin calls 'chains of definability', or at any rate necessary and sufficient conditions for contested facts in terms of facts of the favoured kind (Elgin 1995). The question we take ourselves to be asking is whether Fs exist 'over and above' the favoured entities. If reducibility is not in the cards, we must choose between outright eliminativism—there are no Fs—or realism—Fs exist in addition to, 'over and above', Gs.

We move in this way to a particular conception of realism, one that has obvious affinities with Principle (Φ) (§3.3). In so doing, we saddle realism with an ontological model that falls out of the Picture Theory.

Ought we to accept (A) and the options (depicted in Figure 6.3) springing from (A)? Suppose God sets out to create a world containing statues. God can accomplish this by creating the particles and placing

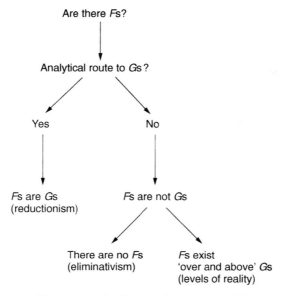

Figure 6.3. Realism on the levels model

them in the right relations to one another.[2] The creation of a single statue could well require the creation of a dynamic arrangement of particles extending over time and incorporating a vast spatial region. Perhaps statues require the existence of intelligent agents with particular kinds of thought. In that case, additional dynamic collections of particles with similarly extended spatial and temporal relations must be added to the mix. There is little or no prospect of a systematic mapping between talk of statues and talk of collections of particles. But it need not follow either that, *in addition to* the particles, the universe contains statues, or that there are no statues.

I am inclined to think that 'this is a statue' can be, and often is, literally true. What makes it true is a complex, dynamic arrangement of particles. A statue's boundaries are, at the particle level, fuzzy. The collection of particles that we might regard as *making up* the statue at a given time can gain and lose member particles over time. We cannot hope to paraphrase, translate, or replace talk of statues with talk of such collections. Even so, it seems clear that, with few exceptions, objects like statues that populate our everyday surroundings owe their

---

[2] I use 'particle' as a placeholder for whatever the ultimate constituents of reality turn out to be. I recognize, though barely, the possibility that nothing is ultimate; see §15.5.

existence to arrangements of more ultimate constituents. We deploy predicates like 'is a statue' to mark off salient features of the world. These features are grounded in properties and arrangements of the fundamental constituents. Their salience is due in part to those properties and arrangements and in part to properties of us *qua* interested observers.[3] (I shall have more to say on this topic in Chapter 16.)

Are statues, then, to be identified with collections of particles? This is not my contention. A statue, at a particular time, is made up of a collection of particles. For these particles to make up a statue, however, they must stand in the right relations to particles that are not parts of the statue. This would be so, for instance, if statues require sculptors. Without these other particles, there would be no statue. This suggests that a statue might be identified with a collection of particles that stand in appropriate relations to other particles. But, of course, particles in the collection can come and go, destroying the collection, but not the statue. Because I reject (A), I see no reason to think that this either casts doubt on the existence of statues or obliges us to regard statues as 'higher-level' entities.

Ontological reduction need not imply analytical or conceptual reduction. The idea that it does, together with the well-supported conviction that such reductions mostly fail, fuels, on the one hand, the view that our world includes levels of objects, properties, and kinds, and, on the other hand, the more daring idea that the world includes *only* the atoms and the void: tables, chairs, human beings, and galaxies do not exist.

6.2 Truth Making and Entailment

I have hypothesized that a conception of the world as including levels of being is traceable, at least in part, to our acceptance of a Picture Theory of language. The Picture Theory (as I am thinking of it) includes a correspondence principle that licenses our 'reading off' features of the world from features of our language (or from features of our language suitably regimented).

I have spoken glibly of truth making and truth-makers. The idea is

---

[3] This is not to locate the observer outside the world. On the contrary, observers themselves owe their nature to the character of the fundamental constituents.

that, when sentences, or utterances, or thoughts, or representations generally hold true of the world, they do so in virtue of ways the world is. If we are not careful, this pleasantly vague idea can issue in Principle (Φ); and Principle (Φ) might be taken to sanction claims of the form

(T) '*a* is *F*' is true if and only if *a* is *F*.

Such claims strike philosophers as innocuous. I am not so sure. C. B. Martin has pointed out, the biconditional read right-to-left appears to imply that for every way the world is there corresponds a truth-bearer—a sentence, for instance. This seems unlikely (see §7.6).

More to the point, the idea that we can explain truth making in terms of entailment (truth-makers *entail* truths) is ill considered. Suppose we think of *ways the world is* as truth-makers for ordinary empirical assertions. The Moon's being roughly spherical might be a truth-maker for 'The Moon is roughly spherical'. It is hard to see how the Moon's being roughly spherical could *entail* anything. The Moon's being roughly spherical belongs to the wrong category. Entailment is a relation holding among representations or statements of particular sorts. If there is entailing here, it is tied to a statement or representation of the Moon's being roughly spherical. And, of course, 'The Moon is roughly spherical' *does* entail 'The Moon is roughly spherical'.

I do not have a positive account of truth making, but I can say with some assurance what truth making is not. Truth making is not entailment. Nor can we explain truth making by a simple correspondence model. If '*a* is *F*' is true, this need not be because there is some entity corresponding to *a*, some property corresponding to *F*, and the entity, *a*, possesses the property *F*. Consider 'This tomato is poisonous' (said of a particular tomato on a particular occasion). The truth-maker for this assertion could be a complex, spatially and temporally extended state of affairs including untold numbers of particles standing in complex relations. I see no hope of translating talk of tomatoes into talk of arrangements of particles, much less of translating talk about the tomato's toxicity into talk of properties of particles and their arrangements. Many different kinds of particle arrangement could answer to 'is a tomato'; and many different properties satisfy the predicate 'is poisonous'. If we are serious about entailment, we will reject *both* the idea that the truth-maker for 'The tomato is poisonous' entails this sentence, or indeed anything at all, *and* the idea that there must be a description of the truth-maker couched in terms of particle arrangements that entails 'The tomato is poisonous'.

Pressure to countenance levels of reality—levels of being—issues from the idea that whatever serves as truth-maker for various assertions must bear an appropriate logical relation to those assertions. Thus, if 'The tomato is poisonous' is true in virtue of the existence of a complex, spatially and temporally extended arrangement of particles, then it must be possible to translate or analyse talk of tomatoes into talk of particles and their arrangements—otherwise there is no entailment. This is what I am questioning. The moves here, though largely unacknowledged, are founded on a misguided conception of the relation of language to the world: a correspondence conception that we have no good reason to accept.[4] (I shall discuss truth making at greater length in Chapter 7.)

6.3 Absolutism, Eliminativism, Relativism

In a discussion of Hilary Putnam's 'pragmatic realism', Ernest Sosa suggests that, in considering the world and its furniture, we appear to be faced with a choice among three alternatives: eliminativism, absolutism, and conceptual relativism (Sosa 1993). An eliminativist holds that reference to human beings, tables, trees, and galaxies is at best 'fictional' and at worst empty; an absolutist affirms the existence of all such things, and many more as well; a conceptual relativist regards objects as existing only 'relative to' a language or conceptual scheme. You can think of the absolutist as a devotee of levels of being. Where an absolutist sees statues, an eliminativist sees only clouds of particles and a relativist sees statues existing relative to our language or scheme. Figure 6.4 provides a schematic representation of the possibilities open to us.

As Figure 6.4 makes evident, Putnam's view of the territory involves the Picture Theory no less than the views of his opponents. Putnam inveighs against what he calls 'metaphysical realism', favouring a 'realism' relativized to 'conceptual schemes': 'internal' (or 'pragmatic') realism. I do not pretend to have a clear conception of what internal realism involves, beyond the fact that it is pretty clearly a form of *anti-*

---

[4] This evidently puts me at odds with Frank Jackson and David Chalmers (Jackson 1998; Chalmers and Jackson 2001).

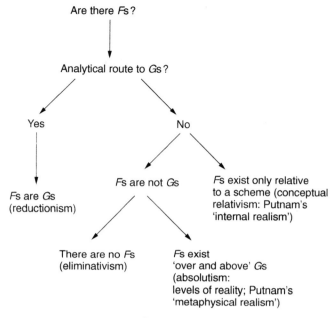

Figure 6.4. Realism according to Putnam

realism, one that makes worldly goings-on mind dependent by making them hostage to 'conceptual schemes' deployed by intelligent agents.[5] I see no reason to embrace internal realism. I have said enough to make it clear that I reject Putnam's metaphysical realism as well. Does this make me an anti-realist?

It would, only if Putnam's options were our only options. Imagine someone who regards the world as comprising dynamic arrangements of particles. These particles possess distinctive properties. Particle complexes exhibit characteristics that stand in an unmysterious relation to properties of their constituents so arranged. Some of these complexes and some of their properties are salient to us as observers and manipulators. These we mark off with concepts expressed by predicates in our language. The concepts and predicates we deploy typically reflect perfectly genuine similarities and differences. In most cases, these similarities and differences do not depend on us, or on our concepts, or predicates included in our language. The bulk of our predicates and the

---

[5] Beware of philosophers defending *kinds* of realism.

concepts they express are in some degree vague or non-specific: the similarities they measure are imperfect; the differences they circumscribe are not sharp. It would be misguided to try to read off from our predicates or concepts hard-edged features of the world; and it would be no less misguided to try to reconstruct those predicates and concepts from descriptions of the basic items, their properties, and their relations.

Someone who thought all this might think, as well, that, while our predicates or concepts often apply—literally and truly—to the world, this need not be taken to imply that these predicates and concepts designate properties shared by everything to which they literally and truly apply. Nor need this be thought to turn familiar objects—tables, trees, human beings, galaxies—into mere shadows cast by the corresponding concepts.

A view of this kind seems not to fit comfortably into Putnam's scheme. It is not a form of eliminativism or anti-realism; it does not imply, as metaphysical realism ('absolutism') is said to imply, a wild proliferation of entities or levels of being; and it does not relativize objects to languages or conceptual schemes. The thought that we must choose from among eliminativism, absolutism, and conceptual relativism depends on a tacit acceptance of a Picture Theory of language. *Given* a Picture Theory, we must find an object, kind, or property corresponding to every significant predicate. This leads in the direction of a layered ontology. When the objects, kinds, and properties prove elusive, we are compelled to choose between eliminativism or relativism. In abandoning the Picture Theory, we are no longer obliged to choose from among these unpalatable isms. We can opt instead for that most maligned of isms: realism.

6.4 Anti-Realism and Ontology

While we are on the topic of realism, it is worth mentioning that anti-realists, too, must be realists (see Martin 1993; Heil 1998*b*). Recall Berkeley's anti-realism about material bodies. Berkeley offers a reductive argument designed to show that talk of material entities could be replaced by talk of ideas—states of mind. The conclusion—that there are no material bodies, only minds and their contents—can be understood as committing Berkeley to an anti-realism about material bodies but a realism about minds and their contents.

If you think of realism about *Fs* as a view according to which *Fs* exist 'mind independently', then Berkeley holds that minds and their contents exist mind independently. This sounds paradoxical. How could minds be mind independent? I believe that what philosophers intend when they hold that objects or properties of objects are mind independent is that these objects or properties are what they are independently of how we might take them to be. Alternatively, a truth, *T*, is mind independent only if *T* is logically (or metaphysically) independent of our believing (or, more generally, taking) *T* to be the case. This leaves open, as it should, the possibility that truths about the world could depend in some other way on minds or their contents. God might form the intention to extinguish the universe when the last conscious being expires. Were that so, the world would be causally dependent on minds; nevertheless the world (or a significant portion of it) would be mind independent in the sense that there is no contradiction in supposing that the world might continue to exist even in the absence of conscious observers.

These points suggest an interesting, largely unremarked standpoint from which to evaluate strains of anti-realism (Martin 1993). Consider an extreme case. Suppose you thought, as some literary theorists apparently have thought, that the world around us is dependent on our theories about it.[6] If you think this, you are, presumably, a realist about theories: if the world is somehow theory dependent, this implies, on pain of regress, that *theories* are not theory dependent. But what then are *theories*? If theories 'carve up' the world, do theories themselves come pre-carved? At the very least, proponents of such a view owe us an account of their ontology. Are theories utterances? Sentences? Thoughts? What is the presumed ontology of these entities? And why should that ontology be unproblematic if the ontology of tables, trees, galaxies, and electrons is iffy?

Anti-realists would like to leave the impression that they are above the metaphysical fray. If you imagine that there is no theory-independent ontology, however, you incur an obligation to provide some account of the ontology of theories. If you think theories

---

[6] Terry Eagleton (1983) provides a readable and sympathetic account of the historical development of contemporary literary theory.

themselves are exempt from strictures on theory dependence, you should be prepared to say what it is about theories that allows them to exist unconditionally. If you go all out—'theories all the way down'—you owe us an explanation of how such a view avoids a vicious regress.

These remarks are not intended as decisive refutations of modern-day forms of anti-realism about the world around us. My aim, rather, has been merely to note that anti-realists must be held accountable for the ontological implications of their views. We must insist on what the Australians call *ontological candour*. Berkeley is clear on the matter. So, in general, are anti-realists about value. The same cannot be said for latter-day anti-realists fond of regarding the world as a linguistic or theo-retical construct. Such theorists hold ontology in disdain, regarding metaphysics generally as belonging to an outmoded philosophical style. There is no evading ontology, however. If you make bold to claim that the world is not as it seems, you are obliged to say what constitutes the seemings.

These observations would strike non-philosophers as obvious. If the world is theory, what is theory? The innocent question ought to give pause to anyone reflecting on any of the more extreme varieties of anti-realism. It is prima facie crazy, for instance, to regard with suspi-cion the independent existence of stones, trees, electrons, and the like while remaining sanguine about the existence of sentences expressing theories. Why should sentences—or whatever vehicles for theories are envisioned—occupy a privileged position in the scheme of things? Here, anti-realists may find it attractive to locate theories in minds and so throw their lot in with Berkeley. In that case, at least, their cards are on the table.

Talk of realism and anti-realism brings us back to the notion of truth and truth making. I have said that truths, or at any rate some of the truths, have truth-makers; I have cast doubt to the thesis that truth making can be understood in terms of entailment. What more can be said about truth making? This is the question to which I shall now turn.

CHAPTER 7
Truth Making

7.1 The Need for Truth-Makers

In the 1950s, C. B. Martin advanced a truth-maker principle that captures a central tenet of realism: when a statement concerning the world is true, there must be something about the world that makes it true.[1] Martin's idea was that there are no 'bare truths'. If the utterance 'There is a tree in the quad' is true, there must be something about the world in virtue of which it is true, in this case a tree's being in the quad. You might have doubts about trees and quads. Perhaps the statement is true because a certain pattern of ideas is implanted in minds by God. This would not show that the statement lacked a truth-maker, however, only that its truth-maker was something immaterial.

The motivation for a truth-maker requirement is easy to understand. Consider Ryle's contention that certain descriptions could hold true of objects without there being anything about those objects in virtue of which the descriptions held. In discussing dispositions, for instance, Ryle asserts that it could be true that an agent is disposed to perform some particular action even though there is nothing about the agent in virtue of which he is so disposed: 'Dispositional statements are neither reports of observed or observable states of affairs, nor yet reports of unobserved or unobservable states of affairs' (Ryle 1949: 120). Such statements do not answer to features of the world, but instead function as 'inference tickets' to 'license inferences'. If I discover that you know Ancient Greek, I am entitled to believe that you could read or translate Greek sentences. This entitlement is not grounded in your mental or physical make-up, however: there is nothing about you, no feature of your mind or brain, for instance, in virtue of which it is

---

: See Armstrong (1997: 2); Jackson (1998: 16 n. 18).

true that you could read or translate Greek sentences. A salt crystal is disposed to dissolve in water: it is true of the crystal that, were you to place it in water, it would dissolve. There is, however, nothing about the salt crystal in virtue of which it is true that it would dissolve were it placed in water.

7.2 What Truth Making Is Not

Nowadays, few philosophers would be willing to endorse Ryle's conception of dispositionality. A large measure of the resistance issues from an implicit commitment to a truth-maker principle: if a statement concerning the world is true, there must be something about the world in virtue of which it is true. But how are we to understand truth making? In describing the truth-maker thesis, I have relied on phrases like 'in virtue of' and 'because' ('There is a tree in the quad' is true because/in virtue of a tree's being in the quad). What exactly is this because/in virtue of relation? One possibility is that truth making is explicable in terms of entailment.

This is the line taken, for instance, by John Bigelow, who follows John Fox in regarding truth making as entailment: truth-makers logically entail truth-bearers.[2] According to Bigelow, 'Whenever something is true, there must be something whose existence entails that it is true. The "making" in "making true" is essentially logical entailment' (1988: 125).

Suppose there to be something which is proposed as a truthmaker for some truth. And suppose it is admitted that the existence of that thing does not entail the truth in question. This means that it is logically possible for that thing still to exist, even if what is actually true had not been true. In the actual world, *a* exists and *A* is true, say; but in some other possible world *a* might still exist, even though *A* is not true. There must surely be some difference between these two possible worlds! So there must be something in one of these worlds which is lacking in the other, and which accounts for this difference in truth. [. . .] If something is true, then *there must be*, that is to say there must *exist*, something which makes the actual world different from how it would have been if this had not been true.   (1988: 126)

---

[2] See Bigelow (1988); see also Mulligan et al. (1984); Fox (1987); Armstrong (1997: ch. 8). Bigelow is concerned to defend what he calls the Truthmaker Axiom.

Let me note in passing a problem for any view according to which, if α is a truth-maker for A, the existence of α necessitates the truth of A. Take the assertion

(P) 'If you drank this cyanide-laced tea, you would die.'

Suppose (P) is true in virtue of some object or fact, α: the existence of a particular cup of cyanide-laced tea perhaps (or this together with your physical make-up and laws of nature). Could we imagine a world that included α, but in which (P) was false?

Think of a world that included the cyanide-laced cup of tea but included, in addition, your having in hand an antidote. In that case, (P) could be false despite the presence of α, the object or fact that might be thought to serve as (P)'s truth-maker in the actual world. More generally, an assertion, A, might fail to hold, not because α is absent, but because α is accompanied by a defeater.

Difficulties of this kind threaten a particular formulation of the truth-maker idea, but not the idea itself. They pose no threat to what I take to be Bigelow's fundamental thesis: if an assertion is true in one situation and false in another, the situations must differ in some way. There is, however, a deeper and more interesting problem for anyone who, like Bigelow, hopes to spell out truth making in terms of logical entailment.

Suppose the pillar box's being pillar-box red is the truth-maker for 'The pillar box is pillar box red'. As we saw in Chapter 6, a state of affairs like the pillar-box's being pillar-box red does not logically entail anything. Both the pillar box and the pillar box's being pillar-box red belong to the wrong category. Bigelow sees the difficulty. Entailment, he notes, is 'a relation between propositions'. The truth-making relation, then, 'should not be construed as saying that an object entails a truth; rather, it requires that the proposition *that an object exists* entails the truth in question' (1988: 126).

As Bigelow says, entailment is a relation holding among 'propositions' or, less mysteriously, among certain kinds of representation. You might doubt this.[3] You might regard entailment as a kind of necessitation relation that could hold between objects, facts, or states of affairs and truth-bearing representations. The relation would mirror

[3] As Michaelis Michael reminded me.

entailment relations among propositions or assertions. Suppose α is some object, fact, or state of affairs—some truth-maker—and suppose A is an assertion made true by α. Now, α entails A in the sense that α's obtaining or being the case necessitates the truth of A: α could not obtain or be the case if A were false.

It is hard to know what to make of this kind of necessitation: a relation putatively holding between non-representational items and truth values of representations. A plausible rendition of a notion of entailment according to which the obtaining of α would entail the truth of A, one that did not run afoul of cases of the sort illustrated by the cyanide-laced tea example, would amount to a restatement (rather than explication) of the truth-making relation.

One possibility is that claims of the form 'α entails the truth of A' (when α is some non-representational object, fact, or state of affairs and A is a representation) should be understood as asserting that a description of α, or an assertion that α exists, could not be true unless A were true.[4] This is Bigelow's idea, and it is what most philosophers seem to have in mind when they invoke entailment in these contexts.[5]

Suppose then, as Bigelow suggests, that allowing that an object, fact, or state of affairs entails the truth of some assertion is just to allow that a representation of that object, fact, or state of affairs logically entails the truth of the assertion in question. If you thought that 'The pillar box is pillar-box red' were entailed by its truth-maker, then, you would be regarding the truth-maker representationally. Bigelow puts this by saying that a truth is entailed by 'the proposition' that the truth-maker exists. But you will want this proposition to be accurate; you will want it to be true! Now it looks as though we have made no progress in explicating truth making.

Quite generally it is hard to see how an account of truth making that invokes propositions as intermediaries between truth-makers and truth-bearers could be thought illuminating. The mediating propositions themselves require truth-makers. Are these mediating propositions made true by virtue of being logically entailed by further

---

[4] Note that α might itself be a representational item. In that case, α's existence, not its representational content, would be taken to occupy the left side of the entailment relation. Your thinking 'I exist' might be thought in this sense to entail your existence quite independently of the significance of that thought.

[5] See e.g. Jackson (1998: 4, 24, 25). For Jackson, a complete description (or 'story') of the world couched in a basic-level vocabulary is what does the entailing (1998: 26–7).

mediating propositions? If so, we have explained nothing; if not, we seem committed to an account of truth making that does not involve entailment. If we have such an account, why not employ it in the first instance? The problem of spelling out the relation between propositions thought to entail truths, and truth-makers answering to these propositions, looks like the original problem all over again.

An appeal to propositions in this context yields at least three problems: (1) the problem of providing an account of propositions consistent with their satisfying their presumed job description; (2) the problem of providing an account of the relation propositions bear to assertions expressing them; (3) the problem of explicating the relation propositions bear to whatever it is that answers to them. Problem (3) is indistinguishable from the truth-maker problem an appeal to propositions was supposed to help solve.

7.3 A Legacy of the Picture Theory

Suppose you regarded these difficulties as negligible. Suppose you persisted in thinking of truth-makers propositionally, imagining that there is an especially intimate relation between a truth-maker for a given truth and the proposition expressing that truth-maker (and entailing the truth). Perhaps the proposition and the truth-maker have the same structure. You might then find it natural to let the proposition 'go proxy for' the truth-maker, replacing talk of the truth-maker with talk of the proposition expressing it (see §1.6). This, I submit, is one more legacy of the Picture Theory.

Assuming that propositions are kinds of representation, it is easy to see how a proposition might logically entail another representation. Trivially, the proposition expressed by 'The beaker contains water' entails 'The beaker contains water'. Similarly, the proposition expressed by 'The beaker contains water' entails 'The beaker contains water or Snoopy is a cat'. The proposition expressed by 'The beaker contains water' might be said to entail as well 'The beaker contains a liquid'. This would be so if an analysis of the concept of water included the concept of liquidity. If you thought of truth making in this way, you might easily be led to the idea that there must be an analytical path between truth-bearer and truth-maker: it must be possible to analyse a given truth-bearer and its corresponding truth-maker in such a way that the truth-maker (more accurately: the proposition that the truth-maker exists) could be seen to include the truth-bearer. This is just the Picture Theory in another of its many guises.

Let me elaborate this last point. Suppose you want to know what the truth-maker for 'Gus is in pain' is. Whatever it is, if truth making is entailment, it will have to entail 'Gus is in pain'. Could the truth-maker be Gus's being in a particular neurological condition? (Could it be true that Gus is in pain in virtue of Gus's possessing some complex neuro-logical property?) Not unless Gus's neurological condition—or, rather, the proposition that this neurological condition exists—entails 'Gus is in pain'. But the entailment could be shown to hold only if 'Gus is in pain' could be analysed in such a way that it could be seen to be included in a fully explicit description of that neurological condition. This is what I meant by saying that this account of truth making requires an analytical path from truth-bearer to truth-maker.

Suppose further, as seems likely, that there is no prospect of analysing talk of pain into talk of neurological conditions or properties. If you insist that truth making is a matter of entailment, you will look else-where for a truth-maker for 'Gus is in pain'.[6] Perhaps Gus's being in pain is not a matter of Gus's possessing some complex neurological property, but Gus's possessing some 'higher-level' property, distinct from, but realized by, Gus's neurological condition. Gus's possession of this higher-level property, or rather the proposition that it is possessed by Gus, will entail 'Gus is in pain'. The higher-level property will, of course, be the pain property. There is no distance at all between this property, or a proposition ascribing it to Gus, and 'Gus is in pain'.

Were you to follow this course, you would be obliged to provide an account of the relation this higher-level property bears to its lower-level realizers. If you are like most philosophers who move in these circles, you might regard this as a mere detail. You will see realism about pain, together with the idea that truth making is entailment as imply-ing that the pain property exists and is distinct from whatever realizes it. You are well on your way to a hierarchical ontology incorporating levels of reality.

---

[6] If you are a certain kind of hard-nosed philosopher, you might regard this as evidence that there are no pains.

7.4 Supervenience

We would, I believe, do better to give up the idea that we can 'read off' features of reality from ways in which we represent reality—the Picture Theory—and with it the idea of truth making as entailment. If we did so (I claim), the currently popular conception of reality as comprising a hierarchy of levels would lose its aura of inevitability. If there are levels, these are levels of complexity or organization or, alternatively, levels of description or explanation, not levels of being. Truth-makers for statements at whatever level are first-order ways the world is (see Heil 1998a: ch. 6; 1999). I have no positive account of truth making to offer. I am doubtful that it is possible to explicate truth making in an illuminating way—that is, in a way that employs simpler, clearer concepts.

Perhaps this is overly pessimistic. Bigelow suggests that we might explicate truth making by invoking the concept of supervenience. 'The essence of Truthmaker, I urge, is the idea that truth is supervenient on being: that you could not have any difference in what things are true unless there were some difference in what things exist' (1988: 132). Bigelow speaks of supervenience as 'a very productive notion'; I am not so sure (1988: 132).[7] My reservations could be put in terms of the truth-making requirement. Supervenience is a modal concept. If As supervene on Bs, then the question is: what is it in virtue of which this is so? What is the truth-maker for the supervenience claim? If all we know is that As supervene on Bs, we know only that As covary with Bs. This could be so because As are Bs, for instance, or because Bs cause As (or As and Bs have some common cause), or because As are made up of Bs. Unless we can say something about what grounds the supervenience claim, an invocation of supervenience does little more than reformulate the truth-maker principle.[8]

---

[7] This point was originally impressed on me by Brian McLaughlin. It is discussed in Blackburn (1984: 186); Kim (1990); Horgan (1993: esp. §8); Heil (1998a); and §4.4 above. Note that you could accept Bigelow's supervenience claim without thereby embracing the further thesis that truth making is entailment.

[8] Bigelow goes on to discuss in detail what might constitute truth-makers for claims about the world, broadly construed. Some candidates: facts or states of affairs, aggregates of universals and particulars, property instances. Bigelow points out that each of these options exacts a price.

7.5 The Totality Fact

A conception of truth making as entailment goes hand in hand with the Picture Theory. According to the Picture Theory, we can 'read off' features of the world from features of linguistic representations of the world (or linguistic representations suitably analysed). This makes it easy to conflate truths about representations and truths about the world: representations (or representations belonging to a certain privileged class of representations) go proxy for the world.[9] Let me illustrate what I have in mind.

Consider two situations:

(A) I have five coins in my pocket.
(B) All I have in my pocket is five coins.

Situations (A) and (B) seem obviously to differ. The first, but not the second, would obtain if I had seven coins in my pocket or if I had five coins and a button. Considerations of this sort have led philosophers to argue for the existence of a 'totality fact'.[10] The fact that all my pocket contains is five coins is in reality a complex fact made up of two facts: (1) the fact that I have five coins in my pocket and (2) the fact that this is all I have in my pocket. This second fact is taken to be an additional fact, something distinct from the fact that I have five coins in my pocket.

You will think complex facts of this kind are needed to serve as truth-makers for statements like (B) above if you conceive of truth making as entailment. Here is Armstrong discussing the world as a whole (and substituting 'states of affairs' for 'facts'):

If it is true that a certain conjunction of states of affairs is all the states of affairs, then this is only true because there are no more of them. If there are more, then the proposition is not true. That there are no more of them must then somehow be brought into the truthmaker. But to say that there are no more of them is to say that they are *all* the states of affairs. This, then, must be brought within the truthmaker. The truthmaker must be the fact or state of

---

[9] In the *Tractatus*, Wittgenstein says, 'In a picture, the elements of the picture take the place of the objects' (Wittgenstein 1922/1961: §2.131; the translation is my own). A reminder: I leave open whether what I am calling the Picture Theory is what Wittgenstein calls by the same name.

[10] See e.g. Armstrong (1997: ch. 13). David Chalmers dubs the totality fact the 'that's all' fact (1996: 85–6); see also Jackson (1998: 26); Chalmers and Jackson (2001).

affairs that the great conjunction *is* all the states of affairs. (Armstrong 1997: 198)

Thus conceived, the totality fact is a distinctive second-order fact: the fact that these are all the facts. Allowing that the world includes this fact along with all the other facts, enables us to envisage a truth-maker for statements like (B), a description of which entails those statements.

In addition to providing an answer to the question 'What is it in virtue of which these are all the *as*?', the postulation of a totality fact is intended to alleviate the need to introduce negative facts to serve as truth-makers for negative existentials. Consider the true assertion,

(C) There are no buttons in my pocket.

What is the truth-maker for (C)? It cannot, it would seem, be my pocket's containing five coins. My pocket's containing five coins (or a statement to that effect) would not entail that there are no buttons in my pocket. Suppose, however, we add to the fact that there are five coins in my pocket a further fact: the fact that this is all I have in my pocket. Together, these facts (or propositions asserting their existence) entail that there are no buttons in my pocket.

David Chalmers presses this point in defending his special brand of dualism:

Certain facts involving negative existentials and universal quantifiers are not logically determined by the physical facts, or indeed by any set of localized facts. Consider the following facts about our world: there are no angels; Don Bradman is the greatest cricketer; everything alive is based on DNA. All these could be falsified consistent with all the physical facts about our world, simply by the addition of some new nonphysical stuff: cricket-playing angels made of ectoplasm, for instance. [. . .] Does this mean that these facts are not reductively explainable? It seems so insofar as there is no physical explanation of why there is no extra nonphysical stuff in our world. That is indeed a further fact. The best way to deal with this situation is to introduce a second-order fact that says of the set of basic particular facts [. . .]: *That's all.* This fact says that all the basic particular facts about the world are included in or entailed by the given set of facts. (1996: 85–6)[11]

Thus, 'to fix the negative facts, God had to do more than fix the physical facts; he also had to declare, "That's all"' (1996: 41).

---

[11] Evidently, facts speak for themselves.

I contend that the need for a totality or 'that's-all' fact is an artiefact resulting from a tendency to conflate representations of ways the world is and ways the world is. This kind of confusion is abetted by the presumption that truth making is entailment. Although it may be the case that (A) and (B) differ as descriptions, it is less clear this implies that what makes (B) true must thereby differ from what makes (A) true. Suppose my pocket is empty. I pick up a coin and put it in my pocket. I repeat this operation five times and stop. I have put five coins in my pocket. I have also made it the case that my pocket contains five coins and nothing more (hence exactly five coins).

Chalmers holds that 'the facts about the world are exhausted by (1) particular physical facts, (2) facts about conscious experience, (3) laws of nature, (4) a second-order "That's all" fact . . .' (1996: 87).[12] He then invokes a 'creation myth':

Creating the world, all God had to do was fix the facts just mentioned. For maximum economy of effort, he first fixed the laws of nature—the laws of physics and any laws relating physics to conscious experience. Next, he fixed the boundary conditions: perhaps a time-slice of physical facts, and maybe the values in a random-number generator. These combined with the laws to fix the remaining physical and phenomenal facts. Last, he decreed, 'That's all.' (1996: 87)

Suppose God had neglected to decree 'That's all'; suppose God had merely stopped creating (just as I stopped in adding coins to my pocket). Would anything have been left out of the world? Would negative existentials like 'There are no Arctic penguins' lack truth-makers? Would our world differ from an identically produced world over which God *had* intoned 'That's all'?

Although it is undoubtedly true that, in order to describe my pocket's contents as consisting of exactly five coins, I must say that it contains five coins, then add, 'and that's all', it does not follow from this that my pocket's containing exactly five coins is a matter of there being a fact that my pocket contains five coins plus some additional 'that's-all' fact. If there is a 'that's-all' fact, it is no addition of being.[13] When I describe my pocket as containing five coins and when I describe it as

---

[12]   For simplicity, I omit a 'dubious' fifth fact, 'an indexical fact about my location'.

[13]   Differently put: once God stops his act of creation, the 'that's-all' fact 'logically supervenes'. See D. Chalmers (1996: 36, 38, 41); Armstrong (1997: 11–13); Ch. 20 below.

containing exactly five coins, the truth-maker for these descriptions can be one and the same object, fact, or state of affairs. (And this is not because the object, fact, or state of affairs that serves as truth-maker for the latter includes as a proper part or constituent the object, fact, or state of affairs that serves as truth-maker for the former.)

In eschewing a totality fact, must we reintroduce negative facts to serve as truth-makers for negative truths or absences? Consider the absence of Arctic penguins.[14] An exhaustive enumeration of Arctic fauna that omits mention of penguins does not entail that there are no Arctic penguins. Such a description could hold of an Arctic that included penguins. To obtain the entailment, we must supplement our description with a 'that's-all' rider. It does not follow from this, however, that, in making a penguin-free Arctic, God must create the Arctic with its assorted fauna (omitting penguins) then do something else: institute a 'that's-all' fact. God will have succeeded in making it the case that there are no Arctic penguins by creating an Arctic bereft of penguins, then stopping.

The imagined need for special 'that's-all' facts stems, I contend, from a tacit allegiance to the Picture Theory, more particularly from the assumption that truth making is entailment. Entailment is a relation among 'propositions', or, more generally, a relation among representations. When we cast about for the truth-maker for 'I have exactly five coins in my pocket', we are led to representations of truth-makers rather than the truth-makers themselves. We note that 'There are five coins' does not entail that there are not more than five coins, or that there are exactly five coins, and so conclude that something more is required: a 'that's-all' fact. Similarly, when we look for a truth-maker for 'There are no buttons in my pocket', we represent potential truth-makers. We recognize that 'My pocket contains five coins' does not entail that it contains no buttons, although 'My pocket contains five coins and that's all' does, and conclude that the truth-maker must be a complex fact that includes my pocket's containing five coins plus a second-order 'that's-all' fact.

My suggestion is that a totality or 'that's-all' fact would involve no addition of being. Once God ceases His creation, once I stop putting objects in my pocket, the totality fact, if there is one, 'logically

---

[14] See Lewis (1992); Martin (1996).

supervenes'. (Think of talk of logical supervenience as a pretentious way of expressing the nothing-over-and-above relation; see Chapter 20.) It is easy to miss this point owing to inherent limitations in linguistic representations of totalities.[15]

7.6 Martin's Objection

C. B. Martin offers a deceptively simple objection to the idea that truth making is entailment.[16] Consider truth-bearers: whatever is made true by truth-makers. What are the bearers of truth? Some say propositions. But what is a proposition? Some say sets of possible worlds. A set of possible worlds is not something that could be true or false, however. Truth and falsehood hold of representations. Whatever propositions are, if they are the sorts of entity that could be true or false, they are representations. Now, suppose truth-makers themselves (and not, on pain of regress, propositions asserting the existence of those truth-makers) necessitate truth-bearers.[17] And suppose, as well, that truth-makers are ways the world is. Then it seems to follow that, for every way the world is, there is a representation of its being that way. This is hard to swallow.

Suppose propositions are the bearers of truth. Presumably, propositions are *abstracta*. Allowing that there is a proposition corresponding to every way the world is or could be involves a multiplication of entities, but in a way many philosophers would find unobjectionable. Propositions take up no space. Propositions do not come for free, however. If you appeal to propositions to explicate truth making, then you owe the rest of us an account of propositions and relations of these to the truth-makers and to ordinary representations, items whose truth and falsity we care about. It is hard to see how an appeal to propositions in this context could be thought illuminating. If truth-bearers are concrete representations, we need some account of the relation these bear to truth-makers. If propositions are introduced as intermediaries con-

---

[15] These limitations may or may not be present in other forms of representation. I can, it would seem, draw a picture of a room containing exactly three chairs—or three chairs and nothing more—by drawing the room, drawing three chairs, then stopping. I need not add a 'that's-all' element to the picture.

[16] The objection is advanced in Martin (2000). See also Musgrave (2001: 49).

[17] Strictly, truth-makers would necessitate the truth of truth-bearers, but it is hard to see how they could perform this feat without thereby necessitating truth-bearers.

necting concrete representations and truth-makers, we need an account, both of the 'downward' relation between propositions and truth-makers, and of the 'upward' relation between propositions and concrete representations.

We could give up the idea that truth-bearers are propositions and return to the simpler thought that truth-bearers are ordinary representations, linguistic or otherwise. If we do this, however, and if we continue to regard truth making as entailment, we are left with the odd idea that, for every way the world is or could be, there is a concrete representation. Unlike propositions, such representations do take up space. No finite world is big enough to hold concrete representations of every way it is or could be.

7.7 Moving Beyond Levels of Being

This concludes my discussion of levels of reality. I have argued that the idea that the world is hierarchical in the sense of containing levels of being (as opposed to levels of organization or levels of complexity) is a philosophical artiefact spawned by a commitment to the Picture Theory. Everyday talk of levels—levels of description, levels of explanation—is unobjectionable. We can describe sociology or psychology as higher-level sciences, chemistry and physics as lower-level sciences. Trouble arises when philosophers introduce levels of reality corresponding to levels thought of in this way. Philosophers then discover difficulties in the resulting picture of the world. These include the problem of causal relevance—how could items at higher levels figure in causal transactions?—and the problem of inter-level relations— what is it for higher-level items to depend on and be determined by items at lower levels?

Having embraced an ontology of levels, philosophers regard attacks on that ontology as attacks on what are taken to be higher-level phenomena, phenomena making up domains of the special sciences. To reject a philosophical account of these domains, however, is not to reject the domains. An ontology that dispenses with levels of being—a 'no-level' ontology—need not be an ontology that dispenses with tables, trees, galaxies, or electrons.

Thus far the project has been largely negative. I have denied the existence of levels of being. Now it is time to advance a positive thesis. If predicates do not line up with properties, what are properties? Are properties universals? What is the nature of a property? What do properties contribute to their bearers? Properties, whatever they are, are properties of objects. But what are objects? Are objects collections or bundles of properties? Or do objects belong to a different ontological category? These are among the questions remaining to be answered. In the chapters that follow, I shall endeavour to answer them, beginning with the question whether properties can be equated with powers.

CHAPTER 8
Powers

I suggest that anything has real being that is so constituted as to possess any sort of power either to affect anything else or to be affected, in however small a degree, by the most insignificant agent, though it be only once. I am proposing as a mark to distinguish real things that they are nothing but power.

(Plato, *Sophist* 247d–e)

8.1 Properties and Powers

In this chapter, and the three that follow, I take up the question of how properties and powers might be related. In the foreground is an idea expressed by Plato's Eleatic Stranger: all there really is to a concrete entity is its power to affect and be affected by other entities. Assuming that an entity's powers depend on its properties, this suggests that there is no more to a property than powers or dispositionalities it confers on its possessors; properties are 'pure powers'.

A view of this kind fits comfortably with the idea that science is the measure of all things. The business of science is to tease out fundamental properties of objects. Properties are what figure in laws of nature, and laws govern the behaviour of objects. Properties, then, are features of the world that make a difference in how objects behave or would behave.

Such a conception of properties faces two difficulties. First, for most English–speaking philosophers, it is an article of faith that powers are contingent. Gelignite is explosive because it possesses a certain chemical constitution, but it could have been otherwise. Had various laws of nature been different, gelignite might have been as benign as pizza dough. If properties *are* powers, however, there could be no question of its being contingent that a given property confers a given power; if all there is to the property is the power it confers, there is no prospect of properties and powers varying independently: what makes gelignite gelignite is its disposition to explode under the right conditions.

Second, it is hard to find room in a world of pure powers for familiar qualities. These include, in addition to much-discussed qualities of conscious experience (the *qualia*), qualities of ordinary material objects. On the face of it, a qualitatively empty world is indistinguishable from the void. The worry here is not just that a world barren of qualities would be dull and listless. A weighty tradition, going back at least to Berkeley, has it that the notion of a world without qualities is incoherent: a wholly non-qualitative world is literally unthinkable.

After discussing these and related issues, I undertake, in Chapter 11, to defend the suggestion that properties (intrinsic properties of concrete objects) might be both qualitative and dispositional. Such a conception takes seriously considerations driving the 'pure power' account of properties, while acknowledging the force of traditional worries concerning a world bereft of qualities. My aim is to convince you that a particular conception of properties—properties as simultaneously qualitative and dispositional—deserves serious consideration. The conception has been advanced recently by C. B. Martin, but I believe it is rooted in Locke's *Essay*. I shall have succeeded if considerations raised here lead you to doubt that the ways we have become accustomed to think about qualities, dispositions, and properties generally are the only ways.

8.2   Properties as Powers

Philosophers of many persuasions have been attracted to the thesis that properties are powers or dispositions.[1] More precisely, the thesis is that intrinsic properties of concrete objects are distinguished by distinctive contributions they make to powers or dispositionalities of their posses-

---

[1] I use 'power' and 'disposition' interchangeably. My focus here is on properties of concrete spatio-temporal objects. I leave aside *abstracta, possibilia*, and their cousins. Philosophers who have regarded properties as powers include, Plato's Eleatic Stranger (quoted above), Boscovich (1763/1966); Priestley (1777/1972); Harré (1970); Harré and Madden (1975); Mellor (1974, 2000); Shoemaker (1980); and Swoyer (1982). Shoemaker has apparently changed his mind; see Shoemaker (1998).

sors. A view of this kind could strike you as inevitable if you began with the thought that impotent properties would be undetectable (assuming that detection requires causal interaction of some kind between detected and detector), hence unknowable; the presence or absence of a flatly undetectable property is not something anyone could lose sleep over. This sounds verificationist. Certainly, it is not obvious how we could have epistemic access to causally inert properties. But doubts about non-dispositional properties outstrip epistemological worries. A property that made no difference to the causal powers of its possessors would, it seems, be a property the presence of which made no difference at all.

Thoughts along these lines lead naturally to a principle of property identity:

(PI) Necessarily, if A and B are properties, $A = B$ just in case A and B make the same contribution to the causal powers of their (actual or possible) possessors.

Sydney Shoemaker, a prominent exponent of the properties-as-powers thesis, provides considerations favouring such a principle:

Suppose that the identity of properties consisted of something logically independent of their causal potentialities. Then it ought to be possible for there to be properties that have no potential whatever for contributing to causal powers, i.e., are such that under no conceivable circumstances will their possession by a thing make any difference to the way the presence of that thing affects other things or to the way other things affect it. Further, it ought to be possible for there to be two or more different properties that make, under all possible circumstances, exactly the same contribution to the causal powers of things that have them. Further, it ought to be possible that the potential of a property for contributing to the production of causal powers might change over time, so that, for example, the potential possessed by property A at one time is the same as that possessed by property B at a later time, and that possessed by property B at the earlier time is the same as that possessed by property A at the later time. Thus a thing might undergo radical change with respect to its properties without undergoing any change in its causal powers, and a thing might undergo radical change in its causal powers without undergoing any change in the properties that underlie these powers.   (Shoemaker 1980: 214–15)

If you find such possibilities hard to swallow, you may be moved to accept something like Principle (PI).

Related to this thought is what Graham Oddie (1982) calls 'the Eleatic Principle' and Jaegwon Kim (1993a: 202) dubs 'Alexander's Dictum': to be real is to possess causal powers. Something akin to the Eleatic Principle appears to underlie the suggestion that predicates like 'is three miles south of a red barn' fail to express genuine properties. Consider Jerry Fodor's *H*-particles: a particle has the property, *being an H-particle*, just in case it is a particle and a coin tossed by Fodor lands heads (Fodor 1988: 33). Such 'properties' are 'mere Cambridge properties'. Their being possessed (or being gained or lost) by objects 'makes no difference' to those objects.

This sounds question begging. Surely causally idle properties would 'make a difference' to their possessors, just not a *causal* difference: such properties would have no effect on what their possessors do or would do. Perhaps it is equally question begging to lump all quiescent properties with 'mere Cambridge properties'. The latter are relational: their possession by an object depends on distal objects (barns on the far side of the county; Fodor and his coin). But this gives us no reason to doubt the possibility of purely qualitative *intrinsic* properties.[2] Indeed, a long philosophical tradition distinguishes categorical properties from dispositional properties precisely on the grounds that categorical properties are intrinsic and dispositional properties are not. An object's being square is intrinsic to the object and (thereby) categorical. A square peg's having the power to pass smoothly through a square hole is, in contrast, a 'relational property', one the possession of which depends on the peg's standing in an appropriate relation to square holes. Or so it is thought.

8.3 Terminological Preliminary

The terms 'categorical' and 'dispositional' are not easy to pin down. Are these meant to pick out kinds of *predicate*? Or are *properties* dispositional

---

[2] Intrinsicality is notoriously difficult to characterize informatively; see Humberstone (1996); Lewis and Langton (1998). Elsewhere (Heil 1992: 24) I have characterized intrinsic properties this way: 'An intrinsic property . . . is *nonrelational* in the sense that its possession by an object does not (logically or conceptually) require the existence of any separate object or the existence of that same object, or a part of that same object, at some other time. An object, o_1, is separate from an object, o_2, just in case o_1 is not identical with o_2 or with any part of o_2.' Whether this, or any other analysis or definition, illuminates the notion of intrinsicality is doubtful.

and categorical? Confusion is abetted by an informal convention whereby 'categorical' has come to mean 'non-dispositional', suggesting that the terms designate mutually exclusive, exhaustive classes of entity (see Mumford 1998).

In an effort to diminish terminological uncertainty, I shall use 'qualitative' to designate intrinsic qualitative properties of objects, properties often classified as 'categorical'. I shall use 'dispositional' to designate properties that bestow powers on their possessors in the following sense: it is solely by virtue of possessing a given dispositional property that an object possesses a given power. Dispositional properties, if there are any, have their powers 'built in'. The idea is to distinguish properties that themselves amount to causal powers from those that bestow powers on their possessors, if at all, only indirectly: via contingent laws of nature, for instance.

If, like Armstrong, you think that objects' possession of causal powers depends on laws of nature that could vary independently of objects' intrinsic properties, then, in my terminology, you are thinking of objects' intrinsic properties as qualitative, but not dispositional. Such properties could bestow a power on their possessors, but only given certain laws of nature. (Armstrong, himself, conceives of laws as higher-order necessitation relations among qualitative properties. The possession of a qualitative property by an object confers a power on the object because the qualitative property bears appropriate relations to other properties.)

8.4 Are Dispositions Relations?

You might be attracted to the idea that dispositions are relations for reasons that have nothing to do with Armstrong. Consider Locke's secondary qualities.[3] These, according to Locke, are powers possessed by objects to produce certain effects in conscious observers.[4] Colours and

---

[3] Locke (1690/ 1978: II. viii); see §§14.10 and 17.3 below. A caveat: although I associate certain views with Locke, my interest is in ontology, not Locke scholarship. If you read Locke differently, so be it. Sophisticated discussions of Locke can be found in Smith (1990) and Lowe (1995: ch. 3). For a pointedly different construal of Locke, see Langton (1998: chs. 7–8).

[4] Locke also mentions tertiary qualities, powers possessed by objects (in virtue of those objects' possession of certain primary qualities) to produce changes in the qualities of other objects. The power of the sun to melt wax is a tertiary quality. Because the difference is irrelevant to this discussion, I shall henceforth follow custom and lump together secondary and tertiary qualities.

tastes are secondary qualities. An object's being red, for instance, is a matter of that object's possessing a power to produce in observers experiences of a particular kind. This might be thought to turn powers into relations.

One of Locke's motives for distinguishing primary and secondary properties can be appreciated by reflecting on how we might explain objects' appearances. Being square is, for Locke, a primary quality. When an object looks or feels square to an observer, this is because it *is* square. Compare an object's looking red. An object looks red because (let us say) its surface incorporates a particular micro-arrangement of primary qualities. These structure reflected light in a particular way. Light thus structured affects our eyes so as to bring about an experience of red.[5] Here, a secondary quality, being red, is characterized relationally: by reference to its actual or possible manifestations. Primary qualities, in contrast, can be denominated non-relationally.[6] An object's being square is an intrinsic quality of the object, a way the object is quite independently of its actual or possible effects on any other object.

It is tempting to assimilate Locke's primary/secondary distinction to a distinction between qualitative and dispositional properties—a distinction between qualities and powers. The temptation should be resisted. Primary qualities, no less than secondary qualities, must be power bestowing. In virtue of being square an object would produce in us an experience of its being square; in virtue of being square an object would leave a square-shaped impression were it pressed against your skin. As I read Locke, primary qualities are *both* intrinsic qualities *and* powers.

What of the secondary qualities? Locke sometimes describes these as 'pure powers'. This suggests that *all there is* to being a secondary quality is being a power. Such properties would be possessed by an object alongside or in addition to the object's primary qualities. What

---

[5] I do not offer this as an account of colour, only as an example of what Locke has in mind.

[6] Locke includes among the primary qualities 'solidity, extension, figure, motion, or rest, and number' (1690/1978: II. viii. 9). Elsewhere (II. viii. 10) he supplements this list by adding bulk and texture. Primary qualities are intrinsic, at least in the sense that they could be possessed by a single particle alone in the void. Locke's inclusion of number among the primary qualities is at first puzzling. Perhaps he had in mind a 'naturalistic' conception of number similar to that advanced in Bigelow (1988). More likely, Locke regards this as a consequence of the view that divisions we find in the world are objective and natural. The question 'How many?' always has a mind-independent answer. What of motion? Locke regards motion as intrinsic to moving objects rather than as a relation between a moving object and something else (a stationary object, for instance, or space).

Locke has in mind might be something quite different, however. A secondary quality is a power possessed by an object in virtue of its possession of certain primary qualities. Philosophers fond of the dispositional/categorical distinction find it natural to think of this in terms of supervenience: an object's secondary qualities supervene on the object's primary qualities. I have argued already that supervenience is a modal notion, however (§7.2). If As supervene on Bs, there can be no A-difference without a B-difference. But then the question is *why*? What grounds the supervenience claim, what is its truth-maker?[7]

One popular idea is that secondary qualities (the dispositions) are *realized by* the primary qualities (the categorical 'grounds' or 'bases' of these dispositions). The realizing relation here is the relation philosophers of mind appeal to in holding that states of mind are realized in sentient creatures by biological states of various sorts (or, more generally, that mental properties are realized by physical properties).

8.5 Dispositions and their Manifestations

I shall return to this conception of dispositionality in Chapter 9. For the moment, note merely that the idea that dispositional properties are realized in, or grounded by, qualitative properties does not itself imply that secondary qualities (dispositions) are relations. Rather it makes secondary qualities out to be 'higher-level' properties, properties possessed by objects by virtue of those objects' possession of certain 'lower-level' properties—their realizers. This thesis is independent of the idea that dispositions are relations. The inspiration for a relational conception of dispositions arises from another source: our practice of identifying dispositions conditionally, identifying them by reference to their possible manifestations.[8]A vase is fragile: it would shatter *if* struck by a solid object or dropped; a pill is poisonous: it would bring about illness or death *if* ingested; a ball is red: it would look red to normally sighted perceivers *if* observed in sunlight.

---

[7] As noted in §7.4, a variety of different kinds of condition can ground a supervenience claim—assuming supervenience to be characterized in the usual way. As will supervene on Bs, for instance if As are Bs, or if As are composed of Bs, if As are caused by Bs, if A and B have a common cause . . .

[8] Martin calls these 'typifying manifestations'; see his (1997) and his contribution to Armstrong et al. (1996).

Such characterizations relate dispositions to their manifestations conditionally: D is a disposition to yield manifestation M if C occurs. Might such conditional characterizations capture all there is to a disposition? Alternatively, what are the prospects of analysing talk of dispositions conditionally?[9] Rather than addressing this vexed question here, let us grant that the practice of characterizing dispositions conditionally is warranted, even unavoidable. The question is whether this should lead us to regard dispositions as relations.

Consider a red object—a red billiard ball, for instance. Suppose Locke is right: the ball's being red is a matter of the ball's having a particular sort of power or disposition: a power to cause experiences of certain distinctive kinds in observers. Is the billiard ball's possessing this power a matter of the ball's (or some property of the ball's) standing in an appropriate relation to observers' experiences? Imagine a world consisting of the billiard ball and nothing else. Is the billiard ball red in such a world? Locke's considered view, I believe, is that the ball *is* red. An object's powers do not fluctuate owing simply to the removal of objects possessing properties requisite for the manifestation of those powers.

Here is an alternative route to the same conclusion. It would be mad to require every actual disposition to be manifested. There might be red objects located in remote regions of the universe that, owing solely to their remoteness, could never look red to anyone. If you agree that an object might possess a disposition it never manifests—and, perhaps because it is outside the light cone of whatever would be required for its manifestation, a disposition it *could* never manifest—then you should not baulk at the thought that this same disposition might be possessed by an object located in a world altogether lacking in whatever might be required for its manifestation.

We deploy conditionals to characterize dispositions, but this does not oblige us to regard dispositions as relations. We might characterize water as a liquid that would look, feel, and taste a certain way were it seen, felt, or tasted by a human being. This does not make water (or, if you prefer, the property of being water) relational. The stuff we pick out in this conditional way could exist in a world altogether lacking in conscious agents.

---

[9] See Mellor (2000). For reasons to doubt the possibility (and utility) of such analyses, see Martin (1994).

8.6 Dispositionality and Reciprocity

To regard dispositions as relations between the disposition itself (or some property grounding the disposition) and its actual or possible manifestations is to confuse a feature of our way of characterizing dispositions—conditionally by reference to their possible manifestations—for the dispositions themselves. (The Picture Theory again!) This is perhaps most clear in cases in which a single disposition is capable of different kinds of manifestation. Suppose an object's being red is a matter of the object's possessing a particular disposition, R. R will manifest itself differently with different kinds of reciprocal disposition partner.[10] R will, for instance, differently affect distinct kinds of ambient light radiation—with the result that objects possessing R will sometimes appear red and sometimes appear brown or grey. (Your visual experience is itself a mutual manifestation of dispositions belonging to light radiation and dispositions of your visual system.) If R is a relation, which of these is it a relation to? Or is R relationally multifaceted? Rather than puzzling out an answer to such questions, we should do better to abandon the thesis that R is a relation.[11]

There is, I believe, no compelling reason to regard dispositions (or, for that matter, Locke's secondary qualities) as relational. Dispositions can be conditionally characterized in a way that invokes their actual or possible manifestations. But this does not turn dispositions into relations. The existence of a disposition does not in any way depend on the disposition's standing in a relation to its actual or possible manifestations or to whatever would elicit those manifestations.

You might agree with all this, yet regard dispositions as relational for an altogether different reason. Suppose you were attracted to Armstrong's idea that an object possesses a disposition in virtue of the object's possessing a certain qualitative property together with that property's standing in an appropriate relation to a contingent law of nature. A vase's being fragile, for instance, might be its possession of a particular kind of microstructure *together with* laws of nature that ensure that anything with this structure would shatter if struck. If you thought

---

[10] The expression 'reciprocal disposition partner' is Martin's; see Martin (1997); Martin and Heil (1999); and Martin's contribution to Armstrong et al. (1996).

[11] I return to the idea that dispositions are relations in Ch. 10.

this, you might regard dispositions as relations between categorical properties—qualities—and laws of nature (laws regarded as entities of certain sorts, and not merely as sentences or statements).

Armstrong's conception of dispositionality, and a somewhat different conception advanced by Elizabeth Prior, Robert Pargetter, and Frank Jackson (1982), have done much to shape philosophers' views on dispositionality. I propose to examine these views in the context of a closer look at the dispositional/categorical distinction. This distinction, often taken for granted, incorporates substantive theses concerning the nature of properties. Because the distinction is taken for granted, these theses can escape notice or, when noticed, appear wholly innocent. In philosophy, no thesis is wholly innocent.

CHAPTER 9

Dispositional and Categorical Properties

9.1 Two Conceptions of Dispositionality

Let us suppose that, while it is convenient to characterize dispositions by reference to their actual and possible manifestations, dispositions themselves are intrinsic to their possessors. This leads us back to the idea that there are two kinds of property: dispositional and categorical. Categorical properties are wholly qualitative; dispositional properties are pure powers.

This division might be thought to coincide with Locke's primary/ secondary quality distinction: primary qualities are intrinsic *qualities* of objects; secondary qualities are powers objects possess. In §8.4 I suggested that it is a mistake to read Locke as denying that primary qualities are themselves powers. If you are tempted to do so, this might be because you embrace a conception of properties according to which properties are *either* categorical *or* dispositional (never both): dispositional properties are non-qualitative; categorical properties are non-dispositional.

The most common variant of this view is expressed in the thought that dispositional properties have categorical 'bases'. On such a conception, dispositional properties resemble functional properties (or indeed might be a species of functional property) in being 'multiply realizable'. Salt, sugar, and lime are soluble in water. Each of these substances is water soluble by virtue of possessing (let us suppose) a distinct microstructural property. Differences in these microstructural properties block the identification of the dispositional property, being water soluble, with any single microstructural property. We are led in this way to the idea that being water soluble is a 'higher-level' property possessed by an object in virtue of its possession of some distinct lower-level categorical property, its realizer.

What accounts for an object's possession of a dispositional property, the property of being water soluble? According to the conception of properties in play, an object possesses this property in virtue of possessing some categorical (presumably microstructural) property. (As will become clear, this 'in virtue of' can be spelled out in at least two distinct ways.) It is thought to be at most contingently true that objects possessing this categorical property are water soluble. Suppose a salt crystal is water soluble. We seem able to imagine worlds in which a crystal with the very same make-up is not water soluble. Perhaps, then, an object's being water soluble is a matter of its possessing some categorical property coupled with certain laws of nature. If these laws are contingent, it is not surprising that the dispositionalities bestowed on objects by their possession of particular categorical properties are contingent.

Two possibilities present themselves. First, dispositional properties might be grounded in (or realized by) categorical properties. This makes dispositional properties 'higher-level' properties relative to their 'lower-level' categorical realizers. Second, dispositional properties and categorical properties alike might be taken to be 'same-level' properties of objects possessing them. A ball, then, could be thought to possess the categorical property of sphericity and the dispositional property of being red. Here, we need not imagine that the redness of the ball has a categorical 'realizer'. Rather, being red would be a pure power co-instantiated, as it happens, alongside a pure quality.

In the previous chapter I noted that there is reason to doubt that properties standardly offered as examples of categorical properties are causally inert: such properties make no difference to the dispositionalities of their possessors. Reflect on paradigmatic examples of categorical properties: having a particular shape or having a particular mass, for instance. These invariably appear to contribute to their possessors' dispositionalities. A ball rolls or could roll in virtue of being spherical; in virtue of being square, a square peg could pass through a square hole, though not (in quite the same way) through a round hole. An object with a particular mass would, in virtue of possessing that mass, depress a scale in a particular way.

What of structural properties? These are sometimes said to be the categorical grounds of dispositions. The microstructure of water molecules, for instance, is sometimes said to ground the disposition of water to take the shape of containers into which it is poured. But this structure would deflect electrons in a particular way in an electron microscope; this structure would resist forces of particular sorts. Why not suppose that water's microstructure itself is what disposes water to take the shape of containing vessels?

Such examples strongly suggest that some categorical properties (so-called) are really dispositional: they need not at any given time be doing all they could do. An advocate of the view that properties are powers can reasonably challenge an opponent to produce a clear example of a purely qualitative property. If such a property is detectable, then it would seem not to be purely qualitative after all. If it is not detectable, it will be tricky to recruit as an example.

A proponent of the idea that dispositions are grounded in categorical properties might concede the point, but insist that, although categorical properties bestow powers on their possessors, they do so indirectly: only by virtue of standing in an appropriate relation to a contingent law of nature. Were the laws different, the very same properties would bestow (indirectly) different powers on their possessors, or even no powers at all. This line of response is available both to those who accept a 'two-level' account of dispositionality and those who side with Armstrong in regarding dispositionality as contingently affixed to categorical properties via laws of nature. Let us look at each of these conceptions in turn.

9.2 Prior, Pargetter, and Jackson

Prior, Pargetter, and Jackson's account of dispositions (1982) has come to occupy what could be regarded as the *default* position on dispositionality. Certainly the account is taken for granted by a large number of philosophers. According to Prior, Pargetter, and Jackson, powers or dispositions are higher-level properties objects possess by virtue of those objects' possession of lower-level qualitative (categorical) properties.[1] Dispositional properties resemble (or perhaps *are*) functional properties. The dispositional property, being fragile, is a property possessed by a given object by virtue of that object's possession of some qualitative—probably structural—property.

Dispositionality might be thought to be a higher-level phenomenon because dispositions appear to be 'multiply realizable'. The argument is a familiar one. Many different kinds of object are fragile: a sheet of glass, a kneecap, an antique watch. In every case, a fragile object is fragile by virtue of possessing some lower-level structural property or other, but these lower-level 'realizing' properties can vary widely across kinds of object. The property of being fragile cannot be reduced to or identified with any one lower-level property. Being fragile, then, must be a higher-level property: a property possessed by objects by virtue of their possession of some distinct lower-level property.

In earlier chapters I maintained that the argument for multiple realizability is founded on a confusion—roughly, a conflation of predicates and properties induced by the Picture Theory. Even on its own terms, however, the idea that dispositional properties are higher-level properties with categorical 'realizers' reveals a number of apparent anomalies. First, and most obviously, it is unclear how higher-level properties could themselves figure in causal relations. This is the so-called problem of causal relevance, a problem that has plagued functionalist accounts of mind. If mental properties are higher-level properties possessed by agents in virtue of their possession of lower-level 'realizing' properties, it looks as though the realizing properties figure in causal relations in a way that pre-empts or 'screens off' higher-level realized properties (see e.g. Kim 1993*a*; Jackson 1997; Ch. 4 above).

You might regard this, not as a difficulty, but merely as a surprising consequence of the view. Consider, however, the peculiar ontological credentials of dispositions regarded as higher-level properties. These properties are introduced in the course of a discussion of powers possessed by objects to behave in various ways under various circumstances. Yet the properties themselves apparently have no part in

---

[1]   Although the terms are frequently interchanged, I have distinguished higher- and lower-*level* properties from higher- and lower-*order* properties. A higher-*order* property is a property of some (lower-order) property. A higher-*level* property is a property possessed by an object in virtue of that object's possession of some distinct, lower-level 'realizing' property.

producing the effects they were introduced to explain! It is hard to credit an account of powers that centres on the postulation of epiphenomenal properties. This is the theoretical tail wagging the ontological dog.[2]

Frank Jackson, himself a proponent of the two-level view, regards the idea that dispositional properties might be causally operative as implying 'a curious and ontologically extravagant kind of overdetermination' (1997: 202). But surely it is the postulation of causally inert higher-level properties that is curious and extravagant. What are these properties supposed to explain? On the view favoured by Jackson, every causally operative qualitative property is accompanied by an epiphenomenal dispositional property. A vase is fragile; it is disposed to shatter if struck by a sufficiently massive solid object or dropped. Its being fragile is a matter of its possession of some higher-level dispositional property grounded in a distinct lower-level categorical property. If the vase should shatter, however, this is not, strictly speaking, because it is fragile, but because it possesses a certain lower-level qualitative property. Why not dispense with the higher-level dispositional property altogether? This would leave us with a qualitative property the possession of which would *itself* amount to the possession of a power. Now, however, we are back to a conception of properties as powers!

Locating the disposition in the qualitative 'realizing' property requires rejecting that idea that being fragile is a single (higher-level) property. Instead, we should suppose that the predicate 'is fragile' is satisfied by any of a family of properties (all those properties, namely, that Prior, Pargetter, and Jackson would regard as fragility's realizers).[3] Fragile objects are fragile, not in virtue of possessing a single higher-level property, but in virtue of possessing any of a family of similar properties. Fragile objects shatter because they are fragile, but not every fragile object is fragile in the same way.

---

[2] Dean Zimmerman points out that some readers will object to my describing higher-level properties so conceived as epiphenomenal. References to such properties might figure in causal explanations and in causally grounded counterfactuals. Explanation is an epistemic concept, however. When a term figures in a true causal explanation, the question remains: what is it about the world that makes the explanation true? The same point holds for counterfactual truths.

[3] A conception of this kind is analogous to the Armstrong–Lewis conception of functional properties, what Ned Block calls the 'functional specifier' conception as distinguished from the 'functional state identity' conception of such properties (see Armstrong 1968; Lewis 1966, 1994; Block 1980a; Chs. 3–5 above).

9.3   Armstrong on Dispositionality

According to Armstrong, a qualitative property bestows a power on its possessors owing to contingent laws of nature. (Armstrong takes laws of nature to be higher-order relations: relations taking properties as relata.) An object is fragile in virtue of its possession of a qualitative property, F, in concert with some law of nature, L. L is contingent in the sense that F could be present in a world lacking L. Thus it is contingent what powers, if any, F bestows on its possessors.

To sharpen the focus, consider a variant of the Armstrong view. A qualitative property, Q, might endow its bearers with the property of being fragile because Q itself possesses a certain property, ϕ. Q possesses ϕ only contingently, however: you could imagine a world in which Q lacks ϕ. In the imagined world, objects qualitatively indiscernible from fragile objects in the actual world would not be fragile. Here, dispositions would be a higher-*order* properties, properties contingently possessed by lower-order qualitative properties.

A view of this kind differs subtly from Armstrong's. For Armstrong, powers do not reside in higher-order properties; powers reside in ordinary qualitative properties. It is just contingent which powers belong to which qualities. Their belonging to these qualities is a matter of their figuring in contingent laws of nature.

Suppose you were attracted to the thought that properties bestow powers on their possessors only contingently. It would be a bad idea, in that case, to embrace the thesis that properties bestow powers by virtue of their possession of higher-order properties. To see why, imagine that Fs necessitate Gs, and that this is because the property, F, possesses a higher-order property, ϕ. The necessitation is contingent, because F might have lacked ϕ. But now consider ϕ itself. If it is in virtue of possessing ϕ that the Fs necessitate the Gs, it looks as though ϕ necessitates non-contingently: ϕ's necessitating Gs is not detachable from ϕ. So ϕ, at any rate, bestows a power non-contingently. This, however, is just the result that an opponent of the idea that properties are powers had hoped to avoid. Further, if the only reason to postulate ϕ was to avoid countenancing properties as powers, then the strategy fails. You might as well assume that the first-order property, being F, bestows a power on its possessors non-contingently.

In §8.4, I suggested that Locke's powers were intrinsic to their possessors. Suppose Cs have the power to produce Es. (Imagine that C is the property of being red, and E is the property of being a visual experience of red.) Imagine a world containing Cs but no Es (the world in question contains no conscious agents, or it contains conscious agents who never encounter red objects). As I read him, Locke rightly supposes that the Cs do not lose their power to produce Es in such a world. I motivated this contention by imagining a world in which Cs did yield Es, but some Cs, owing perhaps to their location outside the light cone of any conscious agent, could not yield Es. If you are inclined to allow that the isolated Cs have the power to yield Es in this case, why not in a world in which all the Cs are unaccompanied by conscious observers?

What of Armstrong? Armstrong must deny that Cs have the power to cause Es in worlds either lacking conscious agents or containing conscious agents none of whom encounter a C.[4] Why so? Armstrong takes properties to be universals, and believes that there are no 'uninstantiated' universals. In a world in which conscious agents never encounter a red object, E is not instantiated. If E fails to be instantiated, then the higher-order universal linking Cs to Es fails to be instantiated. Cs having the power to produce Es is contingent on the instantiation of this higher-order universal, however. So, in a world lacking Es, Cs lack a power they would have had otherwise. This diminishes the inclination to read Armstrong as countenancing the idea that powers are intrinsic but contingent. An object possessing C in our world has a power that an intrinsically indiscernible object lacks in a world indiscernible from ours in all but one respect: in that world Cs never encounter conscious beings (and so never in fact yield Es). Tomatoes are not red in worlds in which tomatoes exist, but no conscious agent ever stumbles over a tomato (or any other red object).

This turns powers into relations in at least one sense: an object does not possess a power unless the power has been manifested on at least one occasion. Two worlds could differ in one small respect: in world A, no conscious agent encounters a C; in B, a conscious agent encounters a single, fleeting C (a tomato whizzes past at high speed). In B all Cs have the power to cause Es, in world A none does. Worse, in world B it

---

[4] Martin makes this point forcefully in his contribution to Armstrong et al. (1996).

is true of the *C*s that, were they to be observed by a conscious agent, they would look red; in *A* this counterfactual is false. You may find a view that implies these possibilities hard to swallow. If you do, this may be because you find it more natural to think of powers or dispositions as intrinsic—really intrinsic—to their possessors.

There is a deeper reason to regard Armstrong's view as disquieting. Consider the world in which just one agent, Lilian, on one occasion encounters a *C* and *E* occurs: Lilian has a fleeting glimpse of a jet-propelled tomato and thus an experience of red. Call this the red world, and compare the red world with a world, the grey world, in which, owing to a tiny mishap, Lilian stumbles and averts her eyes at the instant the tomato whizzes past. In the grey world *E* fails to occur, so it is false that *C*s would cause *E*s. It is hard to see how an event like Lilian's stumbling could make it the case that a law of nature fails to hold. Surely, it is tempting to say, had Lilian—or anyone else—in the grey world seen the tomato, she—or anyone else—would have experienced red. But, if Armstrong is right, there are no truth-makers in the grey world for this counterfactual: it would be false that *C*s have the power to produce *E*s.

It is hard not to believe that, in both the red world and the grey world, red objects would produce red experiences: *C*s would cause *E*s. If Armstrong's theory obliges us to suppose that the grey world lacks the requisite higher-order universal and, as a result, it is false that red objects would produce red experiences, so much the worse for Armstrong's theory.

9.4 Humean Contingency

What drives the idea that laws of nature are contingent? What is upsetting about the thought that the possession of certain properties could endow objects with powers or dispositions non-contingently? Might it be possible to reconcile the sense that things might have behaved very differently from the way they do in fact behave with the thesis that properties bestow powers non-contingently?

Nowadays most analytically trained philosophers follow Armstrong in regarding laws of nature as contingent. If dispositionalities were built into properties, if, for instance, properties were characterized as they are in (PI) or as Shoemaker suggests in the passage quoted in §8.2, contingency goes by the board. God does not create the objects and properties then add the laws. Instead, laws of nature 'logically supervene' on the properties: when God fixes the properties, He thereby fixes the laws (see Swoyer 1982; Fales 1993; Elder 1994). If a sugar cube is water soluble by virtue of possessing a certain property, *S*, then it would be flatly impossible for an object to possess *S*, yet fail to be water soluble. This seems too strong, however. We can easily imagine sugar cubes failing to dissolve; we can imagine that the laws of nature might have been different so that gold, but not sugar, was water soluble; bars of steel, but not Micen vases, were fragile.

Not so fast! What exactly are we imagining when we imagine objects behaving in ways we think they could not actually behave owing to laws of nature? An object's dispositionalities depend on its overall make-up. If you encase a sugar cube in Lucite, you will make the cube-encased-in-Lucite impervious to water. In regarding properties as powers, you would be imagining that every property contributes in a distinctive way to the powers of its possessors. What powers an object possesses would depend on its entire complement of properties. Sphericity can provide an object with the power to roll, but only in concert with various other properties. A spherical cloud lacks the power to roll. A sugar cube could be thought to possess the power to dissolve in water contingently in the sense that the cube might have been encased in Lucite with the result that the cube-encased-in-Lucite would not be water soluble.

Similarly, if you vary an object's circumstances, you may affect the way an object's powers are manifested. A match will ignite when raked across an abrasive surface. It would not ignite, however, if oxygen were not present. The presence or absence of oxygen does not affect the match's dispositional make-up, but it does have an effect on how those dispositions would be manifested.

Might such considerations account for the impression we have that objects' dispositionalities are contingent? Balls *could* fail to roll, sugar *could* fail to dissolve, matches *could* fail to light, not because powers are contingent, but because the manifestation of a power can be affected, often dramatically, by the presence or absence of other powers.

This would scarcely satisfy a dedicated Humean, of course. If the laws of nature are contingent, then the very same sugar cube that dissolves in water could have failed to dissolve in the very same liquid under the very same conditions. On this view, properties of sugar cubes and water in virtue of which sugar cubes are water soluble could have been such that they contributed in utterly different ways to powers of their possessors. Given the laws of nature, sugar cubes must behave as they do, but the laws of nature could have been different.

Perhaps the impression of contingency is partly an epistemological matter. For all we know, the laws could be very different from what we at any time believe they are. This, however, does not imply that the laws could have been different from what they are. In imagining worlds indiscernible from ours with respect to the properties, but discernible with respect to the laws, we are perhaps imagining worlds with different (though superficially similar) properties. Laws of nature would be contingent in so far as it is contingent that the actual world includes the properties it includes.

All this is just to say that the apparent contingency of natural processes might be due, not to those processes (or laws governing them) being contingent, but to two other factors. First, our ignorance concerning the processes or laws means that beliefs as to what the laws are are invariably fallible. Second, even on a view that grounds laws of nature in the properties, there is room for a contingency of sorts: it will be contingent what the laws are if it is contingent what the properties are. Thus, it would not be contingent that salt dissolves in water, but it would be contingent that salt or water exists at all. Perhaps this is all the contingency we need.

One worry here is that the dispute between Armstrong and someone like Shoemaker who regards powers as built into the properties is at bottom a dispute over labels. Suppose a property, P, makes a distinctive contribution to the dispositionalities of its possessors. Now consider a merely possible property, P', qualitatively similar to P, but making a different contribution to the powers of its possessors. Armstrong could describe this as a case in which the same property affords its possessors different powers owing to differences in laws of nature ($P = P'$); Shoemaker, in contrast, could describe the case as one in which a different property is on the scene ($P \neq P'$).

Is this all there is to the dispute? I doubt it. The dispute concerns the nature of properties: whether a property's dispositionality is built into the property or whether it is a contingent add-on. On one side are those who regard properties as nothing more than conferrers of powers. If you thought that, you would not think that properties and powers could vary independently. On the other side are those who regard properties as qualities possessed by objects that, *in addition*, affect the dispositionalities of their possessors. I shall attempt a reconciliation of these conceptions of properties presently.

9.5 What *Is* a Law of Nature?

Armstrong takes laws of nature to be necessitation relations holding among properties, which he regards as universals. Laws, on this view, are to be distinguished from statements of laws, just as properties are to be distinguished from predicates. Laws—relations among universals—are truth-makers for law statements.

If you follow Shoemaker and assume that first-order properties themselves incorporate powers or dispositions, it will be these first-order properties that ground the truth of law statements (see Bhaskar 1978; Cartwright 1989; A. F. Chalmers 1993). A view of this kind could be thought of as supporting a mildly deflationary conception of laws. Law statements would hold in virtue of complex necessitation relations grounded in objects' first-order properties. So long as you consider only the properties of very simple things in controlled settings, such law statements could be expected to imply generalizations that would hold with something like perfect uniformity. Once you move beyond the very simple things, however, uniformity gives way to approximation or worse. This is the realm of *ceteris paribus* laws and defeasible generalizations.

A world containing properties with built in powers would be one in which objects are embedded in what Martin calls a 'power net' (Martin 1993a). An object's behaviour, then, would be the result of a confluence of influences grounded in the object's properties and the properties of other objects that influence it and are in turn influenced by it. Alan Chalmers puts it nicely (substituting 'capacity' or 'tendency' for disposition or power):

Once we interpret laws as describing capacities we should not expect them to describe happenings in the world. Happenings in the world are usually the outcome of several capacities acting in conjunction in complex ways, so a law that accurately describes one of those capacities cannot be expected also to describe the outcome of its interaction with other capacities. The fact that the tendency of a leaf to fall is sometimes swamped by the effect of the wind is no reason to doubt that the gravitational tendency continued to act in that circumstance and, moreover continued to act in the exact, quantitative way specified by the law of gravitation.   (A. F. Chalmers 1993: 201)

These matters, which go well beyond the province of this book, lead directly to the topic of the next chapter: properties as powers. If you are attracted to the idea that properties differentially bestow powers on their possessors, are you thereby committed to the idea that this exhausts the nature of properties? Are properties nothing but powers possessed by objects?

CHAPTER 10

Properties as Pure Powers

10.1 Pure Dispositionality

The exciting idea, introduced in Chapter 8, that to be real is to possess causal powers can lead directly to the thought that properties are purely dispositional: *all there is* to a property is its contribution to the dispositionalities of its possessors.[1] (Qualitative properties, if there are any, stand outside the causal order: qualities exist only in the minds of conscious observers.) Joseph Priestley, for instance, echoing Roger Boscovich, held that the world comprises 'certain *centres of attractions and repulsions*, extending indefinitely in all directions, the whole effect of them to be upon each other [. . .] a compage of these centres, placed within the sphere of each other's attraction, will constitute a body that we term *compact*'.[2] What we regard as solid bodies are, in reality, bundles of powers: '*power centres*'. The material world is wholly made up of what, 200 years later, Harré and Madden were to describe as 'an interacting system of powerful particulars' (1975: 7; cf. Martin's 'power net' (1993a)).

A conception of this kind might be read as incorporating a twofold reduction: (1) objects are reduced to bundles of properties; (2) properties are reduced to powers. The result is a conception of objects as power loci. The world is viewed as a network of powers rather than as a system of self-contained interacting substances.

Although a conception of properties as pure powers does not force the abandonment of a time-honoured substance–property ontology, the daring thought that all there is to the material world are 'centres of attractions and repulsions' pushes in the direction of a 'bundle theory' of objects, a theory that promises to banish all but powers from the

---

[1] A reminder: what I have to say is intended to apply to properties of concrete objects, not to *abstracta*.
[2] Priestley (1777/1972: 239), cited in Harré and Madden (1975: 172).

material world. If an object's qualities are reduced to or replaced by pure powers, anything resembling substantial nature fades away. Substances wholly bereft of qualities are difficult to envision (see §10.3). Far from considering this a problem to be overcome, proponents of the thesis that properties are pure powers are more likely to regard the demise of the traditional substance–property ontology as liberating. A dynamic conception of reality replaces the static seventeenth- and eighteenth-century conception of inert substances propelled by external forces (see Ellis 2001).

Despite its appeal in some quarters, many philosophers have been struck by the thought that a properties-as-powers view leads to a debilitating regress.[3] Suppose As are nothing more than powers to produce Bs, Bs are nothing more than powers to produce Cs, Cs are nothing more than powers to produce Ds . . . and so on for every concrete spatio-temporal thing. How is this supposed to work? Imagine a row of dominos arranged so that, when the first domino topples, it topples the second, which topples the third, and so on. Now imagine that *all there is* to the first domino is a power to topple the second domino, and *all there is* to the second domino is a power to be toppled and a power to topple the third domino, and so on. If all there is to a domino is a power to topple or be toppled by an adjacent domino, nothing happens: no domino topples because there is nothing—no thing—to topple.

Or so it appears. Some philosophers disagree. Richard Holton, for instance, thinks that a conception of the world as comprising pure powers is a viable, even attractive option (Holton 1999; see also Dipert 1997). Holton, assuming a relational model of dispositionality, argues that, if we could coherently describe a world consisting wholly of objects 'entirely characterized' by relations they bear to other objects, this would be tantamount to describing a world consisting of objects whose nature is exhausted by pure powers. Let us grant this assumption for the sake of argument and see where it leads.

Holton invites us to imagine a world consisting of four points: A, B, C, D. A is to the left of B and above C; B is to the right of A and above D; C is below A and to the left of D; and D is below B and to the right

---

[3] See e.g. Campbell (1976: 93–4); Foster (1982: 67–72); Swinburne (1980); Blackburn (1990); Martin (1997: 213–17). A related argument is advanced in Armstrong (1961: ch. 15) and in Armstrong (1999).

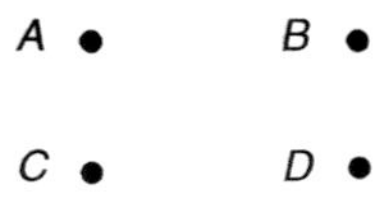

A •   B •

C •   D •

Figure 10.1. A purely relational world

of C. Such a world can be depicted via a diagram (Figure 10.1). Each of the points in the illustration is meant to be 'entirely characterized' by its relations to the remaining points. In one regard the diagram is misleading. The world we are being invited to imagine is not a world of corpuscles or material particles arranged in the way depicted. The world in question comprises entities whose nature consists of *nothing more* than relations they bear to other entities. A description of such a world need not lead to a regress. Entities are constituted by relations they bear to every other entity. The relations in question are weblike, mutually supporting, not linear.

The diagram depicts four points appropriately located relative to one another. According to Holton, 'there really is nothing more to A, B, C, and D than that given by the descriptions [of their relations]. So do not think that, in describing them I have helped myself to the non-dispositional notion of a point' (1999: 10). To get the idea, you would need to subtract the points and keep the relations. This is none too easy. Engaging in Locke's abstraction or 'partial consideration', you could, perhaps, *consider* the relations without considering the points. Subtracting the points, however, and keeping the relations is no less challenging than subtracting the cat and keeping the smile. Relations are, or certainly seem to be, dependent on their relata in a way that excludes the possibility of relata wholly constituted by relations.

10.2 Spatial Parts

Perhaps I am being unfair to Holton.[4] Imagine that A, B, C, and D are spatial points—as distinct from material 'atoms'. In that case, A, B, C, and D might indeed seem to be wholly constituted by relations each bears to the others. If this is right, and if there might be purely spatial

---

[4] Toby Handfield pressed this objection.

worlds, then the possibility of exclusively relational worlds might be vindicated.[5]

I am not so sure. It is hard to see how turning A, B, C, and D into spatial points helps with the matter in hand. First, as Armstrong makes clear in an argument I shall discuss in §10.5, it is hard to see how purely relational worlds would differ from worlds consisting of *nothing but* empty space. Whatever our world is, it is not such a world. Second, space is not *made up* of spatial points in the way a beach is made up of grains of sand. The difficulty is not that spatial points, being infinitely small, could never add up to a spatial expanse. Spatial points are not infinitesimal particles of space. If space were made up of spatial points in the way a beach is made up of grains of sand, it would be false that spatial points are wholly constituted by relations to other points.

I am not denying that space might turn out to be granular, made up perhaps of particle-like entities—as imagined by Plato in the *Timaeus*, for instance. In that case, space itself would be substance-like. Still, we should want to distinguish empty space from a space occupied by material bodies. If we regard bodies as nothing more than relations or as nothing more than powers to affect other bodies, it is not clear that we have left ourselves with sufficient conceptual resources to make this distinction (see §10.5).

The idea here is perfectly general. Spatial parts are not to be confused with substantial parts. Objects with spatial parts are not composites made up of those parts. A particular baseball has a top half and a bottom half, and it can be divided as finely as you please into spatial regions. But these are not what make up the ball: the ball is not the sum of these spatial parts arranged in a particular way. The ball has, in addition to spatial parts, substantial parts: stitches, a cover, a rubber and cork core, and a winding. These, appropriately arranged, constitute the baseball.

Someone who took spatial points to be wholly constituted by relations might be treating space as a simple (indivisible) substance. Fair enough. In that cases spatial points or regions would be like a baseball's spatial parts. The baseball is a complex substance made up of substantial parts (each of which is itself a substance). You can remove or replace a baseball's cover or stitching. You cannot detach a spatial part of the ball,

---

[5] Could there be purely spatial worlds: worlds consisting of nothing but empty space? Not if space requires occupants; see Lowe (1998: 163–4).

however. You cannot remove the top half of the baseball (though, of course, you could remove the portion of the baseball that now occupies the spatial region that includes its top half).

If you thought that space were made up of points in the way the baseball is made up of a cover, stitching, a core, and winding, you would be thinking of space as a complex, granular substance: spatial points (like parts of a baseball) could be moved, removed, or replaced. In that case, however, spatial points had better consist of something more than relations to other points.

10.3 Campbell on Boscovich

Even if, as I believe, powers are not relations, worries about entirely relational worlds extend to worlds comprising objects wholly constituted by powers. These worries are made vivid by Keith Campbell in a discussion of Boscovich's Holton-like ontology (Boscovich 1763/ 1966). Boscovich depicts the world as comprising material points, the intrinsic nature of which is exhausted by their power to accelerate other points. 'What', asks Campbell, 'is at a material point?'

What distinguishes a location in space where there is a point from one where there is no such thing? All we can say is: At a material point there is something which accelerates other somethings which in turn accelerate somethings (including the first) which in turn . . . But what an odd object this is; its *only* feature is to have an effect on things which have an effect on things which have an effect on things which . . . We seem to be caught in a regress or circle, forever unable to say just what these things *are* which have an effect on each other. (Campbell 1976: 93)[6]

Boscovich's world is a world of pure powers located at points. It is not merely that we can know material points only by knowing their effects on other material points, but that this is all there is to being a material point.

When one point moves another, all that has been shifted is a power to shift powers to shift . . . But powers to shift *what*? To be coherent, I consider that Boscovich's points must be *somethings* which have the power to shift

---

[6] Similar reasoning has been deployed by many others; see note 2.

one another. They must have some intrinsic features which make them things in their own right, and they must in addition have the power to shift one another. Then, and only then, will there be something to move about. There must be some answer to the question What is at a point? independent of accelerative capacity.   (Campbell 1976: 93)

Campbell concludes with the observation that 'we do not understand Boscovich's theory until we know just how a universe with exactly one material point in it would differ from a universe containing none at all' (Campbell 1976: 94).[7]

10.4 A World of Relations?

Boscovich's world of pure powers and Holton's purely relational world are alike in being wholly non-qualitative. A non-qualitative world is a world empty of concrete objects—or so it appears. Perhaps I have been too quick. Suppose we accept the idea that a world of pure powers and a world of pure relations stand or fall together, even if it is, as I have argued, a mistake to regard powers as relations. Randall Dipert, inspired by C. S. Peirce, advances an argument to the conclusion that the world is, or could be, wholly constituted by relations (Dipert 1997).

Dipert, deploying technical resources borrowed from graph theory, suggests that a venerable Western tradition of attempting to sweep relations under the rug has led us to the kind of conceptual and ontological impasse we encounter in struggling to reconcile relativity and quantum physics, and accommodate these to everyday experience. Attempts to eliminate relations in favour of monadic properties fly in the face of relativity theory; so we need relations in any case.[8] Suppose every relation we require for a comprehensive account of the world could be reduced to instances of a single determinable ur-relation. And suppose we could express all worldly truths graph-theoretically in terms of this relation. Ordinary objects, even the basic particles of physics, would turn out to be subgraphs of the world graph.[9] What

---

[7] Campbell goes on to consider possible emendations of the theory involving attempts to specify 'that intrinsic quality, whatever it is, which material points have and other points lack', but these appear both ad hoc and at odds with the idea that material points are pure powers.

[8] For a rather different take on these issues, see Mulligan (1998).

[9] Do not confuse graphs with representations of graphs. It is difficult to envision a graph representation components of which did not include monadic properties—size, shape, colour, and the like.

appear to us as monadic properties of objects are in reality paths within subgraphs. External relations among objects (spatial, temporal, and causal relations, for instance) are, in reality, paths connecting subgraphs.

The deep truth, according to Dipert, is that objects are (or at any rate might be) wholly constituted by relations—indeed only the one master relation.

> Our regarding a particle to *have* the 'property' of a certain mass is our explanation of why it interacts in certain ways with other similarly interactive entities. We should perhaps express ourselves in terms of the root phenomenon, rather than its convenient monadistic shorthand, and say that certain entities interact with other entities in certain ways: this relational interactivity (and a 'disposition' for this interactivity over 'time') *is* the underlying phenomenon. Objects supposedly having masses, charges, spins, and so on are much like objects having 'locations': they are our ways of handily referring to deeply relational phenomena using convenient monadic expressions. (Dipert 1997: 340)[10]

Picture the world as a supergraph. 'Objects' are subgraphs. Paths connecting vertices are relations, and objects are wholly constituted by these relations. In representing a graph, we depict points connected by lines. Points, however, are constituted by intersections of lines and lines merely represent relations. There is nothing to the world graph beyond these relations.

You might think that relations require distinct non-relational relata, something to *be* related. You would be wrong. According to Dipert, 'the existence of asymmetric graphs shows conclusively, for the first time in the history of philosophy, that [. . .] distinct relata—vertices in asymmetric graphs, for example—can be distinct (Aristotle: known definitely), and that this distinctness can arise through relations alone' (Dipert 1997: 349).

To what extent does any of this advance the cause of a purely relational world? Everything, Dipert urges, is constituted by relations. But, while objects undoubtedly stand in endless relations to other objects, could this be *all there is* to the objects? In the first passage quoted above, Dipert suggests that, in addition to standing in relations, objects possess

---

[10] In keeping with Dipert's penchant for placing dubious items within quotation marks, I should note that 'particle' is placed within quotation marks in the sentence that occurs immediately preceding the sentences quoted.

dispositions to enter into new relations. But how exactly could a disposition of this kind be constituted by actual relations? Differently put, how could a pattern of relations ground modal truths of the sort expressing dispositional ascriptions? Perhaps a repeated pattern of relations, a pattern that occurs more than once, could be said to have the potential to occur again.[11] It is hard to see how this could substitute for the notion of a power or disposition, however. A disposition need never be manifested. How are unmanifested dispositions to be understood on Dipert's model? It is hard to say.

I have described the world graph as consisting wholly of relations. We represent these relations as lines and vertices as points at which lines intersect. 'Lines', however, are simply relations among points; points arise from the relations: no relations, no intersections, no points. Perhaps this is not quite right. Again, Dipert:

There might at first seem to be no place in these cold graphs for minds, consciousness, and other mental phenomena—unless, that is, everything is mental. [. . .] We should perhaps consider seriously the possibility that something like the pan-psychism of Spinoza, Leibniz, or Peirce is true, and that vertices are pure feelings (Peircean 'firstnesses'), constituting a distinct thought or object only when connected to other such entities.   (Dipert 1997: 358)

It is not easy to square the panpsychism described in this passage with the idea that the world is constituted by relations. Suppose vertices are conscious somethings; this suggests that the world comprises relations among (or within) conscious somethings. Now subtract the somethings but not the relations. This, after all, is the possibility Dipert regards as a momentous consequence of his theory. What is left? What, for that matter, does the presence of the somethings add? And what is it to add a something (or many somethings) to a world of relations? This would not be a matter of adding more relations. The somethings, if they are not themselves relations, must have (or be?) monadic properties. But in that case, there is more to the world than pure relations. A world in which pure relations replace monadic properties is hard to get

---

[11] The world graph is not *in* time and space; time and space are absorbed into the world graph.

a grip on; a world wholly constituted by pure relations but with the possibility of monadic properties is still harder to grasp.[12]

Deipert's view might in fact fall prey to a more fundamental difficulty. Let us suppose (what is almost certainly false) that we could represent all the truths, or all the fundamental truths, using graph theory. Let us suppose, as well, that this involves replacing monadic predicates with relational predicates. We now have a true account of the world expressed in a wholly relational vocabulary. It does not follow from this that the truth-makers for claims made in this vocabulary are relations. That would seem to follow only if you embraced the Picture Theory and imagined that we were entitled to ascribe a relational structure to reality on the grounds that our descriptions of that reality were couched in a relational idiom. The truth-makers for claims expressed in this idiom could be anything at all, however, including ordinary objects with ordinary properties standing in ordinary relations.

Where does this leave us? My suspicion is that proponents of the idea that the world is wholly relational are attracted to a Priestley/Boscovich-like conception of objects as 'power centres', and imagine that powers are relations. If I am right about that, and if my account of dispositionality is correct, then the view is doubly flawed. Powers are both intrinsic to their possessors and qualitative: no world could be a world of pure powers.[13]

10.5 An Argument from Armstrong

Before delving deeper into the nature of properties, let me mention an argument Armstrong (1961: ch. 15) advances[14] against the possibility that all properties might be Locke's primary qualities: shape, size, position, duration, movability, divisibility, and solidity.[15] Think of these as

---

[12] The latter possibility is especially hard to envisage in the light of Dipert's suggestion that there are a priori graph theoretic reasons why 'the actual world graph is the single one that is' (Dipert 1997: 356 n. 45). He continues: 'there is only one alethically "possible" world or graph.' To be fair, the latter assertion is not claimed to be the outcome of an a priori proof, but a 'regulative' or 'pragmatically justified' precept.

[13] If proponents of purely relational worlds regard objects as 'bundles' of relations—if they regard objects as wholly constituted by relations—they may be triply wrong; see §10.6 and Ch. 15 below.

[14] Armstrong no longer endorses the argument.

[15] As Armstrong notes, versions of the argument were advanced by Berkeley (*Principles of Human Knowledge*, §10) and by Hume (*A Treatise of Human Nature*, I. iv. §4). See also Smart (1963: 73–5). I omit number because, Armstrong contends, it does not obviously belong (but see §8.4 n. 6).

properties of the indivisible atoms from which everything else is made. Armstrong asks, 'Do these qualities suffice to give us a physical object?' His answer: they do not. 'These qualities just by themselves do not suffice to differentiate a physical object from empty space' (Armstrong 1961: 185).[16]

Armstrong is thinking of the primary qualities, in the way a physicist might, as wholly non-qualitative. (In this regard, a world made up of objects possessing only the primary qualities resembles a purely relational world or a world of pure powers.) Some of these qualities make up extensive magnitudes, others, perhaps, constitute relational magnitudes. Imagine an exhaustive quantitative description of the world and its contents, a description that mentioned only relations among objects and those objects' non-qualitative, primary qualities. How, asks Armstrong, would such a world differ from a world consisting entirely of empty space? Shape size, duration, and position are primary qualities, but a region of space could have a *shape, size,* or *duration.* If space is absolute, every spatial point or region will have an absolute *position.* If space is a relation among material bodies, then appeals to position, because they presuppose material bodies, cannot be used to distinguish material bodies from regions of empty space. Divisibility is a primary quality, but regions of space are *divisible* into subregions. *Motion,* another primary quality, belongs to bodies moving through space (or moving relative to other bodies). Armstrong takes this to mean that a body is in motion if it occupies adjacent spatial regions over successive intervals. But if this were all there were to motion, motion would be analysable in terms of shape, size, position, and duration. If these other concepts are insufficient to distinguish bodies from empty space, the addition of motion to the list cannot help.

What of *solidity*? Solidity, according to Locke, is what 'hinders the approach of two bodies when they are moving one towards another' (1690/1978: II. iv. §1). This comes close to equating solidity with impenetrability. Impenetrability is a power or disposition, however. If this exhausted the nature of solidity, adding it to the mix would not help. Regions of space are themselves mutually impenetrable in the sense that no region could be 'occupied' by another region. Locke, perhaps recognizing this point, regards solidity as including impenetra-

---

[16] Parenthetical references below are to this work.

bility plus 'something positive'. The presence of this additional ingredient might provide a way of distinguishing impenetrable bodies from
empty regions of space. Armstrong is doubtful: Locke characterizes
solidity as 'that which is impenetrable'. A distinction between pure
impenetrability and impenetrability plus 'something positive' is 'a distinction without a difference' (Armstrong 1961: 187).

We are left, according to this line of thought, without a coherent
conception of material bodies. This suggests that 'objects must have
at least one further quality over and above the [primary qualities]'
(Armstrong 1961: 187). Any such quality must satisfy two conditions.
First, the quality 'must not be analysable solely in terms of the [primary
qualities]' (p. 187). Second, given that relations among material bodies
presuppose material bodies, 'the new quality or qualities must not be
relations that physical objects have to other physical objects' (pp.
187–8).[17] Armstrong suggests that the only qualities satisfying both
conditions are the traditional secondary qualities: colours, sounds,
tastes, smells, and the like, or as yet unknown counterparts of these.

These reflections exhibit affinities with Berkeley's contention that
the primary qualities are metaphysically dependent on the secondary
qualities. Berkeley parlays this observation into an argument for
anti-realism about the material world: if the secondary qualities are
mind dependent, then so are the primary qualities, and indeed so are
material bodies generally.[18] Armstrong declines the anti-realist option
by refusing to accede to the mind dependence of the secondary
qualities. Primary and secondary qualities subsist side by side, neither
being reducible to the other.

Although there is much to be said for it, I believe that this kind of solution is, in the end, unstable. I shall explain why this is so in the course
of sketching an alternative conception of properties in Chapter 11.

10.6 Bundles and Substances

Holton and Dipert depict purely relational worlds. It would seem,
however, that a world comprising pure relations is indistinguishable
from a world consisting wholly of empty space in which nothing

---

[17] For reasons of the sort discussed already, the missing qualities could not be relations of any sort.
[18] For more recent thoughts along these lines, see Foster (1982); Blackburn (1990); Langton (1998).

whatever happens. The thought extends to the thesis that properties are pure powers. This is so even if powers are understood non-relationally (as I have argued they should be understood). In either case, we advance a characterization of everything in terms of everything else. The result is a holism empty of content.

Throughout the discussion I have depicted theorists who endorse a pure powers conception of properties and those who embrace the view that the world might be wholly constituted by relations as *bundle theorists*: particular objects are 'bundles' of compresent properties or relations. A bundle theorist would hold that objects are collections of powers to affect and be affected by other collections of powers or, if objects are bundles of relations, objects are collections of relations borne to other collections of relations. Bundle theories can be contrasted to traditional substance–attribute theories.[19] A substance–attribute theory holds that particular objects are substances possessing various properties and standing in various relations to other substances. On such a view, properties or relations do not make up objects in the way parts of a watch make up the watch. Rather, properties are *possessed by* objects; and objects stand in assorted relations to one another.

I believe it is natural to read Boscovich, Priestley, Holton, and Dipert as bundle theorists.[20] A rejection of intrinsic qualities looks like a rejection of a substance–attribute model of objects. Perhaps this is wrong. One possibility—a possibility I regard as a live option—is that there is but one substance: space, or space–time, or some all-embracing quantum field. Boscovich's powers, then, might be powers *of* regions of space to affect and be affected by powers possessed by other regions; relations might be relations among these regions. Note that a conception of this kind is very different from a view according to which powers are located *in* spatial regions or *at* spatial points.

Suppose Boscovich, Priestley, Holton, and Dipert *are* taken to be substance–attribute theorists. Suppose Boscovich, Priestley, Holton, and Dipert are read as holding that the world includes, in addition to properties or relations, substances: particulars possessing powers or

---

[19] See Ch. 15 below; see also Armstrong (1989: chs. 4 and 5; 1997: ch. 7); for further discussion of these topics, see Martin (1980); Hoffman and Rosenkrantz (1994); Lowe (2000).

[20] Langton (1998) suggests that Kant's 'phenomenal world' is a world of pure relations (see e.g. p. 162), so perhaps Kant should be added to this list (together with Hume).

standing in relations to other particulars. They might hold that there is but a single substance or that there are many distinct substances. Then, on Boscovich's view, particulars would possess only dispositional properties; Holton and Dipert would regard particulars as lacking intrinsic properties but as standing in various relations to one another. Particulars would *have* powers or stand in relations; particulars would not be *constituted by* their powers or relations.

One question is whether it would be possible for there to be substances whose *only* attributes are relations or substances the nature of which was exhausted by dispositions to affect or be affected by other substances whose only attributes are dispositions to affect or be affected by other substances. I would not know how to go about establishing that these options are flatly impossible. Still, it is hard to see how either option could be seen as much of an advance over their bundle-of-powers or bundle-of-relations counterparts. Why would a world comprising particulars the nature of which is exhausted by powers or relations be thought any more believable than a world comprising objects constituted by powers or relations? Worries about views of the latter sort transfer straightforwardly to views of the former sort.

Imagine a world consisting exclusively of particulars whose nature is exhausted by relations these bear to other particulars. Suppose these particulars were regions of space. (Alternatively: they are located in regions of space.) Would such a world differ from a world consisting of a static, empty space? Similarly, a world consisting of spatial regions with powers to affect and be affected by other regions would be hard to distinguish from a spatial world that included no spatial objects.

You might disagree. Physicists tell us that space is not merely an empty, featureless container. Space itself can be bent or warped by its occupants. Perhaps the character of space in purely relational worlds is affected by the presence of these relations. Perhaps objects whose nature is exclusively dispositional would similarly make themselves felt. The 'grain' of such a world might differ from that of a world in which the powers were different or in which powers were altogether absent.

The plausibility of these responses depends on our depicting space (or space–time, or the quantum field) as itself possessing an intrinsic qualitative nature. I have no objection, but it would be hard to square a 'meaty' conception of space with the thesis either that properties are purely powers or that properties are exclusively relational. Intrinsic qualities would be reintroduced through the back door.

Suppose I am right about all this. Suppose a purely relational world is not an option. Suppose properties must be more than pure powers. What conception of properties remains? This is the question to which I shall now turn.

The Identity Theory

11.1 Powers and Qualities

The time has come to offer a positive conception of the nature of properties. The conception I shall discuss is designed to avoid pitfalls associated with competing accounts while accommodating what might seem right about those accounts. I shall postpone until Chapters 12 and 13 the question whether properties are best regarded as universals, as modes, or as something else. Nothing I say here turns on an answer one way or the other to that question.

The conception of properties I have in mind has its origins in the work of C. B. Martin.[1] Martin refers to his conception as incorporating a 'surprising identity'. I call the theory implying this surprising identity the identity theory:

(IT) If P is an intrinsic property of a concrete object, P is simultaneously dispositional and qualitative; P's dispositionality and qualitativity are not aspects or properties of P; P's dispositionality, P_d, is P's qualitativity, P_q, and each of these is P: $P_d = P_q = P$.

This means, in effect, that every property of a concrete spatio-temporal object is simultaneously qualitative and dispositional. A property's 'qualitativity' is strictly identical with its dispositionality, and these are—are strictly identical with—the property itself.

You might regard a conception of this kind as unintelligible. It will strike you as unintelligible, certainly, if you assume from the outset that dispositionality and qualitativity are mutually exclusive, if you assume that every property is either dispositional or qualitative, and no

---

[1] See Martin (1997); Martin and Heil (1999); and Heil (1998b: ch. 6). The identity thesis discussed here is not to be confused with the mind–brain identity theory.

property could be both. Recall, however, Locke's primary qualities. Unlike Armstrong, I take these to be paradigmatically properties of the sort I am envisaging.[2]

Whatever the Mind perceives in it self or is the immediate object of Perception, Thought, or Understanding, that I call *Idea*; and the Power to produce any *Idea* in our mind I call *Quality* of the Subject in which the power is. Thus a Snow-ball having the power to produce in us the *Ideas* of *White, Cold*, and *Round*, the Powers to produce those *Ideas* in us as they are in the Snow-ball I call *Qualities*.   (Locke 1690/1978: II. viii. 8)

Being spherical is a manifest quality of a snowball. But it is in virtue of being spherical that a snowball could, for instance, roll: sphericity is, it would seem, a power possessed by the snowball. Recognizing this, you might be inclined to reason (as philosophers have been wont to reason): if sphericity is a power, then it cannot be a quality. On the contrary; the snowball's sphericity *is* a quality possessed by the snowball and *is* a power. Locke is right to think of primary qualities as *qualities*.[3]

As in the case of the thesis that properties are pure powers, it is convenient, although potentially misleading, to describe properties as powers, or as qualities, or as both powers and qualities. Rather, properties are taken to contribute in distinctive ways to the dispositionalities and qualities of their possessors. The dispositionalities and qualities possessed by a given object depend on its ensemble of properties. A key of a certain size and shape will open a lock, but only if it is sufficiently rigid; a ball made of soft dough at room temperature will not roll.[4]

The identity theory is to be distinguished from theories according to which the dispositional and the qualitative are 'aspects', or 'sides', or higher-order properties of properties. A property's dispositionality and its qualitativity are, as Locke might have put it, the selfsame property differently considered. The identity theory diverges as well from the popular thesis that dispositionality is somehow grounded in the non-

[2] For a very different view, see Langton (1998: ch. 7).

[3] This enables us to make sense of Locke's otherwise puzzling insistence that solidity is not pure impenetrability. *Contra* Armstrong (1961: 187), solidity endows its possessors with qualities and with powers, and so for any property.

[4] Shoemaker speaks of 'conditional powers': something possessing the property of being knife-shaped has a conditional power to cut butter if it is made of wood or steel. See Shoemaker (1980, 1998). I prefer to think of powers as powers *simpliciter*. The powers possessed by an object are the result of powers bestowed by the object's total complement of properties.

dispositional. Sometimes this is put by saying that dispositional properties supervene on categorical properties (or categorical properties
together with laws of nature). An identity theorist need have no objection to the supervenience claim—nor for that matter the claim that
every property is a power. These follow as trivial consequences of the
identity thesis.

We have seen already that it is easy to turn examples of qualities into examples of powers. Think of a quality: being white, for
instance, or being sweet. It is surely in virtue of its being white that a
cupcake would look white and in virtue of its being sweet that the
cupcake would taste sweet. Being white and being sweet are powers of
the cupcake to affect us in particular ways. The mistake—not, I like to
think, a mistake made by Locke—would be to conclude from this that
whiteness and sweetness are *mere* powers. Admittedly, Locke does from
time to time describe the secondary qualities as mere powers. But what
are the secondary qualities? These are powers possessed by an object
(owing to its possession of particular primary qualities) to produce
certain kinds of experience in us. Secondary qualities are qualities distinguished by reference to certain of their manifestations: their effects
on conscious observers.

The resulting conception is straightforward. Objects have various
(primary) qualities. Arrangements of these yield experiences of particular kinds in conscious observers. In some cases, experiences can be
reliable guides to the qualities that produce them: the experiences,
Locke says, 'resemble' the qualities. This is so for shape, size, and (if
Locke is right) the remaining primary qualities. In other cases, experiences are less reliable indicators of their causes. A red triangle looks triangular because it has a triangular shape. It looks red because its surface
exhibits (Locke speculates) a certain kind of micro-texture.[5] Describing secondary qualities as powers is Locke's way of bringing this point
home. If you identify an object's colour with the micro-texture of its
surface, you cannot then say that this texture is a pure power. On the
contrary, the surface has complex qualities and powers, among these
the power to produce in us experiences of distinctive sorts.

---

[5] This does not mean that the triangle is not really red. If Locke is right, the triangle's being red is its
having a particular kind of surface texture: the truth-maker for 'the triangle is red' is the triangle's having a
particular kind of surface texture.

11.2 Identity All the Way Down

The sciences are sometimes said to be in the business of identifying and classifying powers. The mass of an electron, its spin and charge, could be regarded as powers possessed by the electron. Science is silent on an electron's qualities. (Perhaps, in so far as an electron could be thought of as occupying a fuzzy region of space, an electron could be thought of as having something rather like a shape.) We should be mistaken to interpret silence as outright denial, however. Your failure to perceive something need not be a matter of your perceiving its absence (see Armstrong 1968). Analogously, physics' silence on qualities does not amount to an affirmation that there are no qualities. Physics aims at a description of the world centred around quantifiable relations among objects. In this regard, physics reflects our capacity for partial consideration.

I can think of two reasons to suppose that properties of the elementary constituents are (as I have claimed every property is) simultaneously qualitative and dispositional. First, the denial of this view apparently leads to a conception of properties of the fundamental things as pure powers; I have argued that such a conception is prima facie implausible. Second, although you may find it difficult to imagine how charge or charm could be a quality, you probably find it natural to ascribe qualities to ordinary middle-sized objects: tables, stones, trees. It would be comforting to think that qualities of these middle-sized items are what you get when you combine elementary things in the right ways. The mechanism here is broadly combinatorial: the qualities of wholes are built up from qualities of the parts (and the arrangement of these).[6] This suggests that there must be some route from qualities of parts to qualities of wholes. Such a route need not be analytical or available to us a priori. The idea that qualities of complex objects owe their character to qualities of their constituents is something we acknowledge in everyday life. Cooks explain qualities of dishes they have prepared by citing qualities of the dishes' ingredients; painters explain the qualities of different colours and textures of paint by reference to

---

[6] Might qualities 'emerge'? I have nothing against emergence, but I do not think that the properties of wholes emerge in any sense that involves an addition of being to the properties of parts of a whole (suitably organized). Properties emerge 'horizontally' when new kinds of particles are produced—in an accelerator, for instance (see Martin 1997).

qualities of constituent pigments; audiophiles trace the qualities of amplified sounds emitted by loudspeakers to qualities of the components.

Is it outrageous to think that the mass and charge of an electron are qualities? Evidently not. Many philosophers have been attracted to the idea that powers are grounded in categorical properties. If an electron's mass and charge are powers then, on this familiar view, mass and charge are grounded in qualities of the electron. If mass and charge are taken to be purely categorical bases of powers, they are no less qualities. In either case, the mass and charge of an electron are associated with qualities of the electron. The identity theory interprets this association as strict identity: the quality associated with the mass of an electron is strictly identical with the power associated with that mass. Neither is 'reducible to' nor grounds the other.

The identity theory implies that you could not vary an object's qualities without varying its dispositionalities; and you could not vary an object's dispositionalities without changing it qualitatively. In altering a ball's shape, a quality, you alter its disposition to roll; in changing its colour, another quality, you change its disposition to reflect light in a particular way. Altering the ball's disposition to roll or to reflect light in a particular way involves changing the ball's qualitative make-up.

11.3 The Legacy of Functionalism

The widespread influence of functionalism on our conception of properties has made it especially difficult to appreciate the force of such examples. A central tenet of functionalism is that objects can be dispositionally indiscernible but differ qualitatively as much as you please. Functionalists make this idea plausible by describing functional processes at an elevated level of abstraction. Egg-beaters share causal powers vis-à-vis eggs, but could be utterly different with respect to their qualities. This sounds uncontroversial, however, only because we have elected to describe egg-beaters—and their inputs and outputs— in a relatively 'abstract', non-specific way.

The point applies to the Prior, Pargetter, and Jackson (1982) 'default' conception of dispositionality, according to which a disposition is a higher-level property possessed by an object by virtue of its possession of some distinct lower-level qualitative property. One consideration thought to favour this conception is that dispositional properties appear to be 'multiply realizable'. Consider being fragile. Objects can be fragile in virtue of having very different compositions and very different structures. So: same disposition, different qualitative (or structural) basis.

All this will seem plausible only so long as you remain content to characterize fragility in a relatively non-specific way. If being fragile is characterized as shattering when struck by a massive solid object, for instance, this is something shared by a light bulb, an ice cube, and a kneecap: same higher-level dispositional property, different lower-level realizing properties. Light bulbs, ice cubes, and kneecaps shatter in very different ways, however. These 'ways' reflect these objects' possession of distinct, though similar, dispositions. We need not posit a higher-level property here. We have, rather, a range of similar properties all satisfying a single, moderately imprecise predicate, 'is fragile'. Functionalists mistake a non-specific predicate satisfied by a range of imperfectly similar states or properties for a specific predicate satisfied by a unique higher-level 'multiply realized' state or property.[7] Putative lower-level realizers of fragility are really just different ways of being fragile.

If this is right, then it is less obvious that dispositions and qualities *could* vary independently. Try changing a fragile object qualitatively, without altering it dispositionally. The object might remain fragile but become fragile 'in a different way'. Of course, you could change a fragile object qualitatively in a way that has no bearing on its fragility. If you dye an ice cube pink, you do not affect its disposition to shatter. But, if I am right, dyeing the ice cube must change it dispositionally in *some* way. And, indeed, it does: a pink ice cube reflects light differently from a colourless ice cube: a pink ice cube, but not a colourless ice cube, would look pink.

To be sure, Armstrong could agree with all this: qualitativity and dispositionality go hand in hand—but only contingently, only given contingent laws of nature.[8] What advantage might the identity theory offer over the contingency thesis?

---

[7] The Picture Theory encourages us to view abstract, non-specific descriptions satisfied by ranges of determinate properties as determinate descriptions satisfied by non-specific properties; see Ch. 5 above.

[8] Dean Zimmerman made this point. I am grateful to David Armstrong and David Robb for discussion.

The identity theory provides a straightforward account—indeed, the simplest account imaginable—of the connection between an object's powers and its qualities. For Armstrong, the connection requires distinct laws of nature. Why, we might ask, do such laws connect qualities and dispositionalities as they do? The answer, in so far as the question concerns the fundamental qualities and powers, is that they just do. An identity theorist agrees that there is no further explanation for the fact that certain qualities endow their possessors with certain powers (that is, for the fact that actual properties are what they are), but, if powers and qualities are identified, this is not something that could require explanation. The brute fact is that these properties *are* properties of objects in our world. If you are keeping score, an identity theorist is committed to a single brute fact: that these properties are instantiated. Armstrong is committed to a pair of brute facts: that these properties are instantiated and that these laws of nature obtain.[9]

A proponent of an Armstrong-style view would no doubt insist that this is a price well worth paying in order to preserve the contingency of the relation between qualities and powers. To this, an identity theorist might reply that the contingency is only apparent, or, perhaps better, that the source of the appearance resides, not in the power–quality connection but in which properties are in fact on the scene.

11.4 Dispositional and Categorical Pluralism

Many readers will remain unmoved. You might agree that it is a mistake to regard dispositional properties as higher-level properties extruded somehow by categorical properties, and you might even be willing to concede that it is a bad idea to regard every property as a pure power or disposition. But you might draw the line at the thought that properties are simultaneously dispositional and qualitative. Why not embrace a pluralistic approach, allowing that there are two mutually exclusive kinds of property: dispositional and categorical/qualitative? The actual world (and maybe any imaginable world of concrete objects) includes a mix of both.

The idea that dispositions and qualities are kinds of property could

---

[9] A worry about the Armstrong view I shall mention but not discuss concerns the puzzling nature of the necessitation relation introduced by Armstrong's higher-order universals.

seem altogether natural. Cases I have offered to illustrate the identity theory—a ball's sphericity or colour, for instance—might be reconstrued as cases in which property pairs are present: one qualitative and one dispositional. Perhaps properties making up these pairs co-occur as a matter of natural necessity: a contingent law of nature ensures that, whenever the one is on hand, the other is as well. There is no question of every property's being purely dispositional; but, so long as some objects possess properties that are not purely dispositional—properties that would, presumably, be purely qualitative—this should be enough to block the kinds of regress associated with the thought that properties might be 'pure powers' (discussed in Chapters 8–10).

Here I can only fall back on previous observations. A pure quality, a property altogether lacking in dispositionality, would be undetectable and would, in one obvious sense, make no difference to its possessor. Even if you conceive of such properties as nomologically connected to dispositions (even if, as a matter of natural law, purely qualitative properties co-occurred with dispositional sidekicks), they would remain idle.[10] The whole notion of purely qualitative properties appears misconceived and unnecessary.

Where, then, does this leave the idea that some properties might be purely qualitative and some purely dispositional? We should have to suppose that a world containing such a mixture of properties would be a world of pure powers mixed with undetectable, wholly idle qualities. I am not prepared to argue that such a world is flatly impossible. It does strike me, however, as combining two ill-considered conceptions of properties (properties as pure qualities and properties as pure powers or dispositions) into a single ill-considered whole. Philosophers who have grown accustomed to thinking of properties on the categorical–dispositional model might find this a remarkable claim. My contention, however, is that the categorical–dispositional model, despite its comfortable familiarity, is deeply flawed.

11.5 A Dual-Aspect Account

Before moving on, let me belabour a point touched on earlier. I have heard the identity theory described (not by its proponents) as a 'dual-

---

[10] And, of course, the question remains: what *is* it to conceive of such properties?

aspect' conception of properties: every property has a dispositional aspect and a qualitative aspect. I am not sure what aspects are, but one possibility is that aspects are properties.[11] If this were so, then we might imagine that qualities and dispositionalities were bestowed on objects by properties in virtue of those properties' themselves possessing higher-order properties. These higher-order properties would be the original property's aspects.

Such a position strikes me as objectionable for at least two reasons. First, and most simply, it is hard to see how this is an advance over the idea that there are two kinds of property, categorical and dispositional. Why should the promotion (or is it demotion?) of dispositional and qualitative properties to the status of higher-order properties render this bifurcation more plausible?

Second, although it is easy to talk the talk, it is not clear to me what a property's possessing the envisaged higher-order properties could amount to. We are trying to imagine a property, sphericity say, having the property of (as it were) qualitative sphericity and the property of dispositional sphericity. Call the base property P, and P's higher-order properties Q and R. Bearing in mind that P is a property, not an object, what is there to P beyond Q and R? (In that case, the truth-maker for ascriptions of properties to P would be P itself.) But, if P just is Q and R, then either P is composite (in which case the idea that Q and R are higher-order properties of P drops out and we are back with the categorical–dispositional property model) or the double-aspect view collapses into the identity theory: P is Q and P is R, so Q is R (alternatively: Q and R are not different components or aspects of P, but P itself, differently considered).

You might object that a capacity for partial consideration presupposes distinctions in the world, and distinctions are a matter of differences in properties. If a property, P, could be considered both as a disposition and as a quality, then, unless we are suffering an illusion, P must incorporate distinct features answering to these two modes of consideration. Talk of distinguishable features, however, is just an oblique way of indicating distinct properties.

Thoughts along these lines maintain an air of plausibility so long as the model for P is an object. Ordinary objects have multiple properties. Considering the same object in different ways (now as something

---

[11] This seems to be what proponents of Spinozistic double-aspect accounts of the mind–body relation have in mind. See e.g. Hirst (1959: ch. 7).

Figure 11.1. Necker cube

round, now as something pink) is often a matter of considering distinct properties possessed by the object. In the case before us, however, the focus is on properties, not objects. The model, if you want one, is an ambiguous figure—a Necker cube, for instance—that can be seen now one way, now another (Figure 11.1). This need not be a matter of attending to different properties of the figure. Rather, we consider the figure as a whole in different ways.

To my mind, the identity theory is independently attractive, but, even if it were not, it appears to win by default! Purely qualitative properties lack appeal, as do pure powers. Mixing these does not help matters, nor does turning dispositionality and qualitativity into aspects or kinds of higher-order property.

11.6 Armstrong's Thesis

How does the conception of properties I have defended here—Martin's identity theory—stack up against Armstrong's conception? The chief difference is that the identity theory (in common with conceptions of properties as pure powers) builds powers into properties. Armstrong, a good Humean in this respect, regards powers as contingent: the fact that a given property makes a particular contribution to the dispositionalities of its possessors is a purely contingent fact. There could be worlds indiscernible from ours with respect to properties they contain, yet utterly different from ours with respect to the powers these properties bestow on their possessors.

A view of this kind distinguishes first-order properties and laws of nature. Properties bestow powers only because of the addition of laws. Laws themselves are second-order properties resembling my first-order powers. Properties and laws might vary independently: the same qualitative properties combined with different laws yield different dispositionalities. In our world, for instance, the property of sphericity has the property of disposing its possessor to roll; but this is a property the property of sphericity might have lacked. This key has the power to turn a particular lock. Were the laws of nature different, however, the key (or a key with precisely similar properties) could lack this power.

Philosophers who follow Hume in regarding laws of nature as contingent will find such a view attractive. I have addressed this point already (§9.4), suggesting that there are ways to accommodate the apparent contingency of laws of nature without giving up the idea that properties' dispositionalities are built in. The dispute here strikes me as close to a wash. The question remains whether an Armstrong-style view enjoys further, as yet unmentioned, advantages or liabilities.

I cannot speak for its advantages, but I would like to mention a possible liability of Armstrong's position. I have spoken of properties as contributing differentially to dispositionalities of their possessors. Armstrong can accept this description. He will differ, however, in regarding the powers bestowed by a property as conditional on laws of nature. Laws of nature are second-order necessitation relations of the form: Fs necessitate Gs.[12] Suppose F and G are properties and that Fs have the power to produce Gs: objects possessing F are disposed to yield Gs, or disposed to yield Gs under certain conditions. One way to understand this view is to think of Fs having the power to yield Gs as Fs having a second-order property, $F^\star$, the property of disposing Fs bearers to produce Gs. $F^\star$ is a property the Fs might have or lack. Thus, although an object's being F disposes that object to behave in a particular way, this is a contingent fact.

What is emerging is a picture of properties as possessing a certain nature, where this is partly a matter of the property's possessing particular higher-order properties. Suppose F is a simple, non-composite property. F might be thought to have a certain nature: this would be F itself. In addition, F itself has $F^\star$, the property of affecting the dispositionalities of its possessors in a distinctive way. $F^\star$ does not belong to the nature of F; F is $F^\star$ only contingently. If a property is a way an object is or might be, then a higher-order property is a way a property is or might be. $F^\star$, then, is a way F is (but might not have been).

Talk of higher-order properties—properties of properties—comes

---

[12] Armstrong takes properties to be universals. Because this embellishment makes no difference to the point I want to make here, I ignore it in what follows.

cheap, but, as I have suggested already, it is far from clear what such talk amounts to. We can distinguish objects, from ways those objects are. A ball can be distinguished from its shape, or colour, or mass. But it is not clear to me that we can so easily distinguish ways a property is from the property itself. If some of these ways are contingent, this is to say that the property itself might have been different. Note, however, that this is something an identity theorist (or, for that matter, anyone who thought that 'properties are powers') could readily accept! Thinking that a property, *F*, 'could have been different', is just to envision a different property, similar perhaps to *F*.

I do not want to put too much weight on these considerations. If nothing else, however, they make clear that an account of powers that invokes second-order properties needs to be scrutinized carefully before being embraced. In the end, talk of second-order properties may prove unilluminating.

11.7 Meinongianism

Before moving on, let me consider an objection Armstrong has raised to the identity theory (see Armstrong 1997: 79, 250; Armstrong credits J. J. C. Smart with calling the objection to his attention). Suppose that dispositions are always dispositions *for* certain manifestations with particular kinds of reciprocal disposition partner. (In fact, typical dispositions will be dispositions for many different kinds of manifestation with many different kinds of disposition partner.) This feature of dispositions, their 'pointing beyond' themselves, resembles the 'intentionality' associated with states of mind (see Martin and Pfeifer 1986; Martin and Heil 1998; and Chapter 18 below). This, however, suggests that every disposition brings with it endless 'Meinongian' objects: non-actual possible manifestations to which the disposition 'points.' The flame of the match I am holding would scorch the tip of a unicorn's horn, were a unicorn present.

Here we have a pair of worries. First, and most obviously, worries about the unwelcome existence of spooky non-actual possibilia. Second, there is a suggestion that, in so far as a disposition is always *for* some manifestation (with some reciprocal disposition partner), no disposition could be simple. This is bad news if you think that some properties (the charge of an electron, for instance) might be simple. If powers or dispositions are, by virtue of being *for* various manifestations with various reciprocal disposition partners, invariably complex, then no simple property could be a power. This is an embarrassment if you subscribe, as I do, to the thesis that properties are powers.

Let me explain how I think these misgivings might come about. Suppose you thought that powers or dispositionalities bestowed on objects by properties were contingent. It might be that Fs, in concert with Gs, yield manifestation M. This is contingent, we are pretending, so there is nothing in the Fs or Gs themselves that necessitates M. To obtain M we need something further: a law of nature, perhaps. Think of this law of nature as a higher-order property, a property possessed by the Fs (or perhaps a higher-order relation between the Fs and the Gs or between the Fs, the Gs, and the Ms). Call this second-order property or relation N. Powers bestowed by F and G are contingent because they are detachable from F and G, 'external' to F and G. Fs together with Gs yield Ms only given N. If we want to speak of a power to yield M, here, we have three elements: (1) F, (2) G, and (3) N.

Now imagine this is your starting point and you want to know what it could mean for powers to be 'built into' properties. In that case, you have the properties, items (1) and (2). You do not have the 'connecting' item (3), however. If properties include powers, then this means these connections must be built into the properties: N must be included in F and G. On the view that powers are associated with properties contingently, the connections are external to the properties; if we deny the contingency, we in effect relocate the connections inside the properties. This makes every property complex (on the assumption that every property is power bestowing). And, because the items we have moved inside the properties are connections with other properties, it means that every property must include all its possible connections: Meinongianism!

Does the identity theory succumb to Meinongianism? Suppose you thought, as an identity theorist thinks, that properties were powers in roughly the sense that a property is what it is in virtue of the distinctive contribution it makes to the dispositionalities of its bearers. In that case you would not want 'connections' among powers to reside outside those powers. It does not follow, however, that the connections reside inside the properties. The truth-maker for the claim that Fs together with Gs would yield manifestation M is not something in addition to F and G, not even some detachable component of F and G, but just F and G: it is 'of the nature' of F and G to yield manifestation M. This is what it means to say that properties are powers or that powers are 'built into' properties.

Imagine a key with a particular shape. The key would open locks of a particular (complementary) shape. This power is intrinsic to the key. If the key 'points beyond' itself to locks of a particular sort, it does so in virtue of its intrinsic features. This is what it is to be a key of this shape. The key is (as Martin would put it) 'ready to go'. We can say this without committing ourselves to the existence of possible locks. The truth-maker for 'this key would open a lock of kind K' is not the key, a possible lock of kind K, and a relation between the key and K. The truth-maker for the assertion is just the key itself's being a particular way: its being rigid and its possessing a particular shape.

11.8 Moving Ahead

Perhaps I have said enough to persuade previously uncommitted readers to take the identity theory seriously and to regard it as at least within the realm of possibility that every property (that is, every intrinsic property of a concrete object) is at once qualitative and dispositional. There are no purely qualitative properties; there are no pure powers. The human mind, as Locke noted, has a capacity for 'partial consideration'. We can consider an object's properties as dispositions or powers or we can consider them as qualities. In so doing we consider, not two kinds of property, but the selfsame properties in two different ways.

Why should any of this matter? I believe that inadequate conceptions of properties have spawned confusion and despair in the philosophy of mind. Nowadays consciousness is frequently cited as the deepest mystery confronting philosophers and scientists (see McGinn 1989; Chalmers 1996; Nagel 1998). Against this background, it is widely acknowledged that current theories are hopelessly inadequate. What appears to be called for is not more of the same—more neuroscience, more epicycles in going theories—but an utterly different kind of approach.[13]

Perhaps it is time to re-examine certain of our fundamental assumptions. These constrain the space of possibilities we find open to us. Residual dogmas over the nature of properties infect theories that presuppose them. Only by recognizing alternatives and seeing where these lead do we have any hope of moving ahead. If nothing else, perhaps these remarks can serve to direct attention to foundational issues that have been too long ignored in the philosophy of mind. These are topics to be addressed in Chapters 17–20. First, however, a number of loose ends remain to be tied up.

---

[13] David Chalmers (1996) offers *both* more of the same *and* something utterly different. Incidentally, I do not mean to denigrate neuroscience. My point is that a satisfactory way of conceptualizing minds and their place in nature is not something to be deduced from a successful neuroscience.

CHAPTER 12

Universals

12.1 Universals and Modes

The preceding chapter advances a conception of properties as simultaneously dispositional and qualitative. A property makes a distinctive contribution to the qualities and dispositionalities of its possessors. In contributing to an object's dispositionalities, a property thereby contributes to the object's qualities; in contributing to the object's qualities, the property thereby contributes to the object's dispositionalities. In all of this, I have assumed that properties are real. It is now time to make clear what this means.

Properties are *ways*: ways objects are (see Martin 1980; Seargent 1985: ch. 4; Armstrong 1989: 96–8; 1997: 30–1). Properties are not parts of objects. Properties do not make up objects in the way the parts of a table—legs, frame, top, and screws holding these together—make up the table. A table and its parts possess properties. Objects possess properties, but I am sceptical of the idea that properties possess properties. Just as a property is a way some object is, a property of a property would be a way a property is. But a way a property is just is the property itself (or, if the property is complex, a constituent of the property). More generally: truth-makers for claims as to ways properties are are the properties themselves.

Non-philosophers will be ready to move on, but philosophers will want to press a further point: are properties universals? Traditionally, universals are distinguished from particulars. A particular is a one-shot affair. A particular exists at a definite time and place and is distinct from every other particular, however similar. This tree, this table, this galaxy are particulars. Particular objects could be exactly alike with respect to all their properties (or, at least, all their intrinsic properties), yet differ numerically. Universals are, in contrast, repeatable.

Examples of particulars that spring to mind, are, as the examples mentioned above, invariably objects. This suggests a neat ontological division between universals (repeatable ways objects are) and particulars (the objects themselves). Any particular object must be some way or other, and any way must be a way some object is or could be. If that is so, and if properties are universals, then universals need particulars and particulars need universals. A world lacking particulars, like a world lacking universals, is a world in which nothing is any way at all. We are homing in on the idea that universals are constituted by their instances. A different view is that universals remain aloof from their instances. The universal itself resides outside space and time, or at any rate a universal, unlike its instances, does not reside inside space and time. This is sometimes put by saying that universals are located in a Platonic heaven, but it might be better to say that universals, so conceived, have no location at all. If you thought of universals this way, then you would have no trouble imagining worlds containing universals but no particulars.[1]

I shall have more to say about these competing conceptions of universals presently. First, however, let me introduce a rather different way of thinking about properties. This will provide a hint of what is at stake in assessing properties' ontological standing.

Imagine that you are holding a baseball. The ball, let us suppose, possesses the property of sphericity. Now consider this property is, as it were, 'in' the ball: *the sphericity of this ball*. This looks like a particular. There is the particular ball, and the ball's particular sphericity. If this makes sense to you, then you are thinking of properties (as well as objects) as particulars; you are thinking of properties as 'particularized' ways particular objects are. Thus considered, properties are not universals, but what have traditionally been called modes or individual accidents. If properties are ways objects are, then modes or individual accidents are particularized ways objects are: the sphericity or whiteness of this baseball; the greenness of this tree; the mass of this electron.

Nowadays philosophers call particularized properties *tropes*. (Other labels include 'abstract particulars' and 'moments'.) I prefer 'mode' to

---

[1] If you thought that properties were Platonic, transcendent universals existing apart from space and time, you might think, as well, that properties exist 'necessarily', or, as Leibniz would have put it, in every possible world. The idea is difficult to evaluate. Why should an entity's existing, but not in space and time, mean that the entity could not fail to exist?

'trope'. Tropes have come to be identified with views championed by G. F. Stout, D. C. Williams, Keith Campbell, and Peter Simons, among others (Stout 1921/1930; Williams 1953; Campbell 1981, 1990; Simons 1994). These authors regard objects as 'bundles' of tropes. This makes it appear that tropes are parts or ingredients of objects. Objects, however, are not made up of their properties in the way a clock is made up of its parts: screws, gears, a spring, an escapement, and a case. Parts of objects are objects, not properties. Properties—modes—are particularized ways objects are. (I shall say more about modes in Chapter 13 and discuss objects in Chapters 15 and 16.)

12.2 Possible Worlds and Properties as Sets

The chief competitor to the idea that properties are modes is the traditional conception of properties as universals. Both these views can be contrasted to various reductionist or eliminativist accounts of properties according to which properties are taken to be classes or sets of objects or thought not to exist at all. I very much doubt that any of these competing views on properties (including the one I favour) could be established by reasoning a priori. Nor do I think that much is to be gained by imagining that a defence of any one view requires conclusive arguments against its rivals. Each of these approaches to properties evolved as a response to distinctive philosophical pressures. The most straightforward test of an ontological thesis is its overall power relative to its competitors: which thesis best accounts for features of the world we encounter in science and in everyday life?

In this regard, David Lewis has produced an important theory of properties as sets of actual and possible objects (see e.g. Lewis 1983). To appreciate Lewis's theory fully requires negotiating a wide-ranging metaphysical framework, the centrepiece of which is the contention that our world, the *actual world*, is merely one world among infinitely many existing but non-actual *alternative* worlds.[2] These 'possible

---

[2] Martin has convinced me that Lewis's view is best characterized as a view about *alternative*—rather than *possible*—worlds. Lewis's 'possible worlds' are not mere possibilia, but concrete alternative worlds, differing from our own world in various ways. (This is one respect in which Lewis's 'possible' worlds differ from those of Leibniz.) I shall nevertheless honour current practice and refer at times to these alternative worlds as possible worlds.

worlds' are causally isolated from one another. Each is on an equal ontological footing with the rest. Our world—the actual world—is merely one world among an infinitude of sister worlds. The actual world is special only in the sense that we happen to reside in it. Indeed, the phrase 'the actual world' is, like 'here' or 'now', indexical; it picks out the world occupied by the speaker.

The existence of such alternative worlds strikes many philosophers, and most non-philosophers as incredible.[3] Doubts about their existence, however, have not discouraged philosophers from appealing to possible worlds (as implicitly fictional entities) in accounts of many different philosophical theses. This has the severe disadvantage of postponing consideration of what the real truth-makers might be for theses tricked out in the jargon of possible worlds. Lewis has an answer: the truth-makers are the alternative worlds and their relations. But, if alternative worlds are nothing more than convenient fictions, claims explicated in terms of alternative worlds must be grounded in features of the actual world. Why not pursue these features directly?[4]

I shall bracket Lewis's ontology, and bracket as well reductionist accounts of properties, as sets and eliminativist accounts according to which there are no properties. To the extent that we understand what it is for an object to be a member of a set we do so by, covertly perhaps, thinking of objects as differing propertywise. The set of red objects is the set of objects possessing a property: being red. Objects are members of the set in virtue of possessing this property; they do not possess the property in virtue of belonging to the set. As a proof that properties are not sets, this argument suffers the embarrassment of begging the question. But it is not my intention to offer a proof that objects must have properties or that properties are not sets, only to mention one consideration (among many) that could lead someone to find favour with properties as something other than sets or classes. In any case, I

---

[3] Lewis's non-actual, alternative worlds are not to be confused with the 'many worlds' posited by some interpretations of quantum physics (see Everett 1973). If there are 'many worlds', these are all parts of the actual world. If Everett is wrong, there could nevertheless be worlds in which his interpretation held true: worlds comprising many Everett worlds.

[4] A parallel point holds for theorists who do take alternative worlds seriously. Appeals to possible worlds are supposed to illuminate modal claims: the claim, for instance, that you would be ill if you ate this mushroom. We evaluate such counterfactuals by noting how things stand in various 'nearby' alternative worlds (worlds more similar in particular respects to our world than others). But similarity is an internal relation: whether a given world is more similar to our world in relevant ways than another world depends on intrinsic features of our world. These are the features we need to scrutinize.

suspect that many of those who have held properties in disdain have really rejected one or another philosophical conception of properties. You can reject a conception without rejecting what it is a conception of.

What is to be said for properties, and, in particular, what is to be said for properties as modes? Consider this beetroot. We can say truly:

(1) The beetroot is red.
(2) The beetroot is spherical.

Following Martin (1980), I suggest that (1) and (2) do not hold of the beetroot *holus bolis*. Rather (1) is true of the beetroot in virtue of something about the beetroot. Similarly, (2) is true of the beetroot in virtue of something—something *else*—about the beetroot. These 'somethings about' are properties of the beetroot, ways the beetroot is. It is in virtue of its possession of these properties that the beetroot falls into the class of red things and into the class of spherical things.

What the beetroot does or could do depends on its properties. The beetroot rolls (or would roll) because it is spherical, not because it is a member of the class of spherical things; the beetroot looks (or would look) red because it is red, not because it is a member of the class of red things.[5] The causal powers or, as I prefer, dispositionalities of the beetroot depend in this way on its properties.

12.3 *In rebus* Universals

The beetroot, let us suppose, possesses properties, but what are properties? One traditional answer is that properties are universals. Some philosophers regard universals as Platonic entities existing 'outside' the world of space and time. Concrete objects are said to 'instantiate' these universals. A concrete object—the beetroot, for instance—is an instance of sphericity and redness, but sphericity and redness themselves are distinct from their instances.

Other philosophers, most notably David Armstrong, regard universals as denizens of the space–time world (Armstrong 1978, 1989, 1997).

---

[5] Again, as in previous chapters, the cases are simplified in order to make the exposition less cumbersome. The dispositionalities and qualities possessed by an object depend on its overall complement of properties.

The universal sphericity is itself present in the beetroot *and* in every other spherical object. Universals differ in an important respect from concrete particulars, however: a universal is *wholly present* in each of its numerically distinct instances. Two numerically distinct spherical objects—these two beetroots—literally share a constituent: the universal sphericity. It is not merely that the beetroots are exactly similar with respect to shape. They are similar, of course, but this similarity is owing to their having a common property: the shape of one beetroot is strictly identical with the shape of the other beetroot.[6]

Transcendent, unworldly Platonic universals existing other than in space and time yet related mysteriously to their instances are an acquired taste. Although resourceful philosophers can adduce considerations favourable to such entities, I shall not try to do so here (see §13.7 below). My focus will be on *in rebus* universals of the sort defended by Armstrong.

Philosophers embracing a view of this kind take literally talk of distinct objects 'sharing' properties or having 'the same' property. 'The same', they contend, means strictly identical (what logicians express by means of the identity sign: '='). This provides a neat solution to the venerable problem of the one-over-many. How could distinct, and otherwise very different, objects be *the same* shape? The objects share a common element: one property, many instances.

Assuming that properties affect the dispositionalities of their possessors, we can easily account for the fact that objects possessing the same property behave similarly (at least with respect to that property). Spherical objects, qua spherical, behave similarly because they possess a common element: sphericity. We sidestep Hume's worry that we have no grounds for the belief that similar objects will behave similarly.[7] If being spherical disposes an object to roll, then every spherical object (qua spherical) will be disposed to roll. There is no question of sphericity disposing one object, but not another, to roll: the sphericity in each object is strictly identical, numerically the same.[8]

---

[6] If α is strictly identical with β, then α *is* β. Charles Dodgson is strictly identical with Lewis Carroll; so-called identical twins are exactly similar, not strictly identical.

[7] We still face an epistemological problem: granted objects sharing a property must behave similarly (at least in respect to that property), what reason could we have to suppose that distinct objects share a property (rather than possessing distinct, but superficially similar, properties)?

[8] A reminder: this is an idealization. What an object is disposed to do depends on its overall intrinsic make-up.

12.4 Bare Similarity

We speak of objects as being similar or different in particular respects. If 'respect' talk is property talk, then the basis of similarities and differences among objects is their properties. If properties are Armstrong-style universals, we can explain similarity in terms of strict identity. If two beetroots are similar in colour and shape, this is because they possess a common element. The alternative is to appeal to bare similarity. Suppose (as a proponent of modes would have it) the sphericity of one beetroot were numerically distinct from (that is, not strictly identical with) the sphericity of another. We might explain the beetroots' similarity by noting that they had similar (though numerically distinct) properties. But what is the basis of the similarity exhibited by these properties? Armstrong has an answer: identity; the properties are strictly identical. In giving up strict identity, we give up this elegant explanation. We would, in that case, need to fall back on primitive or brute similarity holding among the properties.

Many philosophers find the idea that similarity could be a primitive relation unpalatable. Similarities, they contend, if not grounded in identity, must be in the eye of the beholder. If *A* and *B* are similar, they are similar with respect to some measure (and perhaps dissimilar with respect to some other). Someone who regards properties as modes, however, is committed to the idea that modes can be flatly similar; their similarity is built in; their similarity does not depend on any external measure. My own view is that worries about primitive, flat-out similarity are baseless. I shall reserve discussion of this topic for Chapter 14, however.

12.5 Being Wholly Present in Different Places at Once

By taking properties to be universals and universals to be wholly present in each of their instances, you can account for the fact that similar objects behave similarly and at the same time ground similarity in identity. The question is whether these apparent advantages are enough to overcome what otherwise could be regarded as a crippling defect, a commitment to the existence of items wholly present in each of their numerically distinct instances. It is not clear to me that a conception of such entities is coherent.

A proponent of universals would regard this kind of resistance as question begging. Perhaps it would be incoherent to suppose that particular *objects* are capable of being wholly present in distinct locations at once. The Golden Gate bridge is in San Francisco and in Marin County, but it is not simultaneously wholly in San Francisco and wholly in Marin. In contrast, if tourists at opposite ends of the bridge are both wearing teal jumpers, then the property of being teal coloured is wholly present in San Francisco and, at the same time, wholly present in Marin. This, it might be argued, is just one way in which universals differ from particulars. A particular can be wholly present at only one place at a time, perhaps.[9] What is impossible for a particular, however, is definitive of a universal.

This response shows that we can characterize universals as having a remarkable capacity and so distinguish them from particulars. But that goes no way at all towards making it plausible that properties are such entities, or that such entities could exist. Regarding something as being wholly present in a particular place is, it would seem, to regard it as being present at that place *and in no other place* (at the same time).[10] Proponents of universals must have something else in mind, but what could it be?

Perhaps we are meant to take 'wholly' in 'wholly present' as an undefined primitive. In describing universals as capable of being wholly present in many distinct places at once, a proponent of universals could be saying that a universal is present in a place, but not in a way that precludes its being simultaneously present in some distinct locale. This might be unobjectionable if we had some inkling of what this distinctive way of being present amounted to. I, for one, do not. Any theory must ultimately invoke undefined, primitive notions. Ordinarily, a primitive notion is one concerning which we have some prior grasp. This is not so in the case at hand.

---

[9] In the course of softening up his readers to accept a conception of God as a being who is wholly present everywhere at all times, Pascal notes that a point moving infinitely fast could be everywhere at once. See Pascal 1670/1961: §§444–5.

[10] David Robb made this point and the observation in the following paragraph. The multiple location worry has its roots in Plato's *Philebus*, 15b–c and *Parmenides* 131b (see Baxter 2001: 450).

John Bigelow, endeavouring to make plausible the idea that something could be wholly present at distinct locations at the same time, takes another tack. Like Pascal (see n. 9), Bigelow wants to loosen the grip of the idea that this is flatly impossible, an idea he regards as a 'deep-seated prejudice about locality', a 'prejudice against allowing anything to be two places at once' (1988: 143).[11] Bigelow begins by considering a Buddhist doctrine according to which nothing can exist (in the sense of being wholly present) in successive instants of time (1988: 18–19). The billiard ball an instant ago and the billiard ball now might be thought to be distinct parts—distinct temporal parts—of the billiard ball in something like the way contiguous slices of bread are distinct parts of a loaf of bread. If the billiard ball does have temporal parts (and if temporal parts are analogous to slices of bread), then it is not wholly present at any moment (just as a loaf of bread is not wholly present in any of its slices).

If you imagined that objects lack these kinds of temporal part, however, if you regarded objects as 'temporally simple', you could allow that an object could be wholly present at different times. Consider a Democritean atom, a perfectly simple substance, one that lacks parts. Bigelow takes this to imply that atoms lack both spatial and temporal parts. Suppose this is so. Then an atom, unlike our imagined temporally complex billiard ball, is wholly present at distinct times. If you are suspicious of the doctrine of temporal parts, of course, you will not regard this as especially noteworthy. But in that case you will not be troubled by the thought that objects could be wholly present at different times. Does this move us closer to the idea that something could be wholly present at distinct spatial locations (at the same time)?

Although simple and indivisible, Democritean atoms occupy a region of space. Atoms are not mere volumeless points.

Atoms are indivisible because they *do not have* parts. Combine this with the idea that atoms do have shape; and the result is a doctrine according to which it is possible for a thing to occupy a region of space, to be located at various different point-instants, even though it does *not* have distinct parts at each of those point-instants.   (Bigelow 1988: 21)

---

[11] Such 'Unargued prejudices about locality' (1988: 148) block options that would otherwise open the way to solutions to important philosophical problems.

Bigelow takes this to imply that

The same thing can be present at different times, and in two different places at the same time, without being an aggregate of distinct parts. This view can be abbreviated by saying: 'The same thing can be wholly present at different times or at different places at the same time.' The phrase 'wholly present' implies that it is not just a part of the thing which is present at each different place; it does *not* mean that it is present at that place *and no other*. When something occupies a region, in the way in which a partless atom would occupy a region, then that thing is, in the required sense, wholly present at each point in the region.   (Bigelow 1988: 21–2)

What are we to make of this argument? We might begin by distinguishing two respects in which a thing could be said to have spatial parts. The keyboard on which I am typing this sentence is made up of parts: individual keys, switches, wires, and a frame. What of these parts? Each key is a solid, roughly homogeneous lump of plastic. In the ordinary sense, the key lacks parts. Of course, we know that a lump of plastic is itself composed of parts: complex molecules arranged in a particular structure. These molecules themselves have parts: the atoms that make them up (appropriately arranged). We know, too, that the atoms have parts: our atoms are not Democritean atoms.

Let us pretend, however, that the parts of my keyboard are Democritean: they are indivisible in the sense of not being further decomposable into parts. Does this mean that Democritean atoms lack spatial parts? Recall Bigelow's contention that such atoms are not extensionless points: they occupy a volume of space; they have some shape. The atoms would, it seems, have spatial parts in the sense that the region of space they occupied could be divided into endless subregions. An atom's simplicity and indivisibility consist in its lacking *substantial* parts. A Democritean atom could be any size at all. A simple object—an object lacking substantial parts, parts that are themselves objects— could be the size of a planet. If Plato (in the *Timaeus*) and Spinoza are right, the universe is a single simple substance.

If we distinguish (as we did in §10.2) spatial parts of objects from substantial parts, then Bigelow's suggestion that simple substances are wholly present at different places at once is undermined. A (spatially extended) simple object occupies a volume of space. The object is wholly present in the spatial region that coincides with this volume; it is not wholly present in any of the (proper) subregions that make it up.[12]

We are nowhere nearer understanding the possibility that properties are universals, wholly present in each of their instances. I shall return to this idea in §13.2. Meanwhile, I propose an alternative account of properties, one according to which properties are modes, particularized ways objects are. This conception of properties, I claim, provides a plausible alternative to its competitors.

---

[12] Points made here about spatial parts apply as well to so-called temporal parts. Objects are not made up of temporal parts any more than they are made up of spatial parts. (So the loaf of bread analogy is inapt.) To speak of an object as having temporal parts is to speak of it as being temporally extended (persisting through time). A temporally extended simple object—an object lacking substantial parts—could have both spatial and temporal parts.

CHAPTER 13
Modes

All things that exist are only particulars.
(Locke, *Essay*, III. iii. 6)

13.1 Benefits and Costs

Philosophers like to think of properties as universals largely out of
habit. Some philosophers, most notably David Armstrong, have offered
extended arguments in defence of universals. The gist of these arguments is that universals promise a significant explanatory pay-off.

First, and most obviously, if properties are universals, we have an
elegant solution to the one-over-many problem: distinct objects can
share a common element. If the universal answering to the predicate
'is red' is wholly present in a pillar box, a beetroot, and a strawberry
blonde, it is easy to see how these distinct objects could nevertheless be
the same in at least one respect.

Second, and perhaps most importantly, if properties are universals,
we can easily explain similarity relations among objects. Objects *A* and
B are similar by virtue of sharing a common element: similarity is
grounded in strict identity.

Third, strict identity enables us to provide a decisive answer to
Hume's sceptical question: why should we expect similar things to
behave similarly? If objects share a property, then it can scarcely be surprising that they behave similarly, at least in cases in which this property figures in the production of the behaviour in question. Objects
could cease to possess some properties and come to possess others, and,
on that basis, come to behave differently; but, in so far as objects' having
the same property is a matter of their sharing an element, no sense can
be made of the idea that this property might vary across instances.

The question now is whether the theoretical gain accruing to the postulation of universals outweighs the counter-intuitive idea that a universal can be wholly present at many places at once. For some philosophers, this kind of counter-intuitiveness would be a small price to pay for so rewarding a theory. Before we can reasonably weigh up costs and benefits, however, we need some conception of what the options might be. I propose to look at one possibility, the idea that properties are modes: particularized ways objects are. A commitment to modes brings with it an abandonment of benefits arising from the deployment of strict identity as an explanation of similarity. We leave behind the seemingly balmy idea that properties are wholly present in different places at once, but we leave behind as well the explanatory work done by strict identity. What are the prospects of finding modes to be a reasonable replacement?

13.2 Modes and Tropes

Suppose that properties are particularized ways objects are. I prefer the traditional designation of such ways, *modes*, to the currently more popular *tropes*. I resist talk of tropes because trope theorists have by and large regarded objects as made up of bundles of tropes, and this I reject (see §12.1). I shall have more to say about objects in Chapter 15. For the present my focus will be on properties.

Philosophers seem often to assume that the default view—the view that must be shown to be false before any alternative could be taken seriously—is that properties are universals. I doubt it. Default status ought not be accorded a philosophical thesis merely because it is widely, but on the whole unselfconsciously embraced. A more fitting measure of the pretheoretical stature of a thesis is the extent to which it meshes with scientifically informed common sense. I see no reason to think that either science or common sense encourages the thesis that properties are universals. True, we speak of objects 'sharing' or 'having the same' property. A proponent of universals understands these locutions as implying strict (numerical) identity. If α and β share F, then α and β have a common element, F. What is far from obvious is that ordinary talk of 'sharing' properties or of distinct objects possessing 'the same' property brings with it a commitment to universals.

A proponent of modes can freely speak of objects 'sharing' properties, or of distinct objects possessing 'the same' property. In these cases, however, 'same' indicates not self-sameness—strict identity—but exact similarity. We speak of two stockbrokers wearing *the same* tie, meaning only that they are wearing exactly similar ties. Two diners *share* a taste for anchovies, not in the sense that the diners possess a single gustatory system; rather they have similar culinary preferences. Henry, we say, has the same breakfast every morning: each breakfast is not strictly identical with, but is exactly similar to the others. I strongly suspect that this is the sense of 'same' intended by non-philosophers when they speak of distinct objects possessing the same characteristic. At the very least it is not obvious that non-philosophers conceive of properties as things that can be wholly present in different places at once. I confess that I have no clear conception of what this thought could amount to, however, so I refrain from pressing the point here.

As anecdotal evidence against the suggestion that the default conception of properties treats properties as universals, I might cite my own experiences in trying to explain universals to undergraduate philosophy students. Even those willing to suspend judgement on what they regard as loony philosophical theses typically baulk at the idea of universals; this is so even when universals are presented (as I try to present them) in a most favourable light. I do not place much weight on such observations, but I believe it is important that the state of play not be slanted unfairly towards universals.

Once we grant that objects possess properties, and that properties are ways these objects are, we seem to have two choices: to treat properties as universals, wholly present in each of their instances, or to regard properties as modes. It is hard to see properties-as-universals as a viable option unless we can make sense of the idea that a way something is could be wholly present in numerically distinct instances. I have expressed doubts on this score. Perhaps I have been unfair. Consider the property of sphericity possessed by a beetroot. Sphericity seems completely present in the beetroot. No ingredient of sphericity is missing: it is all there. But sphericity can also be wholly present at the same time in a second, numerically distinct beetroot. Sphericity is all there in the second beetroot just as it is in the first.

If this is what is meant by sphericity being wholly present in each of its instances, however, it is entirely compatible with a conception of properties as modes. Both beetroots are spherical; the beetroots possess wholly similar properties. Each beetroot is a particular way—each is a particular shape—and these shapes are similar. The sphericity of the first beetroot is wholly present in the first beetroot; and the second beetroot's sphericity is wholly present in the second beetroot. It is hard to see what more there could be to the thought that sphericity is wholly present in both beetroots at once.

This suggests that the content of the thought that properties are wholly present in two numerically distinct objects at the same time is exhausted by the thought that the first object is some way, the second object is some way, and these ways are exactly similar. A proponent of universals adds to this the idea that the ways are strictly identical. Perhaps this amounts to no more than a rhetorical flourish!

I shall have more to say on the important topic of similarity in Chapter 14. For the present, let us assume a conception of properties as particularized ways objects are, assume as well that these ways can be similar or not, and ask what the resulting conception of properties comes to.[1]

13.3 Individuating Modes

If properties are particularized ways objects are, this suggests a distinction between properties and their possessors. One possibility is that an object's properties (suitably arranged) are all there is to the object. This is the 'bundle theory' favoured by many philosophers who defend a conception of properties as tropes. It is precisely this feature of the most prominent trope theories that makes me reluctant to describe the conception of properties advanced here as a trope conception. I regard it as important to distinguish properties—ways objects are—from objects that are these ways. (Objects will be addressed in Chapter 15.) The point has important implications for the question how properties are 'individuated'. If properties are constituents of objects in anything like the sense that an object's parts are constituents of the object, then we might expect properties to exhibit determinate identity conditions.

---

[1] Readers more partial to universals than I should note that, for reasons hinted at above, much of what I have to say here about properties-as-modes could apply *mutatis mutandis* to *in rebus*, Armstrong-style universals.

Identity conditions incorporate principles whereby entities of a given sort are distinguished and counted.[2] This is especially important if properties are taken to be tropes that can migrate from one object to another (see Ehring 1997).

Can we spell out identity conditions for modes? Perhaps. Here is one possibility:

(MI) α and β are the selfsame mode ($\alpha = \beta$) just in case (1) α and β are exactly similar and (2) α and β spatially coincide.[3]

Aside from the fact that (MI) would fail for immaterial modes (modes of Cartesian souls, for instance), it is not obvious that we should expect to discover illuminating identity conditions for modes. Modes are ways objects are. Their identity depends on the objects. The red of this beetroot is distinct from the red of that beetroot because this beetroot is distinct from that beetroot. The modes do not spatially coincide because the beetroots do not spatially coincide.

Matters are different for trope theorists who regard tropes as 'transferable' modes or tropes. Douglas Ehring, for instance, holds that causal transactions involve the transference of tropes from one object to another (Ehring 1997). When one billiard ball collides with another, the momentum of the first migrates to the second. A conception of this sort, like conceptions of objects as bundles of tropes, makes tropes out to be object-like entities that retain their identity while being affiliated with different objects at different times. Modes, as I am conceiving of them, are non-transferable. The way one object is cannot be transferred to another object. The momentum of one billiard ball might be responsible for a second billiard ball's acquiring a like momentum, but there is no question of the momentum of the first billiard ball (at a given time) *being* the momentum of the second billiard ball (at a later time).[4]

A philosopher might put this by saying that modes belong necessarily to objects of which they are modes. This makes it sound as though modes and objects are bound together by a special necessitation relation. Consider an analogy. Tibbles the cat's smile is non-transferable.

---

[2] Identity conditions or criteria of identity are not epistemic principles. They do not provide techniques for identifying entities of particular kinds; they specify what counts as a given kind of entity.

[3] This, or something like it, was suggested by David Robb.

[4] This is not an argument against the possibility of transferable tropes. I am merely distinguishing my conception of modes from such one competitor.

This is not because the smile is bound to Tibbles by an especially robust necessitation relation, but because Tibble's smile is a way *Tibble's* face is organized. Similarly, if the ball's sphericity, mass, and momentum are ways the ball is, there is no question of the ball's sphericity, mass, or momentum migrating to another object. Thoughts of modes (or tropes) moving from one object to another are manifestations of the same impulse that leads philosophers to posit universals: if one billiard ball imparts 'the same' momentum to a second billiard ball, this must mean that some one thing that formerly belonged to one billiard ball now belongs to a second billiard ball. The move to modes is a move away from this kind of reasoning.

13.4 A 'Sparse' Conception of Modes

Modes endow their possessors with both dispositionalities and qualities. In virtue of being spherical, a beetroot is a certain way—exhibits the quality of sphericity—and possesses certain dispositionalities—it would roll, make an impression of a certain kind if pressed into soft clay, reflect light in a particular way. Modes, then, are simultaneously qualitative and dispositional. (For a defence of this 'Identity Theory' of properties, see Chapter 11.)

What are the modes? Is being red a mode? Being spherical? Although I have written as though these are modes, I believe that the truth of the matter is not discoverable from the armchair. In this regard, I am sympathetic to the idea that the real properties are 'sparse'. More precisely, I am sympathetic to this idea provided it is properly understood. The basic properties are those possessed by the basic objects (whatever these should turn out to be). Properties of complex objects result from combinations of simpler objects. Different ways of combining similar elements yield different complex kinds of property. These complex properties are perfectly real. If, in counting kinds of property, we include complex properties as well as simple properties, the image of sparseness evaporates.

If properties are modes, sparseness is not a measure of the number of properties. The properties will outnumber the objects. We can, however, speak of kinds or types of property: modes are of the same kind or type if they are similar. Kinds or types of precisely similar modes are hard to distinguish from *in rebus* Armstrong-style universals. The simple properties—the mass possessed by electrons, for instance— are, so far as we know, precisely similar across the electrons. These form tight classes of precisely similar properties. Complex properties can be precisely similar as well. More often, however, complex properties will be less-than-perfectly similar: *im*perfectly similar.[5]

Any complex object will have a multitude of perfectly real complex properties. In virtue of possessing these properties, ordinary objects satisfy predicates we deploy in the special sciences and in our everyday commerce with the world. What I deny is that these complex proper- ties are very often named, or designated, or 'expressed' by these predi- cates. Suppose 'is red' holds of objects in virtue of properties those objects possess. It need not follow that 'is red' designates, 'expresses', or names a property in the sense that every object to which the predicate applies is exactly similar in some way (and the predicate applies to the objects in virtue of the objects' being this way). The predicate is satis- fied by objects possessing any of a range of, presumably complex, less- than-perfectly-similar properties. Each of these properties is entirely real; each answers to 'is red'. What is not the case is that every property satisfying 'is red' is exactly similar. Unlike the class of properties answer- ing to 'is the mass of an electron', the class of properties answering to 'is red' is not an 'equivalence class', but a class of properties that resemble one another to a greater or lesser extent (for more on colour, see Chapter 17 below). This is not to say that 'is red' is a covertly disjunctive predicate, much less that 'is red' names a 'disjunctive property'. 'Is red' is a perfectly ordinary predicate satisfied by a sprawling class of objects possessing broadly similar properties.[6]

13.5 Modes and Explanation

How do modes stack up against universals in explanatory contexts? In §13.1, I mentioned three important theoretical advantages thought to follow from the postulation of universals:

[5] I do not rule out the possibility that simple properties could be imperfectly similar; see Ch. 14.

[6] I speak of classes here and elsewhere. Does this mean I am committed to the existence of classes? I am not sure. It is hard to see classes as an 'addition of being'. God does not create the world, then add the classes.

(1) universals provide a solution to the one-over-many problem;
(2) universals provide an explanation of similarity in terms of strict identity;
(3) universals warrant inductive inferences, expressing our expectation that similar objects will behave similarly.

We account for the fact that distinct objects can be the same in various respects by taking these respects to be universals and taking sameness literally: distinct objects share components. Sameness guarantees behavioural similarity where these components are concerned. Thus two objects, α and β, might share a property F. It is because α and β share F that they are similar F-wise and that they behave similarly in F-respects. Suppose α and β are both spherical. Then α and β share a property, sphericity. This accounts both for their similarity in shape and for their behaving similarly in so far as their shape affects their behaviour.

What might a proponent of modes offer in place of these explanatory virtues? In rejecting universals, you reject the idea that similarity could be explicated in terms of identity. If two balls possess 'the same' shape, the balls are exactly similar in a particular way, but this similarity is not further reducible or explicable.[7] Similarity, on this conception of properties, is a primitive relation holding among properties. Thus, sameness in the midst of difference is explained by reference to a primitive similarity among properties: the balls are similar by virtue of possessing similar properties; the properties are similar *tout court*. All of this suggests that appeals to universals to explain sameness in the midst of difference is really an extension of the idea that sameness amounts to identity. The first two advantages attaching to the postulation of universals stand or fall together. In substituting primitive similarity for identity we sacrifice both advantages at once.

I shall have more to say about similarity in the next chapter. For the moment, let us ask how a conception of properties as modes copes with the remaining advantage thought to attach to universals.

Why should objects possessing similar properties behave similarly? If we build causal powers or dispositionalities into the properties (as I

---

[7] Similarities among complex modes could be explicated by reference to similarities among their simpler constituents, perhaps, but there is no getting beyond similarity to anything more fundamental.

have urged), then it can scarcely be cause for wonder that objects possessing similar properties behave similarly. Properties are similar only if their contribution to the dispositionalities (and qualities) of their possessors is similar. Objects could behave differently in the future because they cease to possess properties similar to these, of course, but this point applies equally to the hypothesis that properties are universals. So long as α and β both possess F, α and β will continue to behave similarly (F-wise). But identity is doing little or no work here. If dispositionalities are built into properties, then, if α and β possess similar properties, they will behave similarly in similar circumstances. This provides no guarantee at all that α and β could, at some future time, come to possess different properties, and so come to behave differently.

What all this makes clear, I think, is that advantages universals might be thought to enjoy over modes boil down to whatever advantage strict identity as a basis of similarity might be thought to have over brute, irreducible similarities among modes. Suppose for a moment that identity trumps brute similarity. This is a point—a significant point—in favour of universals. But this advantage must be weighed against the apparent strangeness of a theory according to which properties can be wholly present at different places at once. It is easy to regard this strangeness as a compelling reason to doubt the coherence of the thesis. Indeed, it is hard to distinguish the content of the thesis from the thesis that properties are modes with the rider that precisely similar modes are in fact strictly identical. This rider is at once the advantage thought to accrue to universals, and a source of profound puzzlement.

I consider the issue, thus framed, a stand-off. In the next chapter, I shall argue that the advantage a theory according to which properties are universals apparently enjoys over a theory according to which properties are modes, namely the reduction of similarity to identity, is merely apparent. Before turning to these matters, one or two further points bear discussion.

13.6 Parsimony

In addressing the comparative advantages and disadvantages of universals and modes, I have omitted mention of a topic that might be thought to have deserved top billing: parsimony. In comparing theories, the principle of parsimony (Ockam's Razor) advises us to prefer simpler theories. Often the principle of parsimony is interpreted as counselling us to prefer theories that postulate fewer entities (or perhaps fewer kinds of entity).

Parsimony should be understood as a methodological precept, not an ontological decree. A commitment to parsimony is not a commitment to a conception of the world as simple. The idea, rather, is that we should not complicate our theories about the world unnecessarily. In some cases this could mean that we should not posit entities without good reason, and it is easy to interpret this as a directive to prefer a theory that posits n entities to a theory that posits m entities, where $m > n$.

Even if we accept this interpretation of the principle of parsimony, it is unclear how it bears on the question whether properties are modes or universals. Someone might reason as follows. If properties were modes, then there would be at least as many properties as there were objects possessing those properties. If properties were universals, however, then many objects would share a single property. So a theory of universals is to be preferred to a theory of modes on the grounds that it posits fewer entities.

This line of reasoning is questionable for at least two reasons. First, although it is true that modes must outnumber universals, there would be as many *instances* of universals as modes. Although these instances are supposed to be strictly identical, it is nevertheless true that they are also diverse. (This is just what makes universals so puzzling.) So, if we are bent on counting entities, we must count each instance of a universal just as we must count each mode. For every mode there corresponds an instance of a universal; the thought that a theory that posits universals is less profligate than a theory that posits modes is misleading.

A second reason to doubt that universals are ontologically more economical than modes becomes obvious when you look more closely at what might be involved in counting entities. I have suggested that the principle of parsimony advises against complicating theories unnecessarily. It is by no means clear that this is best interpreted as a recommendation to prefer one theory, T_1, to a competitor, T_2, if T_1 posits fewer entities than T_2. It could well turn out that a simpler theory—a theory with fewer fundamental principles—posits more entities than a more complex competitor. But, even if simplicity is linked to numbers of entities posited, this surely must be understood as pertaining, not to the number of particular entities, but to the number of *kinds* of entity. You do not simplify physics by cutting down on the number of electrons, but you might simplify physics if you could show that dozens of different kinds of particle are actually made up of particles of a half-dozen different kinds in varying combinations. Here we end up with more fundamental particles, but fewer kinds of fundamental particle.

In this regard, it is far from obvious that theories appealing to universals *do* posit fewer kinds of entity than do theories appealing to modes. Both sorts of theory require that we distinguish a category of properties—ways objects are. If properties are modes, then these ways will, like the objects, be particulars; if properties are universals, then the ways will not be particulars. This suggests that, if anything, a theory of universals complicates the ontology. I do not want to place too much emphasis on this possibility. Both theories incorporating a commitment to universals and theories committed to modes embrace an ontological framework that distinguishes properties from property-bearers. If properties are ontologically distinctive, however, perhaps there is no special economy in their being particulars as opposed to universals.

The upshot is that it is not easy to see how considerations of parsimony could be thought to favour universals over modes. Of course, if universals themselves are problematic (as I have suggested they certainly are), then considerations of simplicity would be altogether beside the point. In any case, where fundamental ontological issues are concerned, appeals to parsimony are at best premature.

13.7 Transcendent Universals

In discussing universals here and in Chapter 12, I have concentrated on Armstrong-style 'immanent' universals: universals *in rebus*. Before leaving the topic, however, I should comment on my hesitation to consider Platonic, transcendent universals: universals *ante res*. Some philosophers will regard my reluctance to discuss these as especially egregious in light of my expressed doubts about the coherence of talk of universals as immanent. If universals are to be given a fair hearing, it might be thought, the Platonic option deserves a hearing as well.

My reluctance to discuss transcendent universals stems, not from ill will on my part, but from simple ignorance. I have no idea what it might mean to say that universals residing ('in some sense') outside space and time have instances in the here and now. This page 'instantiates whiteness'. Although whiteness (the universal) is not present in the page or anywhere else, *instances* of whiteness are. I can talk the talk, but I have no notion of what it means. Here is the universal and here are its instances. We have a name for the relation the latter bear to the former: instantiation. But what is the instantiation relation? This is not a veiled criticism, merely an admission of ignorance.

One facet of such a theory I can appreciate is that it is the instances of universals that make a difference to us. It is not the universal whiteness, but the whiteness of this page, that reflects light in a particular way so as to make the page look white. Indeed, our whole commerce with universals—our route to them intellectually—is exhausted by encounters with their instances. You have all the individual whitenesses, the instances of whiteness, plus whiteness itself. Subtract this last element—the whiteness itself—and you have a conception of properties as modes. A devotee of transcendent universals will regard the whiteness itself as crucially important. But is it? Imagine a pair of worlds, one in which there are the universals and their instances and one in which there are just the instances (a world of modes). How would the absence of universals make itself felt?

A common thought is that, if universals exist, they exist necessarily (they could not fail to exist).[8] In that case, we could not coherently imagine a world minus the universals. But my point does not depend on there being worlds including universals and worlds lacking them. I am not appealing to subtleties associated with alternative worlds. The idea is much simpler. The postulation of transcendent universals is a purely theoretical manœuvre. It differs in this regard from the postulation of objects and properties in the sciences. In positing quarks or properties of quarks—colours and flavours, for instance—we posit objects or properties the existence of which would make a difference to the way objects behave in the world, hence a difference in the way

[8] But see §12.1 n. 1.

we experience the world. But transcendent universals, residing as they do 'outside' the spatio-temporal world, could make no difference to it or our experience of it.

Is this unfair? Transcendent universals, after all, are not *in* the world. It would be unreasonable for us to expect them to make the kind of difference a material entity or property might make. My aim, however, is just to emphasize that transcendent universals are creatures of philosophical theory. But how very odd! How very odd that we could arrive at the existence of entities solely on the basis of philosophical theorizing!

We philosophers can be cavalier about such things precisely because we recognize that the existence of a purely philosophical posit could have no discernible effect on the world as we experience it. In defending the existence of transcendent universals, then, we need not worry that experience will confute us. We must look elsewhere for exoneration. We incur a special obligation to provide evidence that the entities we posit yield an explanatory pay-off, theories in which they figure exhibit more power than competitors.[9] A measure of power is the extent to which a given theory assists us in making sense of the world as we encounter it. And here the postulation of transcendent universals is a positive liability, something to be overcome by demonstrable explanatory success across the board. Explanatory ties go to the advocate of modes.

13.8 'All Things that Exist are only Particulars'

Universals, I believe, are an acquired taste. Locke speaks for most of us in contending that whatever exists is particular. Generality lies not in the world but in our thoughts about the world, and in words we use to express those thoughts:

All things that exist being Particulars, it may perhaps be thought reasonable that Words, which ought to be conformed to Things, should be so too. I mean in their Signification: but yet we find the quite contrary. The *far greatest part of Words*, that make all Languages, *are General Terms*: which has not been the Effect of Neglect or Chance, but of Reason and Necessity.   (*Essay*, III. iii. 1)

---

[9] The model here is Lewis's defence of alternative worlds.

We can, according to Locke, entertain general thoughts because we have a capacity for 'abstraction' or 'partial consideration'.

For since all things that exist are only particulars, how come we by general Terms, or where find we those general Natures they are supposed to stand for? Words become general, by being made the signs of general *Ideas*; and *Ideas* become general, by separating from them the circumstances of Time, and Place, and any other *Ideas*, that may determine them to this or that particular Existence. By this way of abstraction they are made capable of representing more Individuals than one; each of which, having in it a conformity to that abstract *Idea*, is (as we call it) of that sort.   (*Essay*, III. iii. 6)

An image of a swerving automobile on a road sign can be used to indicate swerving vehicles generally and so warn us of hazardous conditions. The image does not represent a Platonic form of vehicularity; it is (in our deployment) satisfied by, and so represents, vehicles indifferently. Transferring generality from our use of representations of the world to the world itself is an especially stunning manifestation of the Picture Theory.

From this perspective, the idea of universals lacks appeal. What then accounts for its popularity among philosophers? One possibility is that the postulation of universals explains so much. I have argued that many of the supposed explanatory benefits of universals is illusory. In any case, I suspect that the attraction of universals has more to do with our philosophical education than with putative theoretical advantages. Learning to engage in philosophical discussion at a high level involves learning to play the game. Games are founded on rules. Our inculcation of these rules often involves our learning to think in particular ways.[10] Ways of thinking become second nature, hence largely invisible. They become obvious only when we start to theorize self-consciously or when we endeavour to explain ourselves to non-philosophers. In the end, we may embrace philosophical theses, not because we are convinced by them on their merits, but because, like shoes that once pinched, we grow used to them.

---

[10] Kuhn, in writing about the pursuit of 'normal science', speaks of scientists' inculcation of particular paradigms (Kuhn 1962).

CHAPTER 14

Imperfect Similarity

14.1 Similarity and Identity

Properties, I have argued, are modes: particularized ways objects are. Modes correspond to the property instances postulated by philosophers who regard properties as universals. Objects are similar by virtue of their properties. Two billiard balls are similar with respect to shape and colour: both are spherical and both are red. If properties are universals, then similarity among property instances is explained by reference to strict identity. The billiard balls have elements—a colour and a shape—in common. This comfortable option is not open to someone who regards properties as modes. One billiard ball's shape is numerically distinct from another billiard ball's shape, although the two shapes might be precisely similar. This similarity must, so to speak, be intrinsic to the properties. Similarity, on this view, is not reducible to identity; similarity is basic, primitive, not further explicable.

In the previous chapter I argued that a choice between *in rebus* universals and modes turned in large measure on the plausibility of this kind of fundamental similarity. Advantages alleged to attach to universals boil down to this one advantage: properties regarded as universals provide an account of similarity in terms of strict identity; properties regarded as modes yield a conception of similarity as a primitive, irreducible phenomenon. A proponent of universals would consider the absence of an account of similarity as a steep price to pay for embracing the thesis that properties are modes. The question is whether every case of similarity can be explained in terms of identity. If not, if brute similarity is ineliminable, then this is a price that must be paid in any case; the chief selling point of universals evaporates.

14.2 Objective Similarity

In discussing properties, proponents of universals and proponents of modes alike take similarity to be an objective relation: the similarity (or dissimilarity) of α and β is mind independent. This kind of objectivity is sometimes challenged. Any object (it might be said) is similar to any other object in some ways and dissimilar in some ways. Take any two objects you like: this hairbrush and the Moon. It takes little in the way of imagination to think of ways in which these seemingly dissimilar objects are similar. Both the hairbrush and the moon are material bodies; both have mass; both are visible; both are made up of smaller particles; both are pleasing to look at. We should put this by saying that the moon and the hairbrush are similar *in some respects* (though not in others).

This seems right. Objects are not similar (or dissimilar) *tout court*, but only in particular respects—respects that we can pick and choose. This will be so even for objects that are intrinsically indiscernible. Two identical billiard balls may not be similar with respect to their spatial locations or with respect to their time and place of origin. Indeed, one of the billiard balls may be more similar to the hairbrush than to an indistinguishable billiard ball with respect to place of origin; both were manufactured in Italy; the second billiard ball is a product of Taiwan.

Two points need to be made here. First, I have argued at length against the idea that, corresponding to every predicate that holds true of objects is a distinct property shared (in whatever sense) by those objects (see Chapter 3 above). Second, and more significantly for present purposes, it is a mistake to assimilate similarity among properties to similarity among objects. Objects are similar by virtue of possessing similar properties; properties, in contrast, are not similar in virtue of anything.

This is not to deny that some similarities might be more salient (to us) than others. Nor is it to deny that similarity comes in degrees: α may be more similar to β than to χ; partial or imperfect similarity can grade off imperceptibly into dissimilarity. In these cases, it may be up to us where we draw the line. This need not affect the objectivity of the phenomenon, however.

14.3 Predicates and Similarity

To set the stage, let me return to a topic introduced in §3.4, multiple realizability. Recall the pain predicate: 'is in pain'. This predicate applies to actual and possible creatures in virtue of properties possessed by those creatures. If we survey creatures' material properties, we find it difficult to locate a single property (1) shared by every actual and possible creature in pain, and (2) in virtue of which it is true that the creatures in question are in pain. This, as functionalists like to point out, speaks against 'type identity', the idea that mental predicates designate properties that are identical with material properties (less pretentiously: the idea that mental predicates designate material properties).

A popular response to this line of reasoning is to posit higher-level properties. A higher-level property is a property possessed by an object in virtue of that object's possession of some distinct lower-level 'realizing' property. I have suggested that the felt need for higher-level properties in such cases is an artefact of the Picture Theory. A simpler explanation of the phenomena beloved by advocates of multiple realizability is that predicates taken to designate so-called higher-level properties are in fact satisfied by members of families of *similar* properties. These similar properties are just those properties standardly taken to be realizers of the higher-level properties. The pain predicate applies or would apply to creatures in virtue of those creatures' possession of any of a possibly open-ended family of *similar* properties. These properties fall under the pain predicate because they are relevantly similar: similar, perhaps in the contribution they make to the dispositional and qualitative character of their possessors' states of mind.

Whatever you might think about states of mind, it seems clear that we need to tell some such story for most of the predicates we deploy in everyday life and in the sciences—or at least those predicates for which we take ourselves to be realists. Suppose I am right about all this. Suppose putative cases of multiple realizability are really cases in which a given predicate is satisfied by a range of similar, but not precisely similar, properties. How are we to understand less-than-perfect—or, as I shall call it—*imperfect* similarity?

14.4 Grades of Similarity

As noted earlier, it is vital to distinguish talk about similarity of *objects* from talk of similarity of *properties*. Objects can be described as similar (or not) in particular *respects*. Talk of respects is property talk. A red sphere and a red cube are similar with respect to colour but dissimilar with respect to shape. The sphere and cube possess similar colours but dissimilar shapes. Objects are similar (or not) in virtue of their properties: similar objects 'share properties'.

What of similarity among properties? Consider two similar shades of red. Are the shades of red similar in some respect? Are they similar by virtue of possessing similar properties? To account for similarity among properties, must we appeal to properties shared by properties—second-order properties?[1]

Before attempting to answer this question it might seem that we must answer the further question whether properties are universals or modes. Suppose properties are universals. Then, if objects are similar, this is because they share a property: they literally have something—the property—in common. In that case, if P_1 and P_2 are properties, and P_1 and P_2 are precisely similar, then P_1 *is* P_2 ($P_1 = P_2$).[2] This gives us a way of reducing similarity to identity: objects are similar when they possess one or more properties in common. Exactly similar objects, if there are any, share all of their properties; less-than-exactly similar objects share some, but not all, of their properties.

Now consider similarity among properties. So long as we construe properties as universals, exact similarity among properties amounts to identity. But what of imperfect similarity? Crimson and scarlet are similar, but not perfectly similar. Here are two possibilities. First, this kind of similarity might be explained just as the imperfect similarity of

---

[1] A reminder: I distinguish higher-*level* properties (properties possessed by an object by virtue of that object's possession of some distinct lower-level property) from higher-*order* properties: properties of properties.

[2] Here, as in Chs. 12 and 13, I assume an Armstrong-style *in rebus* conception of universals. Such universals are not Platonic, other-worldly entities. If a particular ball is spherical, and if sphericity is a universal, then sphericity is 'wholly present' in the ball—and simultaneously wholly present in each of its numerically distinct instances. Other accounts of universals distinguish universals from their instances. In that case, Armstrong's unity-in-identity is replaced by unity-under-a-universal: shared properties are instances of a single universal.

objects is explained by supposing that these properties themselves possess properties, some, but not all, of which they share.

I have no clear conception of what exactly a property of a property might be (see §11.6). My suspicion is that the casualness with which many philosophers speak of higher-order properties stems in part from treating property similarity on the model of object similarity and in part from conflating predicates and properties. If objects are similar because they share properties, then (so someone might reason) similar properties must be similar because *they* share properties. Further, we find it natural to say that crimson is red, that red is a colour, and that colour is a property. This way of talking might suggest that the property of being crimson itself possesses the property of being red, that (the property of) being red itself possesses the property of being coloured, and that (the property of) being coloured itself possesses the property of being a property.

An apparent difficulty with appeals to higher-order properties to account for property similarities is that second-order properties themselves bear similarity relations to one another: scarlet and crimson are similar in being red; red, blue, and orange are similar in being colours; and colours, shapes, and textures are similar in being properties. If we invoke higher-order properties to account for these similarities, we shall need a hierarchy of higher-order properties, and this looks like the start of an unhappy regress. Worse, perhaps, as we ascend the hierarchy, we move further away from our original conception of similarity. Shapes, colours, and textures are all properties, but are they thereby similar? (A bad answer: they must be; they all satisfy the predicate 'is a property'.)

A second difficulty for accounts of property similarity that appeal to higher-order properties is that it is unclear how such accounts could accommodate similarities among simple, non-composite properties. We are imagining that distinct properties might be imperfectly similar by virtue of possessing higher-order perfectly similar properties. But could a simple property possess a higher-order property? A property that itself possessed a property would seem to lack simplicity. I have admitted that I find the ontology of higher-order properties obscure, however, so I am prepared to be proven wrong.

In §11.5 I suggested that higher-order properties might be understood as constituents of complex properties of which the lower-order property was itself a constituent. If this were right, and if every property had the property of being a property, then it looks as though every property would be complex. Worse, this higher-level property would itself be a property, so we would face an embarrassing regress. This strikes me as yet another untoward manifestation of the Picture Theory. I prefer to think that the truth-maker for 'ϕ is a property' is ϕ itself (and not a property of ϕ). Similarly, the truth-maker for 'red is a colour' is the property, being red, and not a property (being a colour) of this property.

14.5 Imperfect Similarity as 'Partial Identity'

If we abandon the attempt to explain imperfect property similarity by reference to higher-order properties, what are the alternatives? One possibility invokes what Armstrong calls 'partial identity' (1989: 103–7; 1997: 51–7). A virtue of this approach is that it avoids a commitment to ranks of higher-order properties. Return to crimson and scarlet. Suppose crimson and scarlet are complex in the following sense: each of these properties comprises a collection of properties. As a crude model, think of the production of colours on a television screen achieved by juxtaposing pixels of different colours. Imagine that every colour is made up in this way of a mixture of simpler elements.

Suppose now that crimson and scarlet share at least one constituent property (they are, as Armstrong puts it, 'partly identical'). Suppose, further, that this property is a constituent of every shade of red, but of no other colour. (Crimson might be a complex property consisting of properties $A + R + D$; scarlet is $B + R + E$; reddish orange is $C + R + F$; and so on.) In this way we account for imperfect similarity by reference to partial perfect similarity; and perfect similarity reduces to strict identity. Further, we can see how crimson objects and scarlet objects could be said to share the property of being red (and do so in virtue of being crimson and scarlet, respectively): the property of being red is a constituent of the property of being crimson and a constituent of the property of being scarlet.[3]

---

[3] This might be the way so-called determinable properties are grounded in determinate properties: determinables are constituents of properties they determine.

It looks as though, by regarding properties as universals, we are in a position to provide an elegant account of similarity, perfect and imperfect, in terms of identity and partial identity. Compare an account that does not invoke universals. Suppose properties are not universals, but *modes*: ways particular objects are. Modes are particularized properties, instances of universals minus the universals. The white of this page is a mode; so is the white of the previous page. These modes, although perhaps precisely similar, are numerically distinct. Assuming properties to be modes, we explain the similarity of objects by reference to the *similarity* of their properties. Someone who endorses universals has more to say about this similarity: the properties are identical instances of the selfsame universal. In rejecting universals, an advocate of modes rejects this account. What then *could* ground property similarity? It is hard to see how an appeal to higher-order properties could help here. Rather, if you think, as I do, that properties are modes, you will be driven to say that similarity among modes is 'built in'. If P_1 and P_2 are precisely similar properties, this is a basic, irreducible fact. In creating P_1 and P_2 God *thereby* creates distinct-but-precisely-similar properties.

A proponent of universals might be thought to have an advantage here. The friend of universals has an account of similarity relations as relations of identity and partial identity; the friend of modes must regard similarity relations as primitive and irreducible. This advantage aside, and substituting precise similarity for identity, the proponent of modes is in a position to explain imperfect similarity exactly as a universals theorist does. Assuming that red and scarlet are complex properties, the crimson of this ball is—imperfectly—similar to the scarlet of that ball because the former includes elements precisely similar to some, but not all, elements of the latter.

14.6 Similarity among Simple Properties

Accounts of imperfect similarity among properties framed in terms of 'partial identity' (or partial perfect similarity, if properties are modes) could well work for many cases of imperfect similarity. This, at bottom, is an empirical issue. Such accounts could not, however, be extended to cases—if indeed there are any—of imperfect similarity among simple, non-complex properties. Simple properties lack constituents; simple properties could not share identical (or precisely similar) constituents. If it is possible for simple properties S_1 and S_2 to be imperfectly similar or for S_1 to be more similar to S_2, than to a third simple property, S_3, then we shall need to appeal to something other than a relation of partial identity (or partial perfect similarity) holding among S_1, S_2, and S_3.

If objective imperfect similarities could hold among simple properties, then one putative advantage of universals evaporates. If properties are universals, it would be possible to reduce similarity to identity (or, in the case of complex properties, partial identity). Such a reduction would not work for imperfect similarities among simple properties. If similarity-as-identity does not work for all cases of similarity, then what might be thought to be an attractive feature of Armstrong-style universals over modes loses its allure. Imperfect similarity among simple properties (whether universals or modes) must be a brute phenomenon: S_1 and S_2 would be imperfectly similar *tout court*; it must be simply of the nature of S_1, S_2, and S_3 to be such that S_1 is more similar to S_2 than to S_3. If some similarities are like this, why not all?

I have put this point in terms of imperfect similarities among simple properties, but there could easily be cases of imperfect (or partial) similarities among complex properties that would resist explanation in terms of identity. Suppose, as before, that crimson and scarlet are complex properties. Now, however, imagine that the simple constituents of these properties are $A + R_1 + B$ and $C + R_2 + D$, respectively. Finally, imagine that R_1 and R_2 are imperfectly similar simple properties. Here the imperfect similarity of a pair of complex properties turns on the imperfect similarity of at least one of their constituent properties. Identity is not an option.

You may doubt that simple properties could be imperfectly similar. But what could fuel such a doubt? Why imagine that imperfect similarity among simples is impossible? If, like me, you are favourably disposed towards modes, then you will accept the possibility of fundamental similarities among perfectly similar modes. Given such fundamental, irreducible similarities, it is not much of a stretch to entertain the possibility of fundamental imperfect similarities. Thus, if P_1 and P_2 are perfectly similar, this is as it were 'built into' P_1 and P_2. But if it can be of the nature of P_1 and P_2 to be perfectly similar, why not allow that it could be of the nature of S_1 and S_2 to be imperfectly similar?

Might the imperfect similarity of S_1 and S_2 depend on the possession by S_1 and S_2 of complex higher-order properties with shared elements? If S_1 and S_2 are simple, what could it mean to say that they possess complex higher-order properties? This would seem to make S_1 and S_2 complex after all. Again, it is hard to see how an appeal to higher-order properties could advance our understanding of similarity among properties.

14.7 Dissimilarity

A proponent of modes regards similarity among modes as an irreducible feature of the modes themselves. If A and B are modes and A and B are similar, then it is of the nature of A and B to be similar. The defender of universals is in a position to account for similarity in terms of identity: A and B are similar because A *is* B or, in the case of imperfect similarity, A and B share some constituent. Imperfect similarity among simple properties poses a difficulty for such a view. If simple properties could be imperfectly similar, a philosopher who favours universals, no less than one who favours modes, must admit brute similarities. If the chief (arguably, the only) advantage of universals over modes is that, by appealing to universals, we can ground similarity relations in a single identity relation, the advantage turns out to be illusory.

You might disdain talk of brute similarity. But consider *dissimilarity*. Suppose properties A and B are dissimilar. It sounds not at all odd to describe it as being of the nature of A and B to be dissimilar. To say that the dissimilarity of A and B is grounded in or reducible to A's failing to be identical with B would seem to reverse the natural order of explanation. A is not dissimilar to B because $A \neq B$; rather $A \neq B$ because A and B are dissimilar.

If this is right, if there is nothing at all untoward in the thought that dissimilarities are of the nature of properties, then why should the complementary thought—that similarities are of the nature of the properties themselves—be regarded with scepticism? I do not think that it should be.

14.8 Functional Similarity

In discussing functionalism, I suggested that the phenomenon of multiple realizability ought not to be regarded as a relation among properties: higher-level properties being possessed by agents in virtue of those agents' possession of distinct lower-level realizing properties. Rather, I argued, cases of multiple realizability are typically cases in which some predicate ('is red', 'is in pain') applies to an object in virtue of that object's possession of any of a diverse range of properties. These properties are similar, just not precisely similar.

It may be that all such cases can be accommodated in one of the two ways discussed above. Perhaps similar properties answering to higher-level predicates are invariably either complex (but contain identical or exactly similar constituents), or simple and flatly imperfectly similar. There is, however, another possibility worth mentioning. Think, first, of functional predicates, and assume for the sake of argument that 'is in pain' is such a predicate: 'is in pain' applies to a creature in virtue of that creature's being in a particular kind of functional state. My contention is that these states need only be broadly similar, but what does this similarity amount to? Functional similarities are causal or, more accurately, dispositional similarities. To a first approximation, functional states are similar just in case they would manifest similar outputs given similar inputs. Functional systems are similar just in case they are decomposable into similar functional states. If functionalist arguments for multiple realizability are right, then functionally similar systems could be built of very different materials and incorporate qualitatively different kinds of mechanism.

In what sense, then, could two functional states F_1 and F_2 be imperfectly similar? Alternatively, given that F_1 and F_2 are imperfectly similar, what might ground this imperfect similarity? Suppose F_1 and F_2 are complex. F_1 and F_2 might be organized in utterly different ways and built from utterly different materials, yet nevertheless possess a range of similar (as we are supposing imperfectly similar) dispositionalities. Dispositionalities possessed by F_1 and F_2 are products of the dispositionalities possessed by their respective constituents and the arrangement of these. Now it could turn out that, owing to interactions among the dispositionalities of a mechanism's parts, its overall dispositional profile resembled the overall dispositional profile of another system composed of very different kinds of component part. Where is the similarity in such cases? The functional similarity of F_1 and F_2 lies in similarities between their respective overall dispositional profiles considered at a suitably lofty level of abstraction.

An atomic-powered egg-beater and an apprentice chef armed with a wire whisk could be said to be functionally similar in so far as we focus on the operations of these two systems at a high level of abstraction. So long as we consider the performance of the chef and the performance of the atomic egg-beater as that of taking runny, liquid egg whites as inputs and yielding fluffy, beaten egg whites as outputs, the systems are 'the same'. Our description 'abstracts' from the details of the process that in each case yields this output from this input.[4] Abstraction involves non-specificity. Describing an object as having a shape is less specific (hence more abstract) than describing it as triangular, which is in turn less specific (thus more abstract) than describing it as equilaterally triangular. It is in virtue of an object's possession of a particular 'maximally specific' shape that it satisfies all these predicates. Just so, two systems describable as egg-beaters are capable of producing (each in its own way) distinctive outputs from certain kinds of input. These outputs themselves have their own 'maximally specific' character (which could well differ on different occasions), but, despite differences, they all satisfy the description 'beaten egg whites'.

Do we need to find a basis for non-specific similarity in some maximally specific similarity? Not, perhaps, if the similarities in question fall under sufficiently abstract descriptions. As a limiting case, think of 'is a thing'. This predicate is satisfied by endless objects (and perhaps non-objects as well) that evidently lack a common element in virtue of which it would be true of them that they are things. The utility of functional predicates is that they enable us to corral very different kinds of state or process by reference to similarity of inputs and outputs. This may involve intrinsic similarity among inputs or intrinsic similarity of outputs, or both (as in the case of an egg-beater). It might involve, as well, a specification of some task for which we possess a

---

[4] It abstracts as well from details of the inputs and outputs. The outputs may differ in their temperature, consistency, and volume, for instance. Under the description 'beaten egg whites', however, these count as the same. Compare: under the description 'is red', a scarlet ball, a crimson pennant, and a head of red hair count as the same.

criterion of success, however vague. Examples include functional descriptions of theorem-proving devices, chess-players, and the like.

14.9 Where this Leaves Us

Let me recapitulate. Similarity is a mixed bag. Objects can be similar because they share one or more properties (or, if properties are modes, because they possess perfectly similar properties) or because they possess imperfectly similar properties. Imperfect similarity can be grounded in partial perfect similarity. Some instances of imperfect similarity might resist this kind of reductive explanation, however. This would be so if simple properties, properties encompassing no constituent properties, could be imperfectly similar. If simple properties could be imperfectly similar, however, I see no reason to doubt that complex properties could be imperfectly similar in the same way. Complex properties might be imperfectly similar, not because they include perfectly similar constituents, but because it is of their nature to be imperfectly similar.

None of this requires an appeal to higher-order properties: properties of properties. Objects are similar in virtue of possessing similar properties, but properties are similar in virtue of their natures. These natures can, but need not, include perfectly similar (or, in the case of universals, identical) elements. Nor, I think, need we imagine that in every case in which items satisfy a single predicate those items must be similar (or identical) in some way. Being red, being spherical, and having a mass of one kilogram all fall under the predicate 'is a property'. Does this mean that these properties share a common element? It is hard to imagine what this element could be. Does it even mean that these properties are imperfectly similar? If properties are ways objects are or might be, 'is a property' is satisfied by any way an object is or might be. The notion that every property could share a common element is not promising. Indeed, once you consider simple properties, this seems patent. An appeal to higher-order properties appears ad hoc: a manifestation of the conviction that, if A, B, and C all fall under a predicate, 'F', A, B, and C must share a common property. In many cases this *seems* false, and I have argued that it often *is* false.

14.10 Secondary Qualities

Locke characterized secondary qualities as powers to produce ideas of certain sorts in us. Some interpreters have taken this to mean that, on Locke's view, secondary qualities are 'pure powers'. I have offered arguments against such an interpretation already (§§8.2, 11.1; see also §17.3 below). For the present I want only to consider how the so-called secondary qualities might fit the thesis I have been advancing concerning similarity. On the face of it, secondary qualities pose an obvious problem for that thesis. I have argued that predicates like 'is red' hold of objects by virtue of those objects' possessing any of a range of similar properties. Colours, however, are secondary qualities. They seem, then, to depend on observers in some essential way. Where does this leave my remarks on similarity? My answer will be that it complicates, but does not fundamentally alter, the position I have been defending.

A prefatory note. My interest here is not in doing justice to the physics, physiology, and psychophysics of colours and colour perception, but to envision a case that is apparently at odds with my account of similarity in a way that reflects more general worries about secondary qualities. I take up colour in more detail in Chapter 17.

At the outset, let me reiterate that I am doubtful that it is useful to regard secondary qualities as kinds of quality (or property).[5] Secondary qualities are just ordinary properties—roughly, Locke's primary qualities—considered in the light of their effects on us. One way to think of the primary/secondary distinction is in terms of explanation. An object's looking square or feeling solid is explained, in part, by its being square or solid. In contrast, an object's looking red, or tasting sweet, or feeling warm, might be explained by reference to complex primary qualities possessed by that object together with the effects of these on observers. An object feels warm, perhaps, because its micro-constituents are in a state of agitation. This agitation is transmitted to sensors in our fingers when we pick it up, and ultimately to the brain, producing, in the process, a feeling of warmth. An object looks red (let

---

[5] I shall use 'quality' and 'property' interchangeably here, but note in passing that I regard Locke's use of 'quality' as both premeditated and felicitous.

us pretend) because particles on its surface are arranged so as to reflect light in a particular way. Such light, in collaboration with our distinctive visual system, yields experiences we should describe as experiences of something red. What holds for warmth and colour holds as well for other secondary qualities.

Such properties threaten my account of similarity in so far as the pertinent similarities appear to depend on us. Secondary qualities apparently lack the kind of robust mind independence exhibited by paradigmatically objective similarities. I have suggested that 'is red' might hold of objects possessing any of a range of imperfectly similar properties. When we look closely at red objects, however, we do not in fact find well-behaved objective similarities. To locate those, we must, it seems, move to a consideration of the human colour-detection system. Considered in their own right as physical structures, red things seem not, as a matter of fact, to share similar properties (or at least none in virtue of which they answer to the predicate 'is red').

By way of illustration, let us imagine that ranges of properties of objects describable as being red include 'gaps' (the so-called metamers). Imagine, for instance, that objects possessing P_1, P_2, and P_3 all look red to us and uncontroversially satisfy 'is red'. P_1, P_2, and P_3 are, let us grant, similar but imperfectly so. Imagine, in addition, that objects possessing P_5, P_6, and P_7 all look green to ordinary observers under ordinary conditions. Suppose, now, that objects possessing P_4, a property not at all similar to P_1, P_2, or P_3, look red to ordinary observers under ordinary conditions.[6] Further, P_4 is at least as similar to P_5, P_6, and P_7 as P_5, P_6, and P_7 are to each other. Objects possessing P_4 looking red is explained by reference to features of us: idiosyncrasies of our colour-detection system. The structure of the system disposes it to respond in similar ways to P_1, P_2, P_3, and P_4.

We could say a number of things about such a case. In the first place, we might insist (not unreasonably) that objects possessing P_4 are in fact green, even though, on the basis of their possessing P_4, they look red to normal observers in normal circumstances. The idea would be that, owing to features of our colour-detection system, we are in certain regards colour blind. We are incapable of recognizing—unaided—

---

[6] The kind of case I have in mind is discussed astutely by Edward Averill in his 1985. See also Hilbert (1987); Hardin (1993); Akins and Hahn (2000). William Webster disputes evidence for metamers in his (unpublished) Ph.D. thesis (Webster 2001).

certain 'shades' of green. A second option would be to grant that an object possessing P_4 is not, on that account, green, and to move then to a notion of similarity that includes us as observers. Such a notion would be entirely objective. Thus, we might say that objects are red, not merely in virtue of possessing P_1, P_2, and P_3, but in virtue of standing in a relation that includes these properties together with some complex property of our colour-detection system, D_1. An object satisfies the predicate 'is red', on this account owing to its possessing P_1, say, *and* our possessing D_1. Then it might turn out that, while P_4 is not, on its own, as similar to P_1, P_2, and P_3 as they are to one another, P_4 plus D_2 (the property in play in our colour-detection system when it responds to objects possessing P_4) *is* as similar to P_1 plus D_1, P_2 plus D_1, and P_3 plus D_1, as these are to one another.

Each of these manoeuvres is, in its own way, unpromising. Compare the dispositionalities of P_1, P_2, P_3, and P_4. Objects possessing P_1 are disposed to bring about experiences of particular sorts in human observers. These experiences are *mutual* manifestations of P_1 and reciprocal dispositions of our colour-detection system. P_4 is dispositionally similar to P_5, P_6, and P_7, perhaps, but not precisely similar. In concert with our colour detection system it would yield a very different kind of manifestation: an experience we should describe as an experience of something red. Considered as powers or dispositions, then, P_5, P_6, and P_7 *are* in this regard more similar to one another than they are to P_4; and P_4 *is* dispositionally similar to P_1, P_2, and P_3. This similarity is a perfectly objective matter; the dispositional similarity of P_1, P_2, P_3, and P_4 is intrinsic to P_1, P_2, P_3, and P_4.

This is not an attempt to advance a theory of colour, only a suggestion as to how my account of predicates like 'is red' or 'is in pain' might be extended to cover cases in which objective similarities are apparently missing. If something like the imaginary story I have told about colours is apt, we can understand something of the force behind describing colours as secondary qualities. Red's being a secondary quality is a matter of the predicate, 'is red', holding of objects to which it is ascribed in virtue of dispositions possessed by those objects to manifest themselves in particular ways in our conscious experience. The manifestations of P_1, P_2, P_3, and P_4 in our conscious experience are similar. In discovering this, we face a choice. We could continue to insist that objects possessing P_4 are red, or we could say that such objects are green, not red, but (owing to features of our colour-detection system) we are blind to their being green. The choice here has more to do with the use to which we put our colour concepts than to as yet undiscovered facts of the matter. Indeed, all parties might agree on the facts, yet disagree on how best to describe those facts.

14.11 'Projections'

Realism is sometimes said to involve a commitment to the idea that certain of our concepts, those with respect to which we are realists, 'carve reality at the joints'. Do secondary quality concepts like colour do this? When we describe something as red or green are we 'carving reality at the joints'? To focus the question, consider how we might react to the discovery that colour concepts resemble kinship concepts. Suppose 'is red' were like 'is a first cousin twice removed'. Would this show that colour concepts do not 'carve reality at the joints', or that colours are mind dependent, or that they are social constructs? In short, would this oblige us to become anti-realists about colour?[7]

Imagine that we discovered that different cultures conceptualize the colour spectrum in very different, perhaps incommensurable, ways. Thus, we might discover that, when asked to select examples of particular colours from an array of coloured chips, classifications employed by members of different cultures 'cut across' one another in surprising ways.[8] Would this, together with what we know about the physics of colour and the psychophysics of colour perception, lead us to an anti-realism about colour? Would it establish that colours are mere cultural constructs?

In applying colour concepts, we are constrained by the way things stand in the world. A colour concept, C, is satisfied by objects in virtue of those objects' possession of particular properties. What we know about the physical basis of colour judgement suggests that these properties need not form a kind that would easily be identifiable as a kind

---

[7] Familiar forms of anti-realism: cultural relativism, conceptual relativism, internal realism.

[8] For a discussion of these possibilities and some interesting empirical conclusions, see Berlin and Kay (1969). Berlin and Kay argue that, while colour classification systems disagree as to colour boundaries (where one colour ends and another begins), there is remarkable agreement on central cases and an apparently universal hierarchy of colour terms. In the case I am imagining, cultures do not agree even over central cases, and no hierarchical ordering is observed.

of physics or chemistry. Inevitably, there will be borderline cases in which there is just no clear answer to the question whether C applies. Our colour concepts 'carve reality at the joints', but the joints in question are salient to us owing to features of our visual system and perhaps owing as well to culturally induced classificatory practices. Given C, and setting aside vague or indeterminate borderline cases, there is a perfectly objective fact of the matter as to whether an object is C. In this regard, kinship concepts resemble colour concepts. Given the concept of a first cousin twice removed, it is a perfectly objective matter as to whether Fred is Gordon's first cousin twice removed.[9]

Cases like these differ from those in which concepts are supposed to exhibit a 'projective', mind-dependent character. Philosophers have thought that values are 'projective'. I take this to mean, roughly, that your regarding this apple as having a certain value is a matter of your having a particular kind of attitude towards the apple. To be sure, your attitude towards the apple turns on the apple's possession of certain qualities. You value it (let us suppose) because it is crisp, tart, and juicy. I might have a very different attitude towards the apple. The very qualities that recommend the apple to you repel me. Here, the apple satisfies your application of an evaluative predicate in virtue of its possession of certain qualities. The apple's possession of those very qualities, however, prevents it from satisfying my application of the very same predicate.

These points are worth making explicit because it is easy to be misled by the suggestion that we are realists about Fs in so far as we take 'is F' to apply literally and truly to objects in virtue of properties possessed by properties.[10] After all, you literally and truly apply 'is good' to the apple in virtue of the apple's possession of certain properties. This need not imply value realism, however. We can exclude such cases so long as we note that an agent's application of a projective predicate, 'is F', to an object applies to that object in virtue of properties it possesses *only* given that agent's attitudes towards objects with those properties. You and I can reasonably disagree over an object's value without disagreeing over qualities it possesses. This is not so for colour concepts. Doubtless, our colour concepts reflect idiosyncrasies of our visual

---

[9] He is if he is the (first) cousin of one of Gordon's grandparents.
[10] Stephen Schwartz called my attention to this point.

system. But, given those concepts, it is an objective matter which properties satisfy them. Given the concept of red (and ignoring borderline cases), it is an objective fact that this apple is red regardless of how it might look to me.

This concludes my discussion of properties and property-ascribing predicates. I have argued that properties are modes, particularized ways objects are. But, if modes are ways objects are, what are objects? This is the topic to which I shall now turn.

CHAPTER 15
Objects

15.1 Particular Substances

Properties, I have argued, are modes: particularized ways objects are. But what are objects? Some philosophers take objects to be bundles of properties. Trope theorists, in particular, seem partial to the idea that there is nothing more to an object than its constituent properties appropriately arranged.[1] One motivation for such a view stems from a consideration made salient by Hume. When we think about or describe any object, we inevitably bring to mind or mention the object's properties. The beetroot I hold in my hand is red, spherical, and pungent. In perceiving the beetroot, I apparently respond to these and other of the beetroot's qualities. What else could there be to the beetroot?

One possibility is that objects like beetroots result from combining properties and what Armstrong calls 'thin particulars' (Armstrong 1989: 94–6; 1997: 123–6). A beetroot is a 'thick particular': a thin particular plus whatever properties it 'instantiates'. Differently put, a thin particular is what you get when you start with an object and (mentally) subtract its properties. This calls to mind Locke's conception of 'substrata'. Ordinary objects—beetroots and the like—are, on this view, substrata plus properties. Properties require substrata. Modes, ways objects are, cannot exist independently of objects. This is one way of understanding Locke's insistence that an object's properties must 'inhere in' or be 'supported by' a substratum. A substratum is not another property, but an ontologically distinctive bearer of properties.

If (like Armstrong, and unlike Locke) you thought properties were universals, substrata would introduce into the world elements of

---

[1] Examples of trope theorists so inclined include G. F. Stout (1921–3, 1936); D. C. Williams (1953); Keith Campbell (1981, 1990); Peter Simons (1994).

particularity absent otherwise. It is hard to see how particular objects could result from the bundling of universals. Bundles of universals would evidently amount only to a complex universal.[2] The problem is solved by attaching universals—somehow—to particulars. Two distinct beetroots (or, more realistically, two distinct electrons) might share all their intrinsic properties and differ only numerically. This difference is supplied by their respective substrata.

15.2 Substrata

Although substrata are especially appealing to proponents of universals, you need not regard properties as universals to find substrata attractive. Think of Locke. Locke views properties as modes. He recognizes a need, however, for substrata, something 'underlying' or 'supporting' properties. This sounds like a variant of Armstrong's conception of 'thick' and 'thin' particulars: a beetroot, what I have called an object, is a 'thick' particular, a 'thin' particular plus the beetroot's properties (now regarded not as universals, but as modes).[3] In this case, however, the function of a 'thin' particular is not to provide an otherwise missing element of particularity. Modes are themselves thoroughly particular. Rather, substrata (or 'thin particulars') provide a 'support' for properties, something for properties to 'inhere in' or belong to (see LaBossiere 1994).

A view of this kind ought to be an embarrassment for an empiricist like Locke (see Lowe 2000). Agents' 'ideas' of objects seem always to be ideas of objects' properties. How then could an agent form an idea of a substratum 'underlying', but distinct from, these properties? This is Hume's worry. For just the reason we cannot describe objects without describing their properties, we cannot think of substrata without thinking of *their* properties. Hume, a good empiricist, concludes that the conception of a substratum, a bearer of properties, is empty. Berkeley comes close to the same conclusion, but draws back. Ideas,

---

[2] Some philosophers (including Leibniz and Russell, among others) have sought to extract particularity from bundles of universals. One ploy (not deployed by either Leibniz or Russell) is to include among bundled universals making up a particular by including *haecceities*, single-instance universals designed to insure uniqueness: the *x* such that *x* = Socrates. This is the kind of move that gives philosophy a bad name.

[3] I have in mind Armstrong's account (1989) of 'thin particulars'. The account in Armstrong (1997) is closer to the position advocated here.

he reasons, are mental qualities. Qualities cannot exist apart from a possessor of qualities: ideas cannot exist apart from minds. We have, then, a
'notion' of mental substance, a substratum for mental qualities.

Locke and Berkeley could be read as positing substrata in the way a
physicist might posit an unobservable particle to explain observable
occurrences. This would turn substrata into 'theoretical entities'.[4] Such
a move might be a natural one to make if you started with the conviction that properties or modes—mental or material—are neither the
kinds of entity that could exist independently of objects possessing
them; nor the kinds of entity out of which objects could be made. This
implies that, if a mode exists, it must be a mode *of* something. This
something is a substratum: an unobservable support for observable
properties.

You need not be an empiricist to worry about substrata thus conceived. What could substrata (or 'thin particulars') *be*? They support, but
are distinct from, properties. But then it would seem that substrata lack
properties: substrata appear to be 'bare particulars', entities that themselves possess no properties save a capacity to 'support' properties.[5]

Rather than rehearse problems associated with bare particulars, I
should like to offer a somewhat different account of objects, one that
provides an alternative to the idea that ordinary objects (Armstrong's
'thick particulars') are made up of 'thin particulars' plus properties.

15.3 Objects as Basic Entities

Suppose, for a moment, that objects are the basic entities. By this I
mean that our world is a world of objects.[6] If more than one object
exists, these objects are, at a given time, arranged in a particular way.
Objects have properties, and properties belong to objects, but the
world is not a collection of properties—except in the derivative sense

[4] See Lowe (2000: 512). Plato's defence of *khora* (the 'receptacle', space) in the *Timaeus* (roughly,
48e–53b) as 'a third kind', ontologically distinct from the forms and their instances, might be thought to fit
this model. In fact (and leaving aside the forms), I like to think that Plato's conception is compatible with
the somewhat different conception defended in this chapter.

[5] You might think that substrata possess properties, just not the properties they 'support' qua thin particulars. Now we have the makings of a regress, however. We should need to distinguish a 'thick' substratum (the substratum together with *its* properties) from an underlying 'thin' substratum. Does this 'thin'
substratum possess properties? If so, we shall need a substratum for it. If not, it resembles a 'bare particular'.

[6] Compare Armstrong's contention (1997) that the world is 'a world of states of affairs'.

that it is an arrangement of objects, and objects have properties. One way to think about this is to imagine God's creating the world. In creating the world God does not create properties and property-bearers, then glue these together. In creating the objects God creates properties and property-bearers.

I prefer the more colloquial 'object' to the traditional term, 'substance'. By speaking of objects rather than substances, I hope to avoid associations with conceptions of substance some readers might bring with them. An object can be regarded as a possessor of properties: as something that is red, spherical, and pungent, for instance. This, if you like, is to consider the object as a substratum, a property-bearer. You can also attend to or consider an object's properties, ways that object is. The idea of a property borne and the idea of a property-bearer are correlative ideas. Such ideas result from acts of abstraction: selective attention, Locke's partial consideration. Just as an object must be some way (nothing can be no way at all), ways must be ways something is. Property-bearers and properties, then, are equally 'abstractions'. Do we perceive property-bearers? Well, we perceive beetroots, and beetroots are objects. Perceiving a beetroot is a matter of perceiving a red, spherical, pungent object. We can consider (or perceive) the beetroot as a spherical, red, pungent object, something that is these ways and others; and we can consider (or perceive) ways the beetroot is: red, spherical, pungent.

Objects, then, are the basic entities; property-bearers and properties are equally abstractions. Property-bearers require properties—no 'bare particulars'—and properties require property-bearers; neither can exist apart from the other. To ask whether property-bearers themselves have properties is to invite confusion. Property-bearers are not hidden from view, not mysterious entities 'coated' with properties. The beetroot itself is a bearer of properties. When you point to a beetroot, you point to a property-bearer. You can equally point to the beetroot's properties. In so doing, you need not alter the direction you are pointing.

Property-bearers and properties are inseparable. This is not because properties are bonded to property-bearers with an especially powerful metaphysical glue. Rather, property-bearers are objects considered as being particular ways, and properties are ways objects are. In considering an object as a property-bearer, we are considering it partially; in considering its properties, we are considering ways it is, another kind of partial consideration. Properties and property-bearers can be considered separately but they cannot be separated, even in thought.

Let me summarize. Objects are bearers of properties. A property-bearer is not a 'thin particular' to which properties are affixed. A property-bearer itself has all the properties it 'supports' and no more. Property-bearers are not 'bare particulars'. A property-bearer is an object considered as something that is various ways, something that has various properties; properties are ways objects are. On one reading, Locke's substrata are my objects (see Lowe 2000).

15.4 Basic Objects

I have used a beetroot as a model object. If a beetroot is an object, however, it is a complex object, itself made up of objects arranged just so. These constituent objects are themselves made up of constituent objects. Might this division go on indefinitely? In arguing that it is a mistake to regard reality as hierarchical (Chapters 2–6), I committed myself to the idea that reality has at most one level. (For reasons explained earlier, I prefer to describe this as a no-levels view.) Does this mean that I am committed as well to the idea that the world could not be infinitely complex? Am I committed, that is, to the idea that objects are not infinitely divisible, that every object is not made up of other objects?

Although I am inclined to think that reality could not be infinitely complex, that thesis is independent of the thesis that there are no levels of reality. In discussing levels, I noted that a no-levels conception of the world is perfectly compatible with the idea that the world includes levels of organization or complexity. The question now before us is whether levels of this kind bottom out or go on indefinitely. Physics gives us little reason to think that what we today regard as the most elementary constituents of the world might not turn out to be made up of still more elementary constituents. Certainly, in the past, whenever we imagined we had discovered the fundamental building blocks of reality, we subsequently uncovered deeper layers of complexity, boxes inside boxes.

Epistemological considerations of this kind cannot provide an answer to the question whether the world—our world—might not be infinitely complex. If the world is infinitely complex, then every object has parts that are themselves objects with parts: parts 'all the way down'. The denial of this possibility holds that the division of objects into parts 'bottoms out' at some fundamental level of simple objects. Perhaps this is a purely empirical matter. Perhaps we are not in a position to establish a priori that there could not be complexity all the way down.

In so far as you think of ordinary objects—or particles, for that matter—as being *made up of*, in the sense of being *built up from*, other objects, it is not easy to see how this could work. The difficulty here is disguised by the fact that we may find it natural to think of any object that occupies a region of space as infinitely divisible. Earlier (§10.2) I defended a distinction between spatial and substantial parts.[7] A complex object—my beetroot, for instance—is made up of parts that are themselves objects in their own right. An object can have, in addition to substantial parts, spatial parts. The book you are now holding is made up of various parts: a spine, a cover, individual pages. These parts, themselves complex objects, assembled in the right way, make up the book. The book has, as well, a top half and a bottom half. These halves are not parts of the book in the way the cover is a part of the book. You could not remove the book's top half or exchange the book's top and bottom halves using a saw and glue pot (although, of course, you could remove the portion of the book that now coincides with its top half and exchange this with the portion that coincides with its bottom half).

Now, if you thought that a simple object must lack spatial parts, then no object short of a spatial point could be simple. If, however, you regard simple objects as those that lack objects as parts—objects that are not made up of other objects—then there is no reason to think that there could not be simple objects with as many spatial parts as you like. As suggested earlier, a simple object could, on this accounting, be the size of a planet—or indeed encompass the whole of space–time. Similarly, the mere fact that any particle of matter, however slight, could be subdivided spatially goes no way at all towards showing that there are no simple objects. My suspicion is that the casualness with which some

---

[7] Temporal parts of objects, if they exist, resemble objects' spatial parts. A simple object could have any number of temporal parts.

philosophers contemplate the possibility that every object might have parts stems from confusing spatial and substantial parts.[8]

15.5 Considerations Favouring Simple Objects

I know of no wholly convincing arguments to the conclusion that every complex object is ultimately made up of simple objects. As noted above, so long as we think of complex objects as being built up of parts, it is hard to see how this could work unless some objects were simple. A line contains an infinite number of points, but the line is not made up of these points. The idea is difficult to appreciate unless we keep firmly in mind a distinction between substantial parts (parts of objects that are themselves objects) and spatial parts.

Wittgenstein, in the *Tractatus*, offers a more ambitious argument. It would, Wittgenstein contends, be impossible to represent the world at all unless the world included simple objects.

Objects are simple. Every statement about complexes can be resolved into a statement about their constituents and into the propositions that describe the complexes completely. Objects make up the substance of the world. That is why they cannot be composite. If the world had no substance, then whether a proposition had sense would depend on whether another proposition was true. In that case we could not sketch out any picture of the world (true or false).[9]   (Wittgenstein 1922/1961: §§2.02–2.0212)

These uncompromisingly oracular remarks reflect Wittgenstein's conviction that the very possibility of depicting reality requires articulated representations that align with reality in the right way. Ordinary assertions, if they are to be true or false, must be analysable in terms of a basic-level representation. Alignment, however, requires simple, indivisible objects. Otherwise, Wittgenstein seems to be thinking, there could be no definite fact of the matter as to how representational elements lined up with items in the world. Before you could represent anything, you would first need to specify the thing's parts (invoking 'another proposition' that would have to be true); but specifying the

---

[8] The idea that we could read off features of the world from mathematical descriptions is just an application of the Picture Theory. A line segment includes continuum many points. Does it follow from this that an actual line could be made up of 'continuum many' parts?

[9] See Heil (1979) for a discussion of this passage.

parts requires representing them. We face a vicious regress that could be terminated only by the existence of (non-conventionally) simple objects.

I see no need to follow Wittgenstein on this point. I have rejected the Picture Theory and with it any hint that language must align with the world in such a way that features of the world could be thought to be mirrored by linguistic structure. I leave open the question whether proponents of what I have been calling the Picture Theory are, in the end, committed to simple objects. I do not regard a commitment to simple objects as an embarrassment, mind you; I just do not know how to offer an a priori proof that the world must (or, for that matter, must not) be made up of simples.

Here is one possibility. If every object has parts that are themselves objects, if there are no simple objects, then every finite object is made up of an infinitude of objects. To the extent that we understand infinity, we understand that an infinite collection of objects must be one that includes a proper subcollection—a subcollection of objects in the original collection that does not include every object in the collection—that can be placed in one–one correspondence with objects making up the whole collection.[10] It is easy to doubt that this could work for collections of actual concrete objects, the kinds of object that, suitably organized, make up trees, people, and books.

If you are of a mathematical bent, you may find this kind of worry frivolous. Infinite sets are well-defined and well-behaved abstract entities. The question, however, is whether we can be blasé about the application of the concept of infinitude to collections of concrete objects that serve as building blocks of our world. I am not confident that we can—although I am not wholly confident that we cannot either.

In general, it could be a mistake to suppose that what might be true of space (or time) abstractly conceived could be true as well of occupants of space and time. Even if every region of space were infinitely divisible, it need not follow that objects occupying a finite spatial region could themselves be made up of an infinite number of objects. Considered as a spatial entity, a line may be infinitely divisible. But, again, a line is not made up of an infinitude of points in the way a neck-

---

[10] A common illustration appeals to the set of odd numbers, a proper subset of the set of natural numbers, the elements of which can be put in one–one correspondence with the natural numbers.

lace is made up of a string of pearls. Material constitution is not in this regard Euclidean. Or so it would seem.

15.6 What Are the Objects?

Let us suppose that every complex object is ultimately made up of simple objects: objects not themselves composed of objects. I have described these objects as 'building blocks'. This might suggest a seventeenth-century corpuscular picture: the simple objects are billiard-ball-like bits of matter capable of bonding with other material bits to form complex objects.

If physics is on the right track, this picture is highly unlikely. Elementary 'particles', electrons, for instance, behave in a wavelike way. Depictions of electrons as minute billiard balls would be wildly misguided. A commitment to an ontology of objects, however, is not a commitment to material corpuscles. What the fundamental objects are is anybody's guess. The answer is not something to be had a priori, but only by appeal to empirical theories advanced in basic physics. We need not imagine that the fundamental objects are particle-like. Objects could be fields. Perhaps there is but a single object: space, or space–time, or some all-embracing quantum field.[11] If that were so, then ordinary objects would turn out to be modes of the one all-inclusive object. A beetroot, for instance, might be a red, spherical, pungent region of space–time. The question what the objects are, like the question what the properties are, is not one to be answered from the armchair.

Let me emphasize that an ontology of objects—a substance ontology—is not an ontology according to which the things we ordinarily regard as objects must turn out to be objects in a strict sense. For Locke, ordinary objects ('substances') are in reality modes: ways collections of particles are arranged. Similarly, rocks, or beetroots, or electrons could turn out to be local disturbances or thickenings in the fabric of space–time. Suppose this were so. Would we have established that rocks, beetroots, and electrons do not exist? I touched on this matter

[11] Something like this appears to be what Plato has in mind in the *Timaeus*. As C. B. Martin has noted, Locke himself (in *An Examination of P. Malebranche's Opinion* (1706)) entertained the possibility the space might be the substratum (see Lowe 2000: 509 n. 17).

earlier (§§5.2, 5.5), and I shall take it up in more depth in the next chapter. For the moment, however, let me note that it can be perfectly acceptable to use the term 'object' as I have used it in this chapter to designate propertied entities while leaving it open whether what we might ordinarily call objects are objects in this more restricted sense.[12]

Objects might, then, turn out not to be objects. Less mysteriously, we might discover that what we ordinarily regard as objects are not objects in the strict sense, but only modes: ways objects are (or ways some object is). Does this cast doubt on what we ordinarily call objects? In rejecting the Picture Theory, I have rejected this inference. To discover that what we ordinarily regard as an object—the beetroot, for instance—is, at bottom, not a 'continuant', but a thickening of a region space–time, is not to discover that beetroots do not exist; it is to discover that beetroots—surprisingly—just are local thickenings of space–time. This thought leads us directly to the topic of the next chapter: substantial identity.

---

[12] This is what Locke does with 'substance'.

CHAPTER 16
Substantial Identity

16.1 Ordinary Objects

In the previous chapter we encountered the possibility that what we ordinarily regard as objects—human beings, tables, trees, mountains, billiard balls—are not objects 'in the strict sense'. This would be so if, for instance, our world comprised a single object: Plato's *khora*, or space, or space–time, or some quantum ur-field. In that case ordinary objects would turn out to be modes. A beetroot, for instance, might be a disturbance in, or 'thickening' of, a certain region of space–time. One question such a view must face is whether this would mean that beetroots are mere fictions.

You might think this if (1) you took the concept of a beetroot (or the concept of an ordinary material particular) to be the concept of a substance: a possessor of properties not itself a property; and (2) you accepted the idea that realism requires that substances answer to substance concepts expressed by sortals (§5.5 and below). It would turn out in that case that nothing whatever answered to the beetroot concept. The same line of reasoning would apply to human beings, tables, trees, and mountains. If our concepts of these things are concepts of substances, then the possibility I am envisaging would turn out to be one in which there are no human beings, tables, trees, or mountains.

A second, and to my mind more plausible, possibility is that we should grant that human beings, tables, trees, and mountains were not what we might have otherwise thought. In so saying, would we have 'lost' human beings, tables, trees, and mountains? We would have lost a certain conception of what these things are and with it philosophical theories that partake of that conception. But we would not have lost anything we might otherwise have cared about. Our interactions with what we should continue to call human beings, tables, trees, and mountains would be unchanged.[1]

16.2 Sortals

Following Locke, I earlier distinguished sortal terms from characterizing terms.[2] Sortals include ordinary count nouns: 'tree', 'table', 'person', 'statue', 'beetroot', and the like. Part of what it is to understand the meanings of such terms is to grasp conditions of identity they mandate. There is, we imagine, always a definite answer to the question 'how many' when it comes to trees, chairs, persons, statues, and beetroots. Similarly, we suppose there is a definite answer to the question whether a given tree (chair, person, statue, beetroot) is the very same tree (chair, person, statue, beetroot) as this one.[3] Such terms differ from the mass terms, on the one hand ('bronze', 'water', 'butter') and, on the other hand, characterizing terms ('red', 'spherical', 'tall'). You can count lumps of bronze, glasses of water, sticks of butter, but it makes no sense to count bronze, water, or butter. You can count instances of red, sphericity, or tallness, but this requires counting red, spherical, or tall objects of particular sorts.

Much more could be said on these points (see e.g. Lowe 1989). I shall focus here, however, only on ontological puzzles that arise when we look closely at the application of sortals. The quickest way into the territory is to consider an ancient puzzle concerning composition and identity.[4] Consider a statue formed from a lump of bronze. What, philosophers ask, is the relation between the statue and the lump of bronze? The lump, we could say, *makes up* the statue, but what exactly does this mean?

Both 'statue' and 'lump of bronze' are sortals. Each is associated with distinct identity conditions. These identity conditions include synchronic, diachronic, and modal elements: they concern what it is for

---

[1] This is apparently Locke's view in the *Essay* (1690/1978). The only substances in a strict sense are the particles and individual spirits. Ordinary objects (and persons) are modes: ways the basic substances are organized. See §16.8 below.

[2] §5.5 above. 'Sortal' is introduced by Locke in the *Essay* (III. iii. 15) in the context of a discussion of identity. See Strawson (1959: 168); Geach (1980: 63–4); Lowe (1989: 2; 1998: ch. 3).

[3] For a caveat, see §5.5, n. 10.

[4] The literature on this topic is by now voluminous. See Rea (1997) for a representative collection of views and a useful introduction to the central issues.

something to *be* a statue or a lump of bronze; what it is for something to *persist* as a statue or a lump of bronze over time; and what kinds of change *could or could not* befall a statue or a lump of bronze. In speaking of statues or lumps of bronze, we have some idea as to how to count such things, and, in addition, some idea as to what is required for the persistence of a given statue or bronze lump. The easiest way to appreciate such conditions is to observe them in action.

Suppose a particular lump of bronze is moulded into a statue of Abraham Lincoln on Tuesday. On Tuesday, the statue comes into existence, but the lump of bronze existed earlier. Now suppose that, on Wednesday, the statue is melted and formed into a statue of Richard Nixon. The statue of Lincoln ceases to exist, and a new statue comes into existence. The lump of bronze persists through all these changes. We should say that the lump—the very same lump–had changed its shape. Imagine, however, that we remove a portion of the Nixon statue—the nose, for instance—and replace it with a nose moulded from another lump of bronze. The statue persists through this change (just as a watch persists through a replacement of parts by a watchmaker), but the lump of bronze—the original lump of bronze—does not. The lump, but not the statue, would survive dramatic alterations in shape; the statue, but not the lump, would survive replacement of the matter making it up. This is sometimes put by saying that lumps of bronze and statues have different 'modal properties'.

16.3 The Indiscernibility of Identicals

At the core of our concept of identity is the idea that, if α and β are the selfsame object, then, of necessity, every property of α is a property of β and vice versa. It follows that, if α possesses a property β lacks (or β possesses a property lacked by α), α and β must be distinct objects. This is Leibniz's principle of the 'indiscernibility of identicals'. Return to the statue of Lincoln and the lump of bronze that makes it up. Although the lump exists prior to the existence of the statue and exists after the statue ceases to exist, so long as the statue exists, the statue and the lump spatially coincide: every intrinsic property of one is apparently a property of the other. If the lump is shiny, so is the statue; if the statue has a particular shape, so does the lump; if the lump has a certain

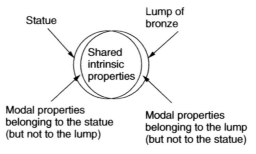

Figure 16.1. The statue and the lump

mass, so does the statue; and so on. This suggests that the statue *is* the lump, or rather that the statue is the lump during a certain temporal interval (the lump is the statue on Tuesday).[5] A view of this kind regards composition as tantamount to identity: if α is composed of β (as the statue is composed of the lump of bronze), then α *is* β.

Suppose, however, modal properties of the statue and the lump of bronze are included in the mix; suppose we extend the idea that α and β are the selfsame object only if every property of α is a property of β and vice versa to include modal properties. Then, if α and β differ in their modal properties, α and β must be distinct (see Figure 16.1).[6] We have seen already that, owing to differences in persistence conditions, the statue and the lump of bronze differ in their modal properties. A statue could undergo certain changes that a lump of bronze could not undergo; and a lump of bronze could undergo changes that would result in the statue's ceasing to exist. Application of the principle of the indiscernibility of identicals apparently obliges us to distinguish the statue and the lump of bronze making it up. On Monday a lump of bronze, but no statue, exists; on Tuesday the lump of bronze continues to exist and the Lincoln statue comes into existence. The statue and the lump coincide and share all of their non-modal intrinsic properties (this is the situation depicted in Figure 16.1). Nevertheless, given differences in their modal properties, the statue and the lump are distinct objects.

This conclusion could be reinforced by including 'historical properties', alongside modal properties in the accounting. (These could be

---

[5] Alternatively: the statue is identical with a particular 'temporal part' of the lump.
[6] The figure, and the idea behind it, is discussed in Paul (forthcoming).

added to the non-overlapping crescents in Figure 16.1.) The statue and the lump of bronze making it up have very different historical properties: the statue exists on Tuesday but not on Monday or Wednesday. The lump of bronze exists on Monday, Tuesday, and Wednesday. The statue, but not the lump, was brought into existence by a particular artisan working in a particular location.

Note, further, that certain properties could be said to be essential to the statue (but inessential—accidental—to the lump of bronze), and other properties could be essential to the lump of bronze but inessential to the statue. The lump is accidentally statue shaped, but the statue is essentially statue shaped. The lump includes a particular portion of bronze essentially, but the statue includes this portion only accidentally: the statue could continue to exist even if this portion of bronze were detached or replaced.

Applying the principle of the indiscernibility of identicals, and including modal and historical properties in the inventory of objects' properties, we can see that the statue and the lump of bronze must be distinct individuals. If the statue and the lump of bronze differ in which of their properties are essential, which accidental, all the more reason to distinguish them. These individuals coincide spatially for a period of time—the period of time during which, as we might put it, the statue is made up of the lump of bronze.[7]

16.4 'Overlapping Objects' and Eliminativism

The idea that objects could overlap in this way would strike non-philosophers as decidedly strange, but strangeness is a matter of degree: alternatives might be stranger still. You could, for instance, hold that there is but a single object: a statue-shaped lump of bronze. This seems to imply that there are no statues, only lumps of bronze (or, more generally, lumps of whatever statues happen to be made of). Worse, perhaps, the very same reasoning that leads us to replace talk of statues with talk of statue-shaped lumps would oblige us to deny the existence of most familiar objects—including lumps of bronze! A lump of bronze is made up of a dynamic collection of electrons and quarks. The

---

[7] Someone who held that objects are bundles of universals would regard statues and lumps of bronze as overlapping, but not perfectly coinciding, even for a particular temporal duration. See Figure 16.1.

lump and this collection have different conditions of identity and persistence, different modal and historical properties. If we doubt the existence of statues, we should equally doubt the existence of lumps of bronze.

This line of argument applies quite generally. Do human beings exist? Human beings are made up of collections of cells in the way statues are made up of lumps of bronze. Considerations leading us to deny the existence of statues would seem to apply in this case: there are no human beings, only collections of cells. More startlingly, the argument apparently encourages us to deny the existence of cells: only collections of elementary particles. Pushed to its limit, the idea we are left with is that all that exists—all that *really* exists—are the atoms and the void.[8]

We seem faced with a choice. Either we can accept the idea that the world is full of overlapping objects, objects that coincide spatially, at least for a time, or deny that familiar objects exist.[9] The latter eliminativist strategy seems crazy. It is patently at odds with common sense. It is at odds as well with scientific practice. The sciences, most particularly the special sciences, are apparently committed to the existence of many of the objects that eliminativism would declare non-existent. Why should practising scientists defer to the philosophers on such matters? Surely it is more likely that philosophers have made a mistake in their reasoning than that there are no statues, human beings, trees, cells. If the alternative—coincident objects—seems a trifle strange, it is surely far less strange than eliminativism.

16.5 Historical and Modal 'Properties'

Must we choose between reductionism (the statue *is* the lump of bronze), eliminativism (there are no statues only statue-shaped lumps

---

[8] Laurie Paul suggested (in conversation) that eliminativism apparently implies that there must be simple objects: there could not be 'parts all the way down'. Yet the latter hypothesis is a live empirical possibility (though see §15.5). I have little sympathy for eliminativism, but I am not altogether convinced that eliminativism does imply that there could not be 'parts all the way down'. Suppose an eliminativist held that the physical world is like space: no matter how far you divide it, further divisions are always possible. This is consistent with there being spatial points. Just as an infinite number of these points constitute any line, so any object will be made up of an infinitude of parts; nevertheless there are simples corresponding to spatial points.

[9] 'Selective eliminativism' is a third alternative. See e.g. van Inwagen (1990); Merricks (2001).

of bronze), and a commitment to coincident objects? I believe there is another, more attractive option. The issue, as I see it, concerns what is required for realism about statues (and other composite entities). Statues and lumps of bronze have different identity and persistence conditions. We grasp these in grasping the respective concepts. In so doing, we are in a position to ascertain a priori certain historical and modal truths that must hold for statues and for lumps of bronze respectively. If we distinguish between objects' essential properties and their accidental properties, we can find differences here as well.

All of this is relatively uncontroversial—or at any rate I shall not challenge it here. What I should like to challenge is the idea that realism about an object answering to a sortal obliges us to suppose that the sortal designates an object or a class of objects in a metaphysically robust sense of object. Before taking up this point, however, it will be convenient to say something about putative historical and modal properties.

Recall that it is differences in the historical and model properties of statues and lumps of bronze that lead to doubts that statues could be identified with the lumps of material making them up: composition is not identity. But what exactly are historical and modal properties? The lump of bronze is said to possess the modal property of being able to undergo a change of shape; the statue is said to lack this modal property and to possess the complementary modal property of being unable to change shape.[10] This makes it sound as though modal properties resemble powers or dispositions: a grain of salt, but not a grain of bronze, would dissolve in water. The modal properties at issue are not dispositions, however. The statue 'cannot' change shape, perhaps, but this is not because it is especially resistant to outside forces in the way a grain of bronze might be said to resist dissolving in water. Rather, a statue cannot change shape in the sense that, were the bronze that makes up the statue to undergo a sufficiently dramatic change of shape, it would no longer count as a statue. Similarly, the lump of bronze cannot lose bronze particles, not because the lump is unusually resistant to forces that would hive off constituent particles, but because, once the lump loses particles, it no longer counts as the very same lump.

---

[10] This is an idealization, I suppose. A statue might undergo *some* changes in shape without ceasing to be the very same statue. Similarly a lump of bronze rolled into a length of thin wire might cease to be a lump.

Where does this leave modal properties? Consider what the truth-maker might be for a claim of the form 'this statue cannot change shape'? Note, first, that the claim appears in fact to be short for something like 'this statue cannot change shape and still count as the same statue'. This seems to point us towards the concept of statuehood. Indeed, this is precisely what we might expect once we enquire as to the truth-makers for ascriptions of modal properties. What makes it true that a lump of bronze can change shape or that it cannot lose bronze particles that make it up? So far as I can see, nothing in the lump of bronze itself makes such assertions true. We can know a priori that these truths hold of lumps of bronze because the truths concern, not properties of the bronze, but the concept of a lump of matter.

Casual mention of modal properties disguises this point. Worse, perhaps, so long as we uncritically tolerate talk of modal properties, we are likely to be misled when we ask the question asked in the previous paragraph: what are the truth-makers for modal truths concerning statues or lumps of bronze? The answer seems obvious: the objects' possession of certain modal properties. If we look beyond this facile answer, however, if we ask in an open-minded way what the truth-makers are, we are led in a very different direction.

Suppose, now, that all the so-called modal properties commonly thought to distinguish statues from the matter making them up are like this. Talk of modal properties is a philosophically pretentious, and potentially confusing, way of describing constraints built into concepts we deploy. To say that statues and lumps of bronze possess different modal properties is just an oblique way of calling attention to the evident fact that our statue concept differs from our lump concept. This implies that talk of statues could not be reduced to, replaced by, or translated into talk of lumps, a point it is easy to concede.

Does this mean that statues are mind-dependent entities? Why should it? We decide what is to count as a statue, but an object's satisfying the statue concept is a matter of that object's being a particular way quite independently of how we take it to be.[11] Statues are no more

---

[11] You might think that statues are mind dependent in the sense that only an artefact, only something created by an intelligent agent, could count as a statue. If this is so, then a mind must figure in the causal process that results in a statue. This is not a form of anti-realism about statues, however, merely a recognition that the conditions required for the satisfaction of the statue concept include minds playing appropriate causal roles.

mind dependent than trees, mountains, beetroots, electrons, or lumps of bronze. In each of these cases, we decide what is to answer to 'tree', 'mountain', 'beetroot', 'electron', 'lump of bronze', but our application of these terms requires cooperation on the part of the world.

16.6 Modal Properties and Dispositions

Am I right in thinking that reference to alleged modal properties is best construed as an indirect way of invoking constraints on the application of sortal concepts? Consider powers or dispositions. These might reasonably be accounted modal properties. In virtue of possessing a disposition to dissolve in water, it is true of this grain of salt (but not that grain of bronze) that it would dissolve in water. I have suggested already that, in discussion of issues involving identity and constitution, talk of modal properties is given a kind of undeserved legitimacy by way of an implicit association with talk of powers or dispositions. Dispositions, however, are intrinsic features of objects (or so I have argued). It is all too easy to slide from talk of modal truths to talk of modal properties supposedly answering to these truths. If I am right, however, the truth-makers for kinds of modal truth invoked in these discussions are not properties at all.

Return to the statue and the lump of bronze. If we exclude what I have identified as fraudulent modal properties from consideration, can we find a difference in properties of a sort that would incline us to distinguish the statue and the lump of bronze (or the lump of bronze on Tuesday)? E. J. Lowe offers the following suggestion.

The statue and the lump of bronze can in fact differ from one another, during the time of their coincidence, even in respect of certain of their *dispositional* properties—the implication being that not *all* of their dispositional properties are simply grounded in the properties and relations of the material particles which compose them. For example, we may say of the statue that it is disposed to cast a shadow of a certain shape, implying that if it were to be set on the ground and exposed to sunlight, a shadow of that shape would be cast on the ground at its foot. But we cannot say of the lump of bronze, without qualification, that it is disposed to cast a shadow of a particular shape. For, whereas the statue, so long as it exists, must retain a certain constant shape, this is not true of the lump of bronze.   (Lowe 2002: 72)

Is Lowe right? Does the statue differ dispositionally from the lump
of bronze during the time the statue exists? The statue exists on
Tuesday, during which time it coincides spatially with the lump of
bronze. The question is whether, during this period, the statue possesses
a power or disposition that the lump of bronze does not possess. The
statue has the power to cast a shadow of a particular shape. Does the
lump of bronze possess this power? It does, so long as the statue does.
At t, the statue and the lump both have this power. Differently put: if
the statue has this power at t, the lump of bronze has it at t, and vice
versa. The lump could lose this power; the statue could not fail to have
it. But this is just to say that the lump that makes up the statue could
count as a statue only so long as it possesses this power. This seems to be
the case with dispositional properties quite generally.[12] If α possesses a
dispositional property, P, at t, and α is made up of β, then β possesses P
at t (and vice versa).

I do not want to put excessive weight on this point. My aim is not to
show that composition is identity (the statue is the lump). I readily
accept that modal and historical constraints on the application of these
concepts ensure that it is a mistake to identify statues with lumps of
matter. The question is, what are we to conclude from this?

16.7 What Does Realism about Statues Require?

Although our statue concept and lump concept differ significantly in
their conditions of application, the very same portion of matter can, on
occasion, satisfy both concepts. In fashioning a lump of bronze into
a statue of Lincoln, an artisan fashions a statue. Now the very same
portion of matter answers to the statue concept and the lump concept.
It is natural to express this fact by saying that the lump *is* the statue.
Does this mean that the lump (or a temporal segment of the lump) is
identical with the statue (or a temporal segment of the statue)? That
appears unlikely for all the reasons opponents of the idea that composition is identity are fond of offering.

Should we then adopt the view that the lump (or a temporal

---

[12] Given the account of properties defended in Chapter 11, every intrinsic property of a material object
is dispositional—*and* qualitative.

segment of the lump) and the statue spatially coincide? Again, there can be no objection to this provided it is understood as meaning nothing more than that, at a particular time, the very same portion of matter satisfies the statue concept and the lump concept.

You might prefer the idea that statues are not objects at all, but merely modes: ways objects are. Statues, on this view, are just statue-shaped lumps of matter. I have already flagged one worry about a view of this kind. If we follow out the reasoning consistently, we risk being left with the idea that neither statues nor lumps exist: there are only the atoms and the void.

What is the truth here? What do we require in order to say that statues (or lumps) exist? What is it to be a realist about such things? Suppose we ask what is required for God to create a universe like ours incorporating statues. God will need to create the atoms and the void (the elementary particles, or the fields, or what have you), and arrange them appropriately. If we are to have statues, and statues require distinctively intelligent intervention, then, in creating a universe featuring statues, God will need to create dynamic, possibly widely dispersed systems of particles. Once this is accomplished, God will have created a world containing statues: it will be true there are statues. The truth-makers for our statue talk will be staggeringly complex and, from the point of view of physics, hideously unruly. Nevertheless, it will be true, literally true, that there are statues (and, for that matter, that there are lumps of bronze).

Does this deflate statues? It deflates a certain conception of what the truth-makers must be for claims about statues to be true. It is an open question what the ultimate truth-makers are for true descriptions of the world we unselfconsciously deploy. Imagine, for instance, that the world consists of a single space–time manifold. What we regard as distinct objects are ways this manifold is organized. Were this so, the deep truth about objects like statues and lumps of bronze would be that such things are in fact modes. Is our ordinary talk of states and lumps of bronze at odds with this possibility? Again, I do not see why we must think so. Many philosophers who would be inclined to think so are, I have argued, beguiled by a Picture Theory according to which features of reality are mirrored in our styles of representation: if 'statue' is a sortal, then either statues are distinct objects or there are no statues. This is the linguistic tail wagging the ontological dog.

16.8 Material Constitution

All of this leads, I think, to a deeper point about material constitution. In so far as you are inclined to think that some objects are made up of other objects, you might be moved to endorse the view that the only objects—or the only *true* objects—are the ultimate objects: the quarks, electrons, the quantum field. This is close to the conclusion at which Locke arrived. Ordinary objects—trees, mountains, human beings— are not strictly speaking objects but modes: ways the ultimate objects are arranged. Locke allowed for the possibility that there are mental objects, souls. Persons are not mental objects, however, persons are mental modes.

Locke believed that material reality was corpuscular. Corpuscularism has long been out of fashion. Nowadays we prefer to think of the material world as a collection of elementary particles, or fields, or perhaps a single field, a single space–time manifold. On any of these views, macroscopic material objects will consist of arrangements of the ultimate constituents or, if you prefer the idea that the world is a single unified space–time manifold, a way this manifold is. This turns macroscopic objects into modes.

Suppose this is right. Suppose that trees, mountains, human beings, and the rest are modes: ways the ultimate stuff is. Does this mean that macroscopic objects do not exist (or do not *really* exist)? Only a philosopher would want to say this. My suggestion is that, were things to turn out in the way described, we would be in possession of the deep story about trees, mountains, and human beings. The truth-makers for claims about such things would be modes: ways the ultimate bits of the world are organized. Indeed, objects thought of commonsensically would, in reality, be modes: this would be the deep story about objects. (The contention here resembles that advanced in §5.2.)

To think that any of this would render ordinary assertions about middle-sized objects false is to misunderstand the nature of truth making. We are in no position to move analytically from concepts to truth-makers for applications of those concepts. To think otherwise is to embrace the Picture Theory.

16.9   Eddington's Tables

In a widely cited passage, the physicist A. S. Eddington (1928) speaks of setting out to write *The Nature of the Physical World*. He begins by drawing up 'my chairs to my two tables'. 'There are', he says, 'duplicates of every object about me—two tables, two chairs, two pens'. Eddington then focuses on the two tables:

One of them has been familiar to me from earliest years. It is a commonplace object of that environment which I call the world. How shall I describe it? It has extension; it is comparatively permanent; it is coloured; above all it is *substantial*. By substantial I do not merely mean that it does not collapse when I lean upon it; I mean that it is constituted of 'substance' and by that word I am trying to convey to you some conception of its intrinsic nature. [. . .] Table No. 2 is my scientific table. [. . .] My scientific table is mostly emptiness. Sparsely scattered in that emptiness are numerous electric charges rushing about with great speed; but their combined bulk amounts to less than a billionth of the bulk of the table itself. Notwithstanding its strange construction it turns out to be an entirely efficient table. It supports my writing paper as satisfactorily as table No. 1; for when I lay the paper on it the little electric particles with their headlong speed keep on hitting the underside, so that the paper is maintained in shuttlecock fashion at a nearly steady level. (Eddington 1928: pp. ix–x)

Eddington is at pains to emphasize the difference between familiar objects and their scientific counterparts.

It makes all the difference in the world whether the paper before me is poised as it were on a swarm of flies and sustained in shuttlecock fashion by a series of tiny blows from the swarm underneath, or whether it is supported because there is substance below it, it being the intrinsic nature of substance to occupy space to the exclusion of other substance.   (Eddington 1928: p. xiv)

Eddington concludes that 'modern physics has by delicate test and remorseless logic assured me that my second scientific table is the only one which is really there' (Eddington 1928: p. xiv).

These remarks suggest that, if we are to accept physics, we must suppose that tables (and along with tables, human beings, trees, and mountains) do not exist. Nothing answers to our table concept, in so far as that concept is of objects possessing a substantial constitution.

All that exists—*really* exists—are swarms of electrons and other particles.

The alternative is to take the scientific evidence as illuminating the nature of tables, trees, and mountains. Eddington makes much of the 'substantiality' of tables. The idea, expressed in the jargon of philosophers, is that substantiality is an essential property of tables. We are meant to take it that modern science has revealed that nothing is substantial—or at any rate no plausible table candidates are substantial—so there are no tables. But what precisely is substantiality? Eddington himself poses this question and answers it as follows: 'I do not think substantiality can be described better than by saying it is the kind of nature exemplified by an ordinary table' (Eddington 1928: p. ix). Substantiality in this sense, however, is most definitely possessed by Eddington's 'scientific table'!

Where does this leave us? The truth-maker for 'This is substantial' is an arrangement of particles. The truth-maker for 'This is a table' is this same arrangement of particles with a particular history and standing in particular relations to other arrangements of particles. Talk of tables and talk of substantiality cannot be analysed in terms of talk of particles. We can—and typically do—speak of tables and their substantiality while knowing nothing of the particles. Eddington is mistaken. Twentieth-century physics did not establish that nothing is substantial or that tables are fictions. Rather physics gives us a deeper understanding of the nature of substantiality and the nature of ordinary objects like tables.

With these thoughts in mind, I now turn from a discussion of issues in fundamental ontology, to its application to three topics that have occupied philosophers of mind: colour, intentionality, and consciousness.

APPLICATIONS

CHAPTER 17

Colour

17.1 Plan of Attack

The account of colour, begun in §14.10 and to be extended here, could be described as broadly dispositionalist. In saying this, I align myself with a long realist tradition going back at least to Locke. That tradition has not fared well in recent years, in large measure because the nature of dispositions has been misunderstood and misdescribed. The result has been confusion on the part both of those attracted to a dispositional account and of their opponents. I begin with a brief summary of the account of dispositionality advanced already, followed by a briefer discussion of the primary/secondary quality distinction. I then turn to the question what might reasonably be expected of a philosophical theory of colour, and conclude with some observations on the state of play.

17.2 Dispositions

An understanding of what is involved in a dispositional account of colour requires an understanding of dispositions. I have discussed dispositionality at length in Chapters 8–11. Here I shall presuppose the account developed in those chapters and summarize certain of its most important aspects, especially as these bear on the topic at hand.

(1) Dispositions are intrinsic properties of objects possessing them.

Dispositions are not relations or 'relational properties'.[1] The tendency to regard dispositions relationally stems in part from a tendency to imagine that the nature of dispositionality could be wholly captured

---

[1] So far as I can tell, to say that an object possesses a relational property is just to say that it, or perhaps a part of it, stands in some relation.

via subjunctive conditionals. An object is fragile if it would shatter when struck by something solid. An object can be fragile when the conditional is false, however. Consider this delicate crystal vase. The vase is fragile, although it is false that, were it struck by a hammer, it would shatter. It is false because the vase is watched over by an angel who would see to it that the glass would liquefy were it struck. Liquefied, the vase would alter dispositionally: it would cease to be fragile. This granite boulder is not fragile, although it is true that, were it struck by a solid object, it would shatter: a boulder-watching angel would see to it that its temperature would be lowered dramatically were it struck, thereby ensuring that it would shatter.[2] Conditionals provide a defeasible, rough-and-ready way to pick out dispositions, not a reductive analysis.

A disposition is not a relation to its actual or possible manifestations or manifestation partners. A disposition can persist unmanifested and, in the right circumstances, be unmanifestable. α-particles are disposed to annihilate β-particles; but no α-particle exists within the light cone of any β-particle. You need not be distracted by fanciful cases, however. A moment's thought should make it evident that most dispositions will never be manifested. I shall say more about the process of manifestation presently. For the moment, I want only to insist on a conception of dispositionality according to which dispositions are intrinsic properties of objects.

Dispositions are ubiquitous. Indeed:

(2) Every intrinsic property of a concrete object is dispositional.

The idea here is that properties contribute in a distinctive way to the dispositionalities or causal powers of objects possessing them. A property that made no causal difference to its possessors would be a property that made no difference at all. Among other things, such properties would be undetectable. This makes it challenging to produce examples of non-fanciful properties altogether lacking in dispositionality. Consider sphericity: the property of being spherical. Being spherical is a paradigm case of what Locke called a primary quality. But it is in virtue

---

[2] So-called finkish cases of this kind are discussed in Martin (1994). See Bird (1998, 2000) for a discussion of cases in which 'antidotes' block the manifestation of a disposition. The cases mentioned here bear an obvious similarity to so-called Frankfurt cases, which have been discussed extensively by philosophers writing on free will.

of being spherical that an object rolls or would roll; it is in virtue of being spherical that an object makes or would make a concave impression in a lump of clay; it is in virtue of being spherical that an object reflects or would reflect light in a particular way (so as to look spherical).

I do not say that properties are purely dispositional. I have already offered reasons to think that every property is at once dispositional and qualitative (Chapter 11). Certainly this appears to be the case for properties of ordinary material bodies. Locke was right to regard the primary qualities as qualities. Readers of Locke have been wrong, however, to imagine that primary qualities are not themselves powers. This is evident in the case of shape. But it is no less evident for the remaining primary qualities: size, position, duration, movability, divisibility, and solidity. All these properties make a difference to what their possessors could and could not do and what could and could not be done to their possessors.

I shall return to Locke presently. First, however, let me call attention to something dispositions are not.

(3) Dispositions are not 'higher-level' properties.

Nowadays many philosophers regard dispositions as higher-level properties grounded in non-dispositional, categorical properties. The idea, familiar to functionalists, is that a dispositional property, D, is possessed by an object, o, in virtue of o's possessing some purely categorical property, C.[3] Recall that, on such a conception, D is not a higher-*order* property: D is not a property of some property—C, for instance. D and C alike are properties of o. C is the *realizer* of D in o.

A view of this kind is partly inspired by the thought that powers bestowed by properties are contingent. Were that so, it might be possible, given different laws of nature, for the very same categorical properties to realize distinct dispositional properties. The chief impetus for such a view, however, is the conviction that dispositions are 'multiply realizable'. A vase, a slate shingle, a pocket watch, and a gramaphone record are all fragile. The features of these objects in virtue of which they are fragile, however, are quite different. A single property, being fragile, is multiply realizable: the property is possessed by objects by

---

[3] See Ch. 9. The classic statement of this view can be found in Prior et al. (1982). The *in virtue of* relation here is standardly explicated by reference to contingent natural laws.

virtue of those objects' possession of distinct, lower-level realizing properties.

I have suggested that this line of reasoning is founded on a confusion (see Chapters 2–6). We find it convenient to say that a vase, a piece of slate, a pocket watch, and a gramaphone record all possess the same disposition: being fragile. These items are examples of things that typically shatter when struck or dropped. But do they, on that account, possess *the very same* disposition? That seems unlikely: the objects shatter in different ways. To be sure, the shatterings are similar enough to fall under a single predicate. But the similarity in question is far from precise. I take it as uncontroversial that, if distinct objects possess the very same property, F, they must be precisely similar F-wise. To assume that 'is fragile' must name a higher-level property is to fall prey to the Picture Theory, the idea that language mirrors ontology.

(4)   The manifestation of a disposition is a manifestation of reciprocal disposition partners.

A salt crystal manifests its disposition to dissolve in water by dissolving in water. But this manifestation is a manifestation of both the salt crystal's disposition to dissolve in water and the water's complementary disposition to dissolve salt. A match bursts into flame when it is scratched across the abrasive surface of a matchbox. The match's bursting into flame is a manifestation of dispositions possessed by the match, the surface of the matchbox, and the surrounding air.

I do not deny that some dispositions could manifest themselves spontaneously. That is evidently how it is with the emission of particles by atoms undergoing radioactive decay. The kinds of disposition at issue here, however, manifest themselves in concert with reciprocal partners. A colour experience, for instance, is a mutual manifestation of complex dispositionalities of our visual system and dispositionalities inherent in structured light radiation.

(5)   One and the same disposition can manifest itself differently with different reciprocal disposition partners.

Principle (5) is an extension of (4). Consider a simple case, the sphericity of a particular ball. The ball's sphericity, in concert with incoming light radiation, structures outgoing radiation in a definite way. The

very same property of the ball disposes it to produce a concave depres-
sion in a lump of clay or to roll; each of these manifestations depends
on the presence of appropriate reciprocal disposition partners: one
disposition, many different kinds of manifestation.[4]

Earlier, I noted that conditional characterizations of dispositions can
lead us to count distinct dispositions as the same. Now it is clear that
over-reliance on such characterizations can result in our counting
instances of one and the same disposition as different.

17.3 Primary and Secondary Qualities

Locke was by no means alone in regarding colours as secondary qualities.[5] What exactly is the force of such a conception? More generally,
what makes a quality a secondary quality, and how do secondary qualities differ from primary qualities?

Locke describes secondary qualities as powers to produce certain
kinds of idea in us. Colours, for instance, are taken by Locke to be
powers to produce experiences of certain sorts in conscious agents.
This kind of view has been widely discussed and, I believe, widely mis-
construed. I make no claim to being a Locke scholar, but I suspect that
the position often associated with Locke—that colours are 'in the
mind'—flies in the face of Locke's considered view.

First, reflect on the question whether secondary qualities are
pure powers. Is the nature of a secondary quality exhausted by the contribution it makes to the dispositionalities or powers of its possessors? I
see no reason to think this is so (see §§9.3, 11.1, 14.10). Consider the
primary qualities, being spherical, for instance. In virtue of its possession of this quality, an object has the power to roll, to reflect light in a
particular way, and so on. Primary qualities must be dispositional as
well as qualitative.

Secondary qualities are powers an object possesses in virtue of its
possession of certain primary qualities. Secondary qualities are not

---

[4] As elsewhere, I offer these cases as illustrative examples only. A careful account of dispositionality
would begin with properties of the fundamental things. Oversimplifying: the charge on an electron, for
instance, might dispose the electron to repel other electrons, but to attract positrons. See also Martin and
Heil (1999: 58 n. 22).

[5] See §14.10. Similar distinctions can be found in Descartes (*Principles of Philosophy*, IV, §§188–203),
Boyle (*The Origin of Forms and Qualities*), and Galileo (*The Assayer*), for instance.

distinct from primary qualities: an object's possession of a given secondary quality is a matter of its possession of a certain complex
primary quality. In virtue of possessing this complex quality, the object
would look, feel, taste, smell, or sound a certain way to an observer.
(How it would look, feel, taste, smell, or sound depends in part on the
observer's make-up.)

This anthropocentric way of picking out dispositions does not turn
those dispositions into something subjective.[6] The dispositions are
there, mind independently, in the objects. They are qualities of the
objects picked out by reference to certain of their characteristic manifestations. What then is the point of the primary/secondary distinction
for Locke? Suppose you ask why an object looks spherical. The answer:
because it is spherical. Now, suppose you ask why an object looks red.
The answer is going to be a complicated dispositional story: the surface
of the object has a certain character; the surface structures light radiation in a particular way; light radiation so structured, in combination
with our visual system, yields an experience of something red. Locke
puts this, not entirely misleadingly, in terms of *resemblance*: experiences
of primary qualities resemble those qualities; experiences of secondary
qualities do not. This is not an anti-realism or subjectivism about the
secondary qualities. Characteristics of objects responsible for structuring the light radiation are perfectly respectable qualities (see §13.4). A
taxonomy in which these qualities feature would be of little interest to
physics, however.

In sum, secondary qualities are not properties objects possess alongside, or in addition to, their primary qualities. This is why, in giving an
inventory of the fundamental properties, physics need do no more than
list the primary qualities. These, suitably combined and picked out via
their effects on us, make up the secondary qualities.

17.4   What Ought We to Ask of a Philosophical
Theory of Colour?

Lack of agreement over fundamental issues in the study of colour suggests that it would be unreasonable to expect a univocal answer to the

---

[6] Here I am disagreeing with Campbell (1993: 257), who describes secondary qualities as 'qualities of the ideas that perception produces in the mind', with Jackson and Pargetter (1987), and with many
others who take Locke to be a 'subjectivist' about colour.

question 'what is colour?' Enough is known about the physics and psychophysics of colour and the mechanisms of colour perception to make it extremely unlikely that colour predicates designate unique properties.[7] A philosophical account of colour should provide a framework that would enable us to make sense of colour experiences in the light of what we know about the physics, psychophysics, and phenomenology of colour, on the one hand, and, on the other hand, what we know about the visual systems of creatures equipped to perceive colours. Theories that take colours to be properties of the surfaces of objects have difficulty accounting for a host of phenomena including coloured light emitted by radiant sources and so-called film colours (the colour of the sky, for instance). Theories that tie colours to features of light radiation fare better on this score, but yield implausible results for the objects. Tomatoes are not red, on such a view, but merely reflect red light. Theorists hoping to defend a realist account of colour find the gappy and disjunctive character of physical properties that give rise in us to unified colour experiences a source of embarrassment.[8]

So regarded, a plausible account of colour need not be framed as an answer to the question whether we ought to be realists or anti-realists about colour. Part of the difficulty here is in getting clear on what realism and anti-realism would amount to in this context. Suppose realism is understood in terms of mind independence: you are a realist about Fs if you believe Fs exist independently of anyone's taking Fs to exist. Note that on such a conception of realism Berkeley is an anti-realist about material objects, but a realist about minds and their contents. Someone who thought colours were states of observers could, on this construal, be regarded as a realist about colour. The interesting question is not whether we should be realists about colours; the interesting question concerns the nature of the truth-makers for colour claims: what must be the case if colour ascriptions are true.

Empirical work on colour suggests that the answer to this question is extraordinarily complicated. Locke might have regarded colours as textural properties of the surfaces of objects. Possession of these properties disposed objects to reflect light in distinctive ways. Light so reflected was disposed to produce particular kinds of idea

---

[7] Colour predicates need not be thought special in this regard. If the argument of previous chapters is correct, very few predicates designate unique properties.

[8] See §14.10. Theorists who take colours to exist only in minds take comfort in such findings.

(kinds of experience) in human observers. Does such a view imply that there is a one–one mapping between colours in objects and kinds of colour experience? Not necessarily. Colour blindness is a familiar phenomenon. We know enough about the visual capacities of other creatures to make it reasonable to think that other creatures can perceive colours human beings cannot perceive (or cannot perceive unaided). Honeybees evidently see colours we cannot see. Some of the apparent gaps in human colour perception might thus be due to selective colour blindness on our part.

Idiosyncrasies of the human visual system dictate that human colour experiences will have a distinctive internal structure. Much has been made of 'colour space' and its dependence on the operation of opponent processes in the visual system (see e.g. Hardin 1988). Ought this to cast doubt on the 'objectivity' of colour perception? Colour experiences, on the view defended here, are mutual manifestations of reciprocal dispositionalities of incoming light radiation and the visual system. All of these items belong to the objective order of things. You could think of light as bearing information as to the colours of objects. Those objects, or their surfaces, are disposed to structure light in a particular way. This 'way' is a function both of the surfaces and of the light.

It seems unlikely, however, that colours could usefully be identified with surface qualities of objects. Objects are coloured no doubt; but we see the sky as coloured, and radiant sources appear to us to be coloured. Perhaps there is a connection among such apparently disparate phenomena. In each case, experiences are produced in observers that are more or less similar to experiences produced by observation of coloured objects. Painters depicting the sky or coloured lights take full advantage of this fact. Experiences of the sky, of coloured lights, and of coloured objects are alike in being mutual manifestations of dispositions of light radiation and dispositions of the visual system. The visual system is such that it is disposed to yield roughly similar experiences in concert with distinct kinds of disposition partner.

If all this is taken into account, it seems clear that the truth-makers for the application of colour predicates will vary widely. 'Is red' could be satisfied by properties of the surfaces of objects, by a radiant source of structured light radiation, and perhaps by internal goings-on (as when you describe an after-image as red). Does this imply a rejection of colour realism? I doubt it.

Some readers will think this misses the point. Colour terms, after all, are notoriously fickle. Colour categories are thoroughly anthropocentric. Granted. But what does this imply? Colour science provides us with a way of spelling out the complex conditions under which colour predicates are satisfied. We notice that these conditions are, from the point of view of physics and chemistry, gerrymandered and gappy. This does not cast doubt on the objectivity of colour, but it does undercut attempts to map colour predicates onto properties of objects or light radiation in a way that relations among the predicates mirror relations among the material properties. Colour predicates are applied on the basis of colour experiences, and colour experiences are mutual manifestations of dispositions of light radiation and dispositions of the human visual system.[9]

None of this should be taken to imply that colour predicates map smoothly onto qualities of colour experiences. Experiences of colours can vary when colours do not. Your experience of a green coat with blue trim alters as the lights dim, but the coat's colours do not change— nor, in all likelihood, do your judgments as to the coat's colour change. Following Akins and Hahn (2000), we might distinguish

(1) colours objects have;
(2) colour appearances: experienced colours of objects;
(3) colours objects are judged (believed, taken) to have.

These can vary independently. The colour an object actually has does not vary, as experienced colours do, with changes in lighting or with changes in observers' visual systems. One of the challenges facing psychological theories of colour is that of providing an account of the relation colour judgements bear to colour experiences. The relation is not a simple one, but neither is it wholly arbitrary or unprincipled.

The task of making sense of colour is made more difficult by a tendency to run together (2) and (3), to conflate talk of the way things look (roughly, the subtle 'phenomenal' character of our visual experiences) and talk of ways we judge or take things to be. You do not take the colour of your companion's blue coat to fade as the light dims, but, in the relevant sense, your experiences do 'dim'. A simple way to see the

---

[9] Hallucinatory or imagistic experiences similar to ordinary colour experiences can be mutual manifestations of wholly internal processes. I ignore this possibility in what follows.

Figure 17.1. The Müller–Lyer illusion

distinction between (2) and (3) is to consider how a painter might go about depicting a scene that includes a variety of coloured objects. In order to depict a uniformly red ball on a white surface illuminated from above, the painter would need to use a variety of pigments. The aim would be to devise an array of colours that would produce in observers the kinds of experience they might have in looking at a red ball resting on a white surface illuminated from above, an experience that would lead them to judge that they are looking at a uniformly red ball.

As Akins and Hahn make clear, an ambiguity in the notion of colour appearance makes discussion of these matters especially tricky. In one perfectly good sense of 'appears', the red ball appears uniformly red. Indeed, you might describe the painter as aiming to depict a ball that looks or appears to be uniformly red. The painter does so by applying a variety of pigments. This sense of 'appears' or 'looks' is closely associated with judgement or belief, item (3) above. You can speak of objects appearing or looking a particular way when your interest lies in how agents judge (or believe, or take) them to be. Matters are made complicated by cases like that of the Müller–Lyer illusion (Figure 17.1). Here, it is natural to say that, although the lines appear to be of different lengths, you need not judge (or believe) them to be of different lengths. In this case, the notion of appearance intended in (2) reasserts itself.[10]

17.5 Divide and Conquer

The suggestion on the table is that we must take care not to run together (1), (2), and (3). If we are to think sensibly about colour, we

[10] I am not suggesting that, in looking at an illustration designed to elicit the Müller–Lyer illusion, observers have experiences—in sense (2)—of lines of different lengths (as a sense datum theorist might put it: sense data of different lengths). Rather, there is something about the experience that disposes observers to judge that the lines differ in length. This disposition can persist when its manifestation is thwarted—for instance, by knowledge that the lines do not differ in length.

need some notion of objective colour, a notion distinct from that of experienced colour, and distinct, as well, from a notion of colour judgements. Suppose talk of the objective colour of objects is made true by objects' dispositions to produce various experiences in observers. It need not follow that colours are subjective or relational. Colours could still be intrinsic features of objects. Looked at as intrinsic features, the colours seem not to form a class of properties salient from the vantage point of physics. It is not that the intrinsic properties are invisible, but that the classificatory system we deploy with respect to these intrinsic properties has as much to do with our physical constitution as it does with the properties themselves. It is founded on the mutual manifestation of the properties in question and properties of the visual systems of conscious creatures.

What of this classificatory scheme? Its basis lies, not in colour experience, what could be called the phenomenology of colour, but in colour judgement. Of course, colour experiences have something important to do with colour judgements, but the relation is messy and ill understood. This is why it can be misleading, as Akins and Hahn (2000) contend, to imagine that we could characterize red, say, as what appears red to the right observers under optimal conditions. If 'appears' is taken in sense (2), this is highly doubtful. To be sure, ordinary observers are likely to agree on judgements as to what is red under optimal conditions; but this is not a promising basis for an analysis or explication of what it is for something to be red.[11]

Where does this leave us? First, we possess a vast body of empirical work on colour and colour perception. Philosophical accounts of colour must make sense in the light of these fundamental empirical findings.

Second, we can treat colours dispositionally: to a first approximation, colours are dispositions of objects to produce experiences of distinctive sorts in observers. Colour experiences are mutual manifestations of structured light radiation and the visual systems of observers. Structured light radiation is itself a mutual manifestation of relatively unstructured radiation and properties of illuminated objects. Such an account can be extended to film colours and colours produced by radiant sources, by noting that, in these cases, the structuring source is

---

[11] A *Euthyphro* moment: objects are not red because well-placed observers agree they are red; the observers agree because the objects are red.

something other than illuminated bodies. A view of this kind can accommodate hallucinatory or imagistic colour experiences. In such cases, experiences similar to those produced veridically have an internal etiology.

Third, it is vital to distinguish colour appearances or experiences (the 'phenomenology of colour') from what I have called colour judgements. The really challenging problem for a psychological account of colour is the explication of the relation colour judgements bear to colour experiences. This is not to say that psychologists should be expected to produce an algorithm or set of principles that takes colour experiences as inputs and yields colour judgements as outputs. Although colour judgements appear to be grounded in some way in colour experiences, colour experiences and colour judgements could, for all anyone knows, be produced by some common, deeper mechanism.

Finally, we should do well to reject the idea, implicit in much philosophical writing on colour, that either (a) colour predicates uniquely designate properties of objects (or light radiation) or (b) colours are subjective, mind dependent. A predicate, 'F', uniquely designates a property only if it applies truly to an object in virtue of that object's possessing a property, F, possessed by every object to which the predicate 'F' truly applies. There is no such simple story available for colour. Colour experiences are mutual manifestations of properties of structured light radiation and properties of the visual systems of conscious creatures. Colour judgements are in some fashion related to these experiences. Very different properties of objects can result in the very same colour judgements, and similar properties can yield different colour judgements. This does not show, however, that colours are subjective or mind dependent. On the contrary, the story here is objective at every stage. What it does show is that, in order to understand the basis of colour classifications, we need to know a great deal about both the propensities of objects to structure light radiation in particular ways and the visual systems of perceivers. None of this would come as a surprise to colour scientists.

Where does this leave philosophical theories of colour? It does not bode well for accounts that attempt to turn colours into simple properties of objects, or light radiation, or experience. Colour experiences, their relation to colour judgements, and the relation of these to properties of objects and light radiation, are a complex affair. Philosophers are in no position to improve upon colour science in explicating these relations. What philosophers can do is show how what we know about the mechanisms of colour comports with our pre-theoretical conception of colour.

More significantly, philosophers are in a position to spell out the ontology of colour and colour experiences. What are colour experiences? How are colour experiences related to objects' colours? Does a commitment to colour experiences bring with it a commitment to non-material properties? These are the kinds of question a satisfactory ontology of colour ought to answer. It would be futile to seek answers to such questions by focusing exclusively on colour. Answers, if we are to have them, can come only from work in basic metaphysics.

CHAPTER 18

Intentionality

18.1 Ontology and Intentionality

Human beings, and doubtless other creatures as well, have a capacity to represent their surroundings. What is the basis of this capacity? When you entertain the thought of a beetroot, what is it about you in virtue of which your thought concerns the beetroot—and not, for instance, a nearby tomato or a visually indistinguishable wax beetroot? These are contentious matters. It would be foolhardy to attempt a definitive account of our representational capacities in the space of a chapter. Instead, I shall indicate how the ontological scheme defended in earlier chapters affords a framework within which we might hope to make sense of 'intentionality'—the capacity for representational thought—in a way that honours both common experience and the demands of science.

Many philosophers would regard this as putting the cart before the horse. Surely, they would argue, it is a mistake to hold intentionality hostage to ontology. Ontology is an endlessly contentious domain. If accounts of intentionality must await agreement among the ontologists, we risk having to wait forever.

On the contrary. The prospects of a naturalistic grounding for intentionality can be appreciated only if we have some sense of what the natural world has to offer. I shall freely appeal to a conception of properties (defended already) that holds a key to a plausible understanding of intentionality (and, as I shall argue in Chapter 19, consciousness).

18.2 Internalism and Externalism

Nowadays philosophers concerned with intentionality divide into two camps. One camp, the internalists, epitomize a traditional approach to the character of thought: thoughts owe their significance to intrinsic features of thinkers. This is the kind of view Descartes, for instance, presupposes in discussing the possibility that we are under the sway of an evil demon. The demon has the power to alter (or even eliminate) the world around us without affecting the contents of our thoughts. This is the source of Descartes's central epistemological conundrum: what assurance can we have that our thoughts 'match' a mind-independent 'external' reality?

A second, less tradition-bound camp, the externalists (or 'anti-individualists'), contend that thoughts owe their character to contextual factors: what your thoughts concern depends on causal relations you bear to your surroundings, perhaps, or on relations in which you stand to your linguistic community. Your twin in the demon world might intrinsically resemble you in every detail, in particular both you and your twin could have qualitatively indiscernible mental lives, yet the contents of your thoughts would differ utterly from those entertained by your twin.

The idea can be illustrated by means of a simplified example. Suppose (as many philosophers really do suppose) your thoughts of trees concerned trees because they were caused by trees. In that case, your twin in the demon world might have thoughts qualitatively indistinguishable from your tree thoughts, yet your twin's thoughts would not concern trees. How so? We are pretending that the contents of an agent's thoughts depend, not on intrinsic features of agents, but on those thoughts' causes. In the demon world, your twin's 'tree' thoughts would concern whatever caused them. Whatever that is, it would not be a tree. (Your twin's 'tree' thoughts are brought about, not by trees, but by an incantation on the part of the demon.) One consequence of a view of this kind is that occupants of the demon world are not, *pace* Descartes, deceived! When an agent in the demon world entertains a thought he might express by 'uttering' the sentence 'That's a tree', the agent is not entertaining a false thought about trees, but a true thought about something else—a particular demon incantation perhaps.[1]

---

[1] Some readers will recognize this as a component of Putnam's Brain in a Vat argument (1981: ch. 1), an early version of which was advanced by O. K. Bouwsma in the 1940s (Bouwsma 1949). For an account of Putnam's arguments see Heil (1987). A more sustained attempt to motivate externalism can be found in Heil (1992: ch. 2), which draws on Burge (1979, 1986); Millikan (1984, 1989); Baker (1987); Davidson (1987); Dretske (1988). The roots of externalist accounts of mental content lie in Wittgenstein (1953/1968),

Externalist conceptions of mind have been inspired by 'Twin Earth' thought experiments. Imagine a remote planet resembling Earth in every obvious respect but one: the clear, colourless liquid that fills lakes, rivers, oceans, and ice trays on Twin Earth is not H_2O, but *XYZ*, a liquid exhibiting a superficial resemblance to water, but possessing an utterly different chemical composition. Inhabitants of Twin Earth (at least those who speak Twin English, a language indistinguishable from English) call this liquid 'water'. Water is H_2O, however, so when inhabitants of Twin Earth speak of 'water' or entertain thoughts they would express with utterances in which (the word) 'water' figures, they would not be speaking or thinking of water but of (as we should call it) *Twin* water. The moral we are invited to draw from imagined cases of this kind is that the significance of what we think and say depends on contextual factors; in particular it depends on causal relations we bear to our surroundings.

18.3   The Dart-Tossing Model

What exactly do Twin Earth thought experiments show? Do they, for instance, establish that internalism is false? That depends on what internalism encompasses. What if the intentional character of states of mind were tied to their dispositionality? Were that so, what makes a thought about a tree a thought about a tree would be the difference it makes to tree-directed dispositionalities of the thinker. What kind of difference? The thought might be an internal manifestation of a disposition to interact with trees in characteristic ways, to describe trees as trees, to utter sentences in which 'tree' figures, to assent to queries 'Is this a tree?' and so on.[2] The thought's dispositionality takes advantage of the built-in projective character of dispositions.[3] A salt crystal is soluble in water. The salt possesses a disposition *for* dissolving in water (and water possesses a reciprocal disposition *for* dissolving salt).

---

but Hilary Putnam's 'The Meaning of "Meaning"' (1975*a*) is the inspiration for much subsequent work on the topic.

[2] This is a caricature. An agent's dispositional make-up is interconnected, focused, and unimaginably complex.

[3] George Molnar called this 'physical intentionality'. See Martin and Pfeifer (1986); Martin and Heil (1998).

Intelligent agents are, whatever else they are, complex dispositional systems; a thinker is an agent with an appropriately focused dispositional make-up. Dispositionality underlies the projective character of thought. What of the agent's environment? Return to Twin Earth. An inhabitant of Twin Earth who entertains thoughts he would express by uttering sentences containing 'water' is entertaining thoughts about *XYZ*, not thoughts about water. In this the externalists are right. But what is it in virtue of which inhabitants of Twin Earth are thus characterizable? On a dispositional account of intentionality, the projective character of thought—its of-ness, or for-ness, or about-ness—stems from its dispositional nature (or the dispositional nature of the agent entertaining it). What the thought concerns, however, can depend on context in something like the way in which what 'here' or 'now' designates depends on the location of the speaker or the time of utterance. Wittgenstein was right: thoughts *do* 'reach out' to the world! What they find there depends on the world.[4]

On a view of this kind, the externalist is right in supposing that what a thought designates often depends on what there is to be designated. The designation need not turn on incoming causal connections, however. Thoughts entertained by inhabitants of Twin Earth concern *XYZ*, Twin water, not water. This is not because the thoughts are *caused* by *XYZ*—although they could very well be. The thoughts 'project to' Twin water, rather than water, because Twin water, not water, is on the scene. If you wanted a model for this, think of a dart-thrower. A dart-thrower is responsible for the direction taken by a dart. What happens to the dart once it is released, however, what the dart hits, depends on what is 'out there' to be hit.

Does this imply that the 'water' thoughts of an inhabitant of Twin Earth instantaneously transported to Earth would suddenly become thoughts of water? Not obviously. In so far as the Twin Earth native's 'water' thoughts are bound up with endless other thoughts—including the thought that this watery stuff is no different from the watery stuff encountered yesterday—we need not suppose his 'water' thoughts become water thoughts merely by virtue of a shift in locale. Compare a case in which a person is transported to another room while asleep and who, when questioned on awakening, thinks: 'I am still here.'

---

[4] Wittgenstein (1922/1961: §§2.1511, 2.1515).

18.4 The Self

Let us allow that intelligent agents represent their surroundings: think-ing, in its many guises, is representational. If this is right, then we are in a position to grasp the significance of the 'I', the *self* or *ego*. Like Hume, you could doubt that the self is an object of inward observation. What role then might a self-concept have? Perhaps the self comes into play in acts of representation. You represent your inner states, your environ-ment, and goings-on around you. Your representational capacities equip you to represent, as well, non-local and purely imaginary states of affairs and events. In so far as you deploy representations to negoti-ate your world, however, you will have need of a self-concept.

To see why this is so, consider a simple analogy. As a first-time visitor to Manhattan, you venture out of your hotel clutching a detailed street map you hope will enable you to find your way about. The map con-stitutes a representation of Manhattan. Before you can put the map to use, however, you must locate yourself on it, you must be in a position to recognize that 'you are *here*'. In representing the world around us, we take up a point of view. Our taking up a point of view is a matter of our orienting or locating ourselves within the world as we represent it. Our self-concept includes as an essential element this egocentric orienta-tion: you are the agent with *this* point of view.

In this regard, a point of view is not something included in repre-sentations; not one more representation. As Wittgenstein puts it in the *Tractatus*, the self's relation to its representations of the world is like the relation of the eye to the visual field: the eye is not part of the visual field, but its limit. To get the idea, substitute 'representation of the world' for 'the world' in this quotation (Wittgenstein 1922/1961: §§5.633–5.634):

The subject does not belong to the world: rather, it is a limit of the world.

Where *in* the world is a metaphysical subject to be found?

You will say this is exactly like the case of the eye and the visual field. But really you do *not* see the eye.

And nothing *in the visual field* allows you to infer that it is seen by an eye.

For the form of the visual field is surely not like this

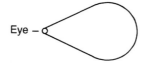

The self emerges in the activity of representing the world. The world is represented as a spatio-temporal manifold to be negotiated by the representor, the occupant of a unique place within the manifold. This is the expression of a point of view, the point of view of the representing agent.

These somewhat oracular remarks are intended only to suggest that intentionality and the self-concept are conceptually entangled. We need not assume that the self is a distinctive, inwardly observed substance in order to account for the significance of the 'I'. Nor need we regard points of view as mysterious, other-worldly, or dramatically at odds with the 'third-person perspective' (Searle 1992). An act of representing can be an act of taking up a point of view. This idea is vigorously promoted by Berkeley and Kant, among others. Berkeley, for instance, insists that an unperceived material object is literally inconceivable: conceiving of a material object is a matter of representing how that object would look, sound, feel, taste, or smell to a perceiving agent. Kant speaks of the 'transcendental unity of apperception', the 'I think' that lies behind all thought.

You can appreciate the force of these suggestions without descending with Berkeley and Kant into anti-realism. The self can be taken seriously without being thought of as an immaterial substance, or indeed as a material substance. Creating a self would require creating a system capable of representing the world from a point of view: representing the world 'self-consciously'. This would be a matter not of including the representor as an element in the representation, but of representing in a particular way.[5]

An unmanned missile might seek out a target by constantly monitoring its location and the location of the target and adjusting its course accordingly. Does such a weapon have a point of view? The

---

[5] Perhaps a system capable of representing in this way would be a system capable of second-order representation: representing representations—*qua* representations. See Heil (1992: ch. 6) for a discussion of second-order representation and its significance.

device, D, represents the location of the target, T, and its own location relative to T. But D could do this without in any sense recognizing that *it* is D. That would require, not a more detailed representation, but a different style of representing. When you use a map to find your way about Manhattan, you engage in this kind of representing. This is so, whether you use a printed map or a 'mental map'. Compare a device like D to a device capable of homing in on a target by making use of what Gibson calls 'optical flow' and adjusting its course accordingly (Gibson 1966: chs. 10, 12; 1979: chs. 7, 12). Here the system's location is given implicitly by changes in the structure of the 'optic array'. A system engaged in representing of this kind is a system with a primitive point of view.

This brings us abruptly back to the topic of intentionality and the question whether intentional states of mind owe their nature to contextual factors as the externalists would have it. I have suggested that intentionality is grounded in the dispositionalities of agents. Dispositions are intrinsic to agents, so this places me on the side of the internalists and against the externalists. Internalism is decidedly out of fashion, but fashions come and go. Perhaps I can say enough here to make a kind of internalism attractive to readers willing to entertain unfashionable possibilities.

18.5 Swampman

In a much-discussed thought experiment, Donald Davidson imagines that, while wandering through a swamp, he is struck by a bolt of lightning and vaporized (Davidson 1987). Simultaneously, another bolt strikes a nearby tree stump rearranging the particles that make it up to produce, wholly by chance, a molecule-for-molecule duplicate of Davidson: Swampman. How are we to describe Swampman's states of mind? It seems natural to say that Swampman has Davidson's thoughts, beliefs, and preferences. Swampman differs from Davidson, not in what he wants and believes, but in the truth value of many of his beliefs. Swampman falsely believes he was a student of Quine's, that he has published papers in *Dialectica*, and that he once visited Terra del Fuego.

I think this natural interpretation is the right one, but philosophers of an externalist persuasion disagree. Swampman, they contend, would lack appropriate causal relations to objects and events in the world.[6] Until these are established, Swampman's thoughts lack content. They resemble marks in the sand traced by a foraging ant that happen to spell out the English word 'HELLO' (Putnam 1981: ch. 1). The marks are intrinsically meaningless. They might come to acquire significance were they given a use by an intelligent agent. (You could photograph the marks, for instance, and use them on a greeting card or on your web page.)

We can agree that marks in the sand (or, for that matter, images, utterances, or signs generally) lack intrinsic significance. Such items take on significance when they acquire an expressive use. An ant does not use marks it traces in the sand to mean anything. Are Swampman's thoughts similarly intentionally inert? Swampman is dispositionally indistinguishable from Davidson. This, I suggest, is enough to endow Swampman's thoughts with significance. Their significance lies, not in the thoughts' intrinsic qualitative nature, but in Swampman's intrinsic dispositional make-up.[7]

I like to think of Swampman as a counter-example to externalism: if, on externalist grounds, we would be obliged to deny that Swampman has endless thoughts, externalism is mistaken. Swampman's thoughts are anchored in his dispositional condition. In virtue of this condition, Swampman is disposed to interact with the world in particular ways. What ways? The very ways Davidson himself would have interacted with the world. Like Davidson, Swampman would call trees trees, water water, spades spades.

18.6 Causally Loaded States of Mind

You may find the view being bruited here incredible. Before dismissing it outright, however, you should be certain you are doing so for the

---

[6] Externalism comes in different flavours. Some externalists focus on causal-historical connections, others emphasize social matters (especially thinkers' linguistic communities), still others focus on biological function. I use a simple causal theory for purposes of illustration, but the points I make here apply, *mutatis mutandis*, to other strains of externalism.

[7] Astute readers will recognize that this way of putting the point is incautious. I have identified the qualitative with the dispositional (Ch. 11). The point here is that signs acquire meaning through use, where use is given a dispositional reading.

right reasons. A view of the kind under consideration does not deny that certain states of mind are 'causally loaded' in the sense that their character depends in part on causal relations involving the agent. Memory and perception are like this. It is apparently built into our concept of what it is for an agent to remember some object or event that the agent stand in an appropriate causal relation to the remembered object or event. Suppose you have a vivid image of a childhood experience. The image counts as a *memory* of the experience only if there is a causal link of the right sort between the experience and your subsequently calling the image to mind. Similarly, your *perceiving* this tree depends on your standing in the right kind of causal relation to the tree.[8] In this way we distinguish memories and perceptions from idle imagery or hallucination.

None of this affects the idea that intentionality works from the 'inside out': states of mind owe their projective character to intrinsic features of agents. Consider referring. Does your successfully entertaining thoughts of a particular object require a causal chain connecting you to that object? This is not obvious. Imagine thinking a thought you would express as follows: 'There is an object at exactly two million kilometres from me in *that* direction.' If there happens to be an object so located, you have succeeded in referring to it!

18.7 A Worry from Kripke

In an intriguing study of Wittgenstein's 'private language argument', Saul Kripke suggests a reason for rejecting dispositional accounts of intentionality (Kripke 1982).[9] The argument is straightforward, but requires stage setting.

Suppose that speaking a language is, as it is frequently claimed to be, a matter of following rules. Rules govern utterances in two senses. First,

---

[8] Suppose you see what appears to be a ghost gum 10 metres in front of you. Suppose, further, that there *is* a ghost gum 10 metres in front of you but that your visual experience is caused by an image of an identical tree somewhere off to the right reflected in a camouflaged mirror (if the mirror were removed you would have an indistinguishable visual experience, but it would be caused by the tree in front of you, not the reflected tree). With the mirror in place, the tree you see is the reflected tree, not the tree in front of you. This is apparently due to the fact that the cause of your tree experience is the reflected tree. See Martin (1959: ch. 6); Grice (1961).

[9] The arguments discussed in this section and the next are examined in much greater detail in Martin and Heil (1998).

a rule underlies agents' actions in so far as these actions are *based on* the rule.[10] Second, rules serve a normative function: they ground distinctions between correct and incorrect actions. A chess move is incorrect only so long as it violates a rule of chess and the agent who makes the move intends to be playing chess (and so undertakes to be governed by the rules of chess).

Kripke's famous example involves addition. Mastering arithmetic includes mastering a rule for summing numbers. The rule guides arithmetical judgements and provides a norm against which such judgements are taken to be correct or incorrect. We judge that $2 + 3 = 5$ and $68 + 57 = 125$ are correct, that is, they accord with this rule, and, that $2 + 3 = 4$ and $68 + 57 = 5$ fail to accord with the rule, and so are incorrect. Similarly, our use of words is guided by rules, and, to the extent that words and concepts words express figure in our thoughts, thoughts themselves are rule governed. The question pursued by Kripke's Wittgenstein concerns what it is to be guided by a rule: what makes it the case that you are following a particular rule?

It will not do to suppose that, if you set out to follow the addition rule, your mathematical judgements must always accord with that rule. Error is always possible, even, for finite agents, inevitable. Suppose, on a particular occasion, you judge that $68 + 57 = 5$ (in the course of balancing your chequebook, say). You have judged incorrectly; your judgement fails to conform to the addition rule, a rule you intended to be following in judging as you did. Any finite device, including a mechanical calculator, could err in this way.[11] Note further that the rule you are following ranges over sequences you will never have occasion to sum. Indeed, the rule pertains to an infinite number of sequences, thereby outrunning the capacities of any finite intelligence.

Now imagine an agent, Dwayne, who grasps, not the rule for addition, but a different rule. This rule yields results that coincide with the addition rule up to a particular point, then deviate. (Following Kripke, we can call this rule the *quaddition* rule.) According to the rule for

[10] Talk of a rule's underlying an action is shorthand for an agent's being motivated by his acceptance or inculcation of the rule.

[11] In the case of a simple mechanical system, talk of intention is misplaced. The point however, is that a device we devise—intentionally—to operate in accord with a particular rule can fail to do so owing to what we would describe as a mechanical breakdown. In one sense, a malfunctioning calculator behaves precisely as it ought to behave: it does whatever laws of nature require of it at the time. The sense in which a malfunctioning calculator malfunctions is tied to the intentions of its creator and users. The challenge is to see how intentionality could have a wholly naturalistic, wholly dispositional basis.

quaddition, $2 + 3 = 5$; 2 quadded to 3 yields 5. Suppose Dwayne subsequently judges that $68 + 57 = 5$? As it happens, 68 *quadded* to 57 *does* yield 5: this is a perfectly correct application of the quaddition rule!

The idea is that addition and quaddition coincide up to a particular point, then diverge. Call this point the *divergence point*. Now, imagine that Wayne has mastered the addition rule, while Dwayne embraces the rule for quaddition. Imagine, as well, that neither of these agents has ever considered (or will ever consider) numbers lying beyond the divergence point. Their judgements largely coincide. On rare occasions when their judgements fail to coincide, they agree that one of them must be wrong, and make corrections accordingly. What, asks Kripke's Wittgenstein, makes it the case that Wayne and Dwayne are following different rules? What is it about Wayne and Dwayne in virtue of which it is true that Wayne has grasped the addition rule and Dwayne has grasped the rule for quaddition?

Kripke proposes that Wittgenstein's own response to this query is sceptical and deflationary: there is no 'fact of the matter' here, or at least no fact about the constitution of Wayne and Dwayne, respectively, in virtue of which it is true that they are following the rules that we have supposed they are following. What rules an agent grasps is largely a matter of the attitudes prevailing among members of the agent's community. The conclusion is supported by the contention that it is hard to see how any 'fact about' Wayne or Dwayne could serve as a basis for a rule with infinite application. There could be no state of Wayne or Dwayne that constituted their grasp of the rule for addition or the rule for quaddition, for instance.

What of the idea that an agent's acceptance of a rule (the addition rule, for instance) is grounded in the agent's dispositional make-up? This might at first seem promising. Trouble arises, however, when we consider cases of error, cases in which an agent 'violates' a rule he accepts. Suppose, for instance, Wayne and Dwayne both enter '125' after writing $68 + 57$. Dwayne, but not Wayne, is mistaken (68 quadded to 57 is 5). Both Wayne and Dwayne are, on this occasion at least, *disposed* to answer '125', however. This will be so whenever anyone answers any question at all in any way whatever. How then could Dwayne's dispositional make-up be such that '125' fails to express the rule he intends to follow, if Wayne's (apparently identical) dispositional make-up makes it the case that he is correctly following the addition rule?

18.8 Individuating Dispositions

A sensible answer to this question requires distinguishing an agent's or system's overall dispositional make-up from its dispositional components. Consider a salt crystal. The crystal is disposed to dissolve in water. Now consider a salt crystal encased in Lucite. Although the encased crystal does not lose the disposition to dissolve, the crystal-encased-in-Lucite is not so disposed. The addition of a Lucite coating blocks the manifestation of the crystal's disposition to dissolve in water, but does not eliminate the disposition. Compare this with a case in which salt is chemically modified so as to lose its disposition to dissolve in water (see Chapters 8–11 above; Bird 1998, 2000).

In general, we shall want to distinguish

(A) object o possesses disposition D at t_0, and, at t_1, o loses D;
(B) o possesses D at t_0, and at t_1 acquires a disposition, D', that blocks one kind of manifestation of D.

Suppose now that an agent who has mastered a rule—the rule for addition, say—has acquired a particular disposition, D_a. D_a manifests itself in various ways depending on its reciprocal disposition partners. Thus, if D_a is the disposition associated with the addition rule, D_a might manifest itself as an utterance of '125' in response to the question 'What is the sum of 68 and 57?'[12] This manifestation might be blocked or modified, however, by the presence of blocking or distorting disposition partners. Given the query 'What is the sum of 68 and 57?', the system comprising D_a together with some other disposition or dispositions, D', might yield an utterance of 'five'. This might be due, not to the absence of D_a, but to the presence of D_a together with D'.

Although Wayne and Dwayne might, on a particular occasion, be similarly disposed to answer '125' to 'What is the sum of 68 and 57?', it need not follow that they are dispositionally indistinguishable. Wayne, but not Dwayne possesses D_a. Dwayne possesses some other disposition, D_q, which grounds his mastery of the quaddition rule. This is perfectly consistent with the possibility that, on occasion, the 'correct'

---

[12] Like any disposition, D_a would manifest itself differently in concert with different reciprocal disposition partners. D_a might yield an utterance, an inscription, a thought, or nothing at all, depending on these reciprocal partners.

manifestation of D_a or D_q could be blocked or deflected by the presence of assorted other factors. We need not embrace 'rule scepticism' of the sort associated with Kripke's Wittgenstein.

18.9 Infinite Use of Finite Means

A difficulty remains. In mastering the rule for addition, Wayne apparently acquires a disposition for an infinite range of responses. Wayne, however, is finite, as is his dispositional make-up. How could a finite agent house a disposition for infinite manifestations?

In one obvious sense, no finite thing *could* yield an infinite number of outputs. Nevertheless, a disposition could be for an infinite number of different kinds of response, even if the disposition itself would not survive the production of more than a handful of these. Imagine a chip in a simple calculator. The chip can sum endless numbers. If the calculator's memory is limited, it—the calculator—will reach a point where numbers it attempts to sum are too large to be contained in its memory. The chip has the capacity to sum these numbers, but this capacity requires additional memory if it is to be exercised. We can fix the problem by adding more memory, but eventually the problem will reoccur; at some point the system will simply fall to pieces.

Here is a simpler example. Imagine a chip capable of summing every number up to 1,000. Now, imagine an identically engineered chip made of a material that would last only long enough for the chip to perform a dozen calculations. Both chips are disposed to sum numbers up to 1,000; but the second chip could never complete the task owing to its frailty. In this case, it would be excessive to deny that the chips were mathematically equivalent, although possessing importantly different physical limitations on the manifestation of their respective competencies.

In general, then, it would seem to be impossible to construct a physical mechanism capable of performing an infinite number of distinct operations. The mechanism would eventually deteriorate, run out of space, or succumb to cosmic catastrophe. Such contingencies, however, need not affect the nature of a component engineered to sum numbers. The operation of the component depends on the presence of mechanisms that, like the component itself, lack infinite staying power.

This, however, need be no bar to the possibility that the component itself has an infinite capacity, a capacity perfectly capable of grounding the mastery of an infinite rule.[13]

18.10 Intentionality and Dispositionality

Dispositionality provides a natural basis for intentionality. Projectability—of-ness, for-ness, about-ness—is built into dispositions. Dispositions are *of* or *for* particular manifestations with particular kinds of reciprocal disposition partner. A disposition can be for a non-existent manifestation: a salt crystal drifting in a universe that lacked water would still be water soluble. Unicorns do not exist, but a soap bubble would burst were it punctured by a unicorn horn. Dispositionality, then, includes the 'mark of intentionality': a capacity to project to the non-existent.

This might lead to new worries. Are we now saddled with Meinongian non-existent entities, *possibilia*, and the like (non-actual, merely possible unicorns, for instance)? That is unlikely (see §11.7). We characterize dispositions by reference to their actual or possible manifestations. Dispositions are not relations to actual or possible manifestations, however. Objects possess dispositions by virtue of possessing particular intrinsic properties. The nature of these properties ensures that they will yield manifestations of particular sorts with reciprocal disposition partners of particular sorts. In this regard, the dispositions 'point towards' non-actual, merely possible manifestations with non-actual, merely possible disposition partners. The 'pointing' is grounded in the disposition, however, not in a relation the disposition bears to anything else.

Consider a simple example inspired by Locke. Locke defends a broadly dispositional conception of colours: a colour is a power possessed by an object to cause experiences of certain sorts in conscious observers. Imagine a universe containing a single ripe tomato. Is the tomato red? I have argued (§17.3) that Locke's view is that the tomato is indeed red. Locke characterizes colours by reference to certain of

---

[13] Linguists describe the human capacity for natural languages as a capacity for making 'infinite use of finite means'. The same could be said of an agent who had mastered the rule for addition—or the quaddition rule.

their manifestations, but the colours exist even when the manifestations do not, even when the manifestations are, owing to the absence of suitable reciprocal disposition partners, impossible.

18.11 Natural Intentionality

Many philosophers today are prepared to accept arguments purporting to establish externalist accounts of intentionality. By and large, these arguments are founded on appeals to intuitions about 'Twin Earth' cases, those in which intrinsically similar agents entertain thoughts with dissimilar contents. We can agree—up to a point—with the intuitions without thereby embracing externalism.

In any case, we have available a resource ideally suited to account for the kind of projection associated with intentionality: dispositionality. Dispositions are *of* or *for* particular kinds of manifestation with particular kinds of disposition partner. Dispositions preserve the mark of intentionality in being of or for particular kinds of manifestation with particular kinds of non-existent—possible, but non-actual—objects. This is not mysterious or spooky; it is a feature of dispositions possessed by rocks, or blades of grass, or quarks.

My suggestion is that we make use of the 'natural intentionality' afforded by dispositions in making sense of the kinds of intentionality we find in the minds of intelligent agents. In so doing, we return to a long tradition that takes the contents of thoughts to be fixed by intrinsic features of thinkers.

Even if you agree that intentionality might be grounded in dispositionality, you might wonder how far this takes us in attempting to understand the mind. States of mind of intelligent agents are representational, and perhaps this could be explained dispositionally. But states of mind can also be conscious. It is much harder to see how consciousness, and, in particular, the qualitative side of consciousness, could be accommodated to the material world. This is the problem to which I shall now turn.

CHAPTER 19

Conscious Experience

19.1 Experiences

Imagine that you are looking at a ripe tomato you have just picked in the garden. You are undergoing a particular kind of visual experience, one you might naturally describe as an experience of seeing a ripe tomato in bright sunlight. Such experiences differ from experiences you are having as you read these words: experiences of reading about experiences of seeing ripe tomatoes in bright sunlight. They differ, as well, from experiences of seeing experiences of seeing ripe tomatoes in bright sunlight. Admittedly, it is not altogether clear what might count as observing or experiencing an experience. Let us suppose, however, that your experiences are occurrences in your brain (where 'brain' is short for your nervous system, perhaps including connections distributed throughout your body). In that case, a technician's observing your experience of seeing a tomato in bright sunlight is an experience of watching some occurrence in your brain.

You might boggle at the thought that your experience of seeing the tomato could be an occurrence in your brain on the grounds that nothing in your brain (as a technician observes it or as you might observe it in a mirror or by way of an 'autocerebroscope') resembles your experience of seeing the tomato.[1] I grant that it is controversial to imagine that experiences are in the brain. A bad reason for doubting that experiences are in the brain is that experiences we have in seeing occurrences in brains are nothing at all like experiences we have in seeing tomatoes. Why on earth should they be? A tomato is round and red. In seeing the tomato, you experience something round and red. Your experience, however, is (or need be) neither round nor red. So

---

[1] Autocerebroscopes are discussed in Feigl (1958: 381, 456–7); see also Meehl (1966).

there is not the slightest reason to think that an experience of seeing your experience of seeing a tomato should resemble your experience of seeing the tomato.

19.2 Mary's Experience

In a famous thought experiment, Frank Jackson provides an argument against the idea that states of mind could be physical states of agents to whom they belong.[2] Jackson imagines a scientist, Mary, who knows everything discoverable about colour using techniques of the natural sciences, including reports of agents undergoing experiences of colours. The catch is that Mary is confined to a wholly black and white environment; nothing she can see is coloured, and she wears spectacles designed to ensure that she sees only black, white, and shades of grey. Although she has observed the brains of others undergoing colour experiences, Mary has never herself undergone visual experiences of colours.

When Mary emerges from her black and white environment, removes her spectacles, and experiences colours for the first time, she learns something new: what it is like to have visual experiences of colours. Jackson argues that this shows that qualities of conscious experiences—what it is like to undergo those experiences—cannot be identified with physical properties of agents to whom the experiences belong.

Does Mary acquire 'new knowledge' when she sees red for the first time? Does she, as Jackson puts it, discover some new, non-physical fact? Mary has experienced reading about experiences of red, and she has (let us imagine) experienced others' experiences of seeing red: she has observed occurrences of colour experiences in their brains. She now experiences something she has never before experienced: red. Following philosophical custom, we can say that Mary, for the first time, 'knows what it is like' to have an experience of seeing red.

It is anything but clear what the phrase within quotation marks is meant to capture. Perhaps at least part of what is intended is incorporated in the idea that your knowing what it is like to be in a given state,

---

[2] Jackson (1982, 1986). Jackson no longer endorses the argument.

S, is strongly linked to your being in, or having once been in, *S*. Cases of the sort discussed by Hume in the *Enquiry*—'missing-shade-of-blue' cases—are those in which an agent can, apparently, be said to know what it is like to be in a given state, despite never having been in that state, but (according to Hume) only because the agent has been in states that closely resemble the 'missing' state.[3] Excluding such cases, it seems safe to say that, in speaking of your 'knowing what it is like' to be in a given state, we mean to include your being or having been in that state. More is included, perhaps, but there is at least this.

If this is right, then it is certainly true that, when Mary first encounters red she acquires knowledge she previously lacked. Does this call into question the idea that all there is to Mary's experience is encompassed by perfectly ordinary material occurrences in Mary's brain? Does it imply that some new kind of non-material fact is on the scene?

I have insisted on distinguishing properties of experiences from properties of objects experienced. Tomatoes are spherical and red, but your visual experience of a tomato is not spherical and red. This does not imply that your experience itself lacks qualities. But your experience's possessing qualities does not mean that your experience or its qualities—the *qualia*—are non-physical. On the contrary; if the conception of properties defended in Chapter 11 is correct, no concrete object or occurrence lacks qualities. There is nothing inherently dualistic, then, in the admission that your experience itself possesses qualities. The tricky question concerns whether qualities of your experience are, or could conceivably be, qualities of goings-on in your brain.

19.3   Qualities of Experiences and Qualities of Objects Experienced

We can get over one hurdle by reminding ourselves that qualities of an experience need not, and typically will not, resemble qualities of things experienced. If experiences are occurrences in the brain, we should not expect to find in the brain of someone undergoing visual

---

[3] See *Enquiry Concerning Human Understanding*, §2. Hume's aim is not easy to discern. I am supposing that Hume believes that it is possible to imagine—form an image of—a particular shade of blue you have never before experienced. Do you thereby 'know what it is like' to experience the shade in question?

experiences of a ripe tomato anything visually resembling a ripe tomato. Granting that qualities of experiences of seeing tomatoes differ from qualities of tomatoes, however, what exactly *are* the qualities of experiences? Some philosophers hold that experiences are representational; what we might naturally regard as qualities of the experiences are at bottom nothing more than qualities we represent experienced objects as having.[4]

Representationalists point to our practice of describing experiences by describing objects experienced. Experiences are, in this regard, 'diaphanous'. If I ask you to describe your experience of seeing a tomato, you will most probably talk about the tomato: your experience is of something spherical and red. These represented qualities are, according to the representationalists, all there is to the 'phenomenology' of an experience. What of dreams and hallucinations? Representations of tomatoes can be present when tomatoes are not. Your visually hallucinating a tomato is a matter of your representing a tomato (that happens not to be present) in a way similar to the way you do when you see a tomato. In the latter case, your experience is brought about by a tomato; in the former case, its cause is presumably some internal occurrence.

The representationalists are partly right. A good deal of what we should describe as qualities of experience are in fact qualities we represent objects of our experience as having. What thrills us about experiencing a sunset over the Grand Canyon are qualities of the setting sun and the canyon. I doubt, however, that these qualities exhaust the qualities of our experience, even when we exclude qualities that do not belong to the experience's 'phenomenology'. These residual qualities can escape notice by representationalists because of the often-cited 'diaphanous' character of experience; we 'see through' our experiences straight to the world.[5] Having a diaphanous character, however, is not the same as having no character at all.

---

[4] See e.g. Armstrong (1981); Harman (1990); Tye (1995); Lycan (1996); Dretske (1997); Jackson (2002). Proponents of representationalist theories of consciousness need not deny that experiences have non-representational qualities, only that these qualities are part of the 'felt character' or 'phenomenology' of the experience. If your experience of seeing a tomato is a neurological occurrence, the neurological occurrence might involve goings-on in a spongy grey mass. Being spongy and grey would be qualities of the experience, but not part of its 'phenomenology'.

[5] On the diaphanous character of experience, see G. E. Moore (1903: 450). For young children, ordinary language appears to be transparent in this way. Children may find it inconceivable that a word might have meant anything other than what it does mean. This is the hypothesis popular among literary theorists that what words mean is wholly arbitrary stood on its head.

Imagine that you have dropped your keys behind the refrigerator. To retrieve them you use a stick to probe in the dark space between the refrigerator and the wall until, passing over clumps of dust, a dried apple core, and a mummified Tim Tam, you feel the keys and rake them out. In this case, you can literally feel the keys through the stick. Your use of the stick is, in Moore's sense, diaphanous. This does not mean, however, that there is no feeling of the stick in your hand as you probe. On the contrary, you *use* these feelings to acquire information about and, if you like, represent the location and character of the car keys. They make up what (following Martin) could be called the *material* of representation.

Your use of sensory input via the stick can be compared to your use over the telephone of certain sounds to tell someone how to find your house—or the caller's use of those sounds to learn the location of your house. The sounds are diaphanous; in uttering—or hearing—them we are largely oblivious to their intrinsic character; our attention is occupied by what they represent for us. The same holds for perception generally. In perceiving, we go into qualitatively distinctive sensory states. We (or our brains) use these states to represent how things stand outside us. So used, qualities of our representations become diaphanous; but they do not thereby disappear. Such qualities are not to be identified with qualities being represented.

19.4 Prosthetic Vision

A nice illustration of what I have in mind is provided by the Tactile Visual Stimulation System or TVSS.[6] The TVSS consists of a television camera (its 'eye') coupled to a mechanism that converts the visual image produced by the camera into an 'isomorphic cutaneous display' in the form of a pattern of vibrations produced by vibrating pins arranged in a 40 × 40 grid. The grid is placed in contact with the skin (usually on the back or stomach) of experimental subjects. Practice in the use of the TVSS enables blind persons to detect reasonably fine distinctions among objects scanned by the camera. One experimental subject, G. Guarniero, provides an interesting account of his use of the device. 'Only when I first used the system did the sensations seem as if

---

[6] White et al. (1970); Guarniero (1974). The account here borrows from Heil (1983: 13–18).

they were on my back' (1974: 101). As he became more skilled in the use of the device, Guarneiro became aware, not of patterns of vibrations on his skin, but of scanned objects: 'Very soon after I had learned to scan, the sensations no longer felt as if they were located on my back, and I became less and less aware that vibrating pins were making contact with my skin. By this time objects had come to have a top and a bottom; a right side and a left' (1974: 104). Subjects, like Guarniero, trained in the use of a TVSS describe the experience—aptly, in my judgement—as 'seeing with the skin'.

Imagine an agent equipped with an augmented TVSS, one capable of representing all that can be visually represented. (If you doubt that such a device is possible, then imagine one capable of representing scenes monochromatically in the way they might be represented visually by a colour-blind agent with poor eyesight.) I suggest that, despite representational parity, the experience of 'seeing' with a TVSS differs qualitatively from the experience of seeing with the eyes. In both cases, the sensory medium is effectively diaphanous and difficult, even impossible, to describe independently of the objects it is used to represent. Indeed there might be no functional difference between an agent equipped with a TVSS and a sighted agent. Both would describe their experiences in exactly the same way; both would be unable to detect the presence of objects if the lights were switched off or if an opaque screen were placed in front of the objects scanned. Nevertheless, I submit that the agents' experiences differ qualitatively. Were a normally sighted agent suddenly forced to use a TVSS while the TVSS-using agent's eyesight were restored, both would find their experiences very different.

I do not know how to prove this. Trials with an actual TVSS would not obviously settle the matter.[7] Representationalists would be keen to emphasize the importance of representational richness, and the representational capacity of an actual TVSS differs dramatically from the representational capacity of the human visual system.[8] Nevertheless, it

---

[7] Note, however, that Guarniero describes his initial experience in using a TVSS as an experience of sensations on his back. Later, he says, these came to be felt as sensations of distal objects. It is natural to understand these remarks as supporting the idea that there is more to perceptual experience than is included in what qualities experience represents experienced objects as possessing. One representationalist response involves taking cases in which agents are putatively aware of qualities of experiences as just more representation. The qualities of Guarniero's sensations are just qualities he represents those sensations as having.

[8] Frank Jackson made this point in conversation.

is hard to understand how merely increasing the representational capacities of a TVSS could result in its producing experiences qualitatively like visual experiences. Rather than attempt a refutation of the representationalist line, however, I shall offer an alternative account.

19.5 Sensation and Perception

In perceiving our surroundings, we go into various perceptual states. I am prepared to accept the representationalists' contention that these states are representational. Unlike the representationalists, however, I contend that this amounts to our (or our perceptual system's) *using* sensory materials representationally. The materials themselves, the representational *medium*, have a character of their own. Indeed, that character could uniquely suit the medium for the representational task it is recruited to perform. The what it-is-likeness of conscious experience stems from the nature of the representational medium and (as the representationalists' contend) what is represented. What it is like to experience seeing a bowl of flowers is not what it is like to experience seeing a sunset. What it is like to experience seeing a bowl of flowers with your eyes is not what it is like to see the same bowl of flowers via a TVSS.

The suggestion here is not that we infer an articulated external reality from observation of colourful sensory episodes. The sensory episodes themselves function to represent an external reality. In fulfilling this function, sensory qualities can recede from awareness, as the representationalists like to remind us. But the qualities are there nonetheless, noticeable, perhaps, only under special circumstances—as when you move from seeing with a TVSS to seeing with your eyes and back again.

Philosophers of mind argue over the existence of *qualia*, qualities of conscious experience. We should do well to avoid the idea, implicit in much of this discussion, that qualities belong exclusively to mental phenomena. Qualities, I have argued at length, are everywhere. The difficulty, then, is not in finding a place for qualities in a qualitatively barren material world, but in finding a place for apparently distinctive mental qualities among those in the material realm. Although philosophers are fond of asserting that mental qualities, the qualities of conscious experience, differ from anything in the physical world, this is far from obvious. Of course, if you thought that there are no physical qualities, then mental qualities would differ profoundly from non-qualitative characteristics of physical systems. Once it is granted that every property is qualitative, however, the chasm diminishes. The question, then, is whether mental qualities differ in some fundamental way from material qualities. An answer to this question requires a clear conception of mental qualities.

19.6 The Representational Medium

A clear conception of mental qualities is precisely what we lack. Once we recognize that it is a mistake to conflate the properties of conscious states with properties of what those states represent (as indeed it is a mistake to confuse the properties of any representation with those of what is represented), we are no longer tempted to imagine that experiences of red spherical objects are themselves red and spherical. But where does this leave us? Representationalists imagine that the properties of an experience are nothing more than these represented properties. I have argued that this is not so. One possibility is that it *could not* be so.

Imagine a painting of a still life that includes an apple and a cucumber. The painting represents the apple as spherical and the cucumber as cylindrical. But nothing in the painting is spherical or cylindrical. This does not mean that the painting itself—the painting *qua* representational medium—does not include shapes. It most certainly does. The painting includes shapes intended to represent the shapes of objects it depicts. These shapes can be described along with colours and surface textures that make up the painting. Not all representations are like this. A bystander's utterance describing the scene includes no shapes or colours, only vibratory motions in the air.

It seems possible to imagine endless representational media. These might include, in addition to paint on canvas and linguistic description (written or spoken), deflections in the grooves of gramophone records, patterns on magnetic tape, optical patterns embedded in DVD disks, coloured sand painstakingly arranged in intricate patterns, and so on. We can use these media to represent objects and their properties. In each case, properties of represented objects must be distinguished from properties of the representational media. But this does not mean that the properties of the media are *nothing but* represented properties of objects. In so far as we can distinguish a representation from what it represents, it is almost always the case that representations will possess properties not possessed by what is being represented.[9] The thought that *every* quality of a representation might be a quality something is represented as having is scarcely coherent.

Perhaps this is not what the representationalists have in mind, however. As noted earlier, representationalists could allow that conscious states have intrinsic, non-representational properties. Suppose conscious experiences turned out to be episodes in the brain. These episodes would include a host of non-representational properties. They might involve spongy grey neurons, for instance. Being spongy and being grey would in that case be intrinsic, non-representational properties of experiences. A representationalist could point out, however, that these properties are not part of the conscious content of the experience. And it is the conscious content of experience that representationalists hope can be accounted for representationally.

This manœuvre does not get representationalists off the hook. The worry, recall, was that the idea that conscious experiences could be wholly representational—there is nothing more to a conscious experience than its representational content—is not obviously coherent. Representation requires a representational medium; the use of a representation requires the use of this medium. You can create a representation using oil paints and canvas, or water colours on paper, but you cannot manufacture a pure representation. When we use a representation as a representation, we typically ignore this medium (the medium becomes diaphanous). But in using the representation we do so through the medium in a way that admits awareness of the medium under the right circumstances. If conscious experiences are representational, then, they cannot be wholly representational. They must have qualities not reducible to represented qualities. These account for at least some of the character of conscious experiences, their what-it-is-likeness.[10]

---

[9] Exceptions include cases of perfect replicas and cases in which an object serves to represent itself: the appearance of Hitchcock in a Hitchcock movie.

[10] An appeal to higher-order experiences is no help here. You can, to be sure, represent qualities of the medium, but this representation must itself have a medium through which we represent in this second-order way. Here, as elsewhere, appeals to second-order items to explain first-order phenomena prove unsatisfying.

19.7 Qualia

Where does this leave the qualities of conscious experience—*qualia*? Philosophers lump very different kinds of occurrence under this rubric. To the extent that our experiences are representational, the *qualia* can include qualities we represent objects as having. There is no special reason to think that these qualities could not be ascribed to a purely physical system. The letters RED, although not red, could be used to represent a tomato's colour. Similarly, a neurological episode, although not red, could be a representing of the tomato's redness. If the argument in the previous sections is on the right track, however, this could not be the whole story. I have followed philosophical fashion in speaking of the what-it-is-likeness of conscious experiences. Even assuming (what is almost certainly false) that conscious experiences are invariably representational, the what-it-is-likeness of consciousness experiences cannot be wholly reduced to the representational content of those experiences. What can we say about these residual qualities? To what extent do they pose a special problem for an opponent of mind–body dualism?

We have seen that it is no trivial matter to say what these qualities are. Imagine, however, that we have got over that hurdle and concluded that the qualities are utterly different from anything we might conceivably observe in a brain. Many philosophers assure us that this is so. Let us concede the point for the sake of argument. How could it be that it is true that you are now undergoing a particular qualitatively rich conscious experience by virtue of your brain's operating in a particular way? How could we hope to locate the pertinent qualities in the brain?

We have seen already that it is a mistake to imagine that the kind of experience I have when I look at your brain when you are undergoing a particular experience ought to resemble your experience. There is no reason to think that my visual experiences of your visual (or auditory, or tactual, or olfactory) experiences need resemble your visual (or auditory, or tactual, or olfactory) experiences. Suppose your undergoing an experience is a matter of your being in a dynamic neurological state with particular qualities. When I observe (visually, say) the occurrence of this experience in your brain, this is in part a matter of my undergoing a distinct experience. It is wholly unsurprising that the character of my experience differs dramatically from the character of your experience: you and I are experiencing very different things.

Consider a familiar kind of conscious experience: visual experience. Your visual experience of a tomato is a mutual manifestation of dispositions present in structured light radiation and reciprocal dispositions of your visual system. We are pretending these manifestations are located in your brain (bearing in mind the extended notion of 'brain' introduced in §19.1). If your visual experiences have qualities, these qualities are present in your brain: they are qualities of neurological goings-on that constitute manifestations of dispositions that themselves constitute your visual system. But how could these qualities, the *qualia*, be qualities of your brain?

I have sided with the representationalists in insisting on a distinction between features of perceptual experiences and features of objects experienced. This nudges us away from the conviction that your experiences could not be identified with anything inside your head. For some readers, this might be enough. Others will resist. Even if we avoid the 'phenomenological fallacy' and distinguish qualities of objects experienced from qualities of experiences, it might seem scarcely credible that the qualities of a visual experience—the experience's what-it-is-likeness—are neurological qualities.[11]

The thought here is that, whatever the qualities of conscious experiences are, they are nothing at all like the qualities we find when we examine brains. This is sometimes put, misleadingly, by contrasting perceived qualities of objects around us with perceived qualities of brains. Thus Colin McGinn despairs of our ever understanding 'how technicolor phenomenology could arise from grey soggy matter' (McGinn 1989: 349). In purporting to compare neurological qualities to qualities of conscious experiences, however, McGinn is in reality comparing qualities of one kind of experience (visual experiences of soggy grey brains presumably) with qualities of another kind of experience (visual experiences of the sort that might be had by the brain's owner in observing a 'technicolour' scene). Are we to take it that we should have no difficulty regarding qualities of our experiences of brains as qualities of brains? But why should that be so? If there is no difficulty on that

---

[11] The term 'phenomenological fallacy' originates with U. T. Place (1956).

score, why should there be a difficulty in regarding qualities of our experiences of other things as neurological qualities as well?

You might wonder how far this advances matters. Consider just a visual experience of a brain. Following McGinn, let us imagine that this will be an experience of something grey and soggy. Can we make sense of the idea that qualities of such experiences are qualities of brains? Differently put: why should qualities of experiences of ripe tomatoes be regarded as problematic qualities if qualities of experiences of soggy grey brains are not?

Someone more sympathetic to McGinn might want to insist that what are being compared here are not qualities of experiences of tomatoes with qualities of experiences of brains but qualities of experiences of tomatoes with qualities of *brains*. I am happy to grant that the force of McGinn's observation depends on our interpreting the example this way. The interpretation is not one to which McGinn is entitled, however. Perceptual contact with brains is not privileged. In McGinn's example, we are comparing two kinds of experience, not experiences with non-experiences.[12]

In contrast, assuming we are acquainted non-perceptually with qualities of our experiences, and assuming our experiences are neurological goings-on, we do seem to have something like 'direct acquaintance' with neurological qualities. Some philosophers would deny this, continuing to insist that qualities of experiences differ dramatically from neurological qualities. It is no longer clear what could support this contention, however. Why should we doubt that qualities we are acquainted with in experience are neurological qualities? Provided we (a) distinguish qualities of experiences from qualities of objects experienced, and (b) check the temptation to compare experiences of our surroundings with experiences of brains, it is difficult to see why this conclusion should be resisted. Simply insisting that it is patent that qualities of experiences differ from neurological qualities is, under these circumstances, unconvincing.

You might be worried that a conception of this kind leads to panpsychism or worse. Might the identification of experiential qualities with qualities of brains lead to the idea that mental qualities are attached to the quarks and electrons?

---

[12] Given that one of the experiences is an experience of an experience, we might say that we are comparing an experience (of a tomato, for instance) with an experience of an experience of a tomato.

The right way to respond to this worry is to resist talk of mental qualities.'Mental' can mean 'non-physical'. Neither of these categories is well defined (see Crane and Mellor 1990). I prefer to think that the qualities of conscious experience are perfectly ordinary qualities of brains. By 'perfectly ordinary' I mean that the qualities owe their existence to the properties of the components of brains and their arrangement. Experiential qualities are not 'higher-level' properties, nor are they, in the usual sense, 'emergent'.Their status is no more remarkable than the status of the qualities like sphericity, liquidity, or warmth.[13]

19.8 The Explanatory Gap

This is the kind of pronouncement that leads to charges of dogmatic materialism. I have said that qualities of conscious experiences—*qualia*, if you like—are unexceptional qualities of brains. But claims of this sort strike many philosophers as expressions of blind faith.We can see how sphericity or liquidity could arise from arrangements of particles. But how is this supposed to work for consciousness? Even if we knew that neural tissue arranged in a particular way yielded a feeling of pain, the reason this arrangement yields pain rather than some other feeling (or no feeling at all) remains an utter mystery.

I concede that we are far from an understanding of the neurological grounding of conscious experiences. I concede, as well, that it could turn out that consciousness is physically inexplicable. Arguments here are bound to be founded on ignorance of matters concerning which we as yet have little understanding.We are in the position of primitive beings who encounter for the first time automobiles or televisions. How could such devices work? For these beings, there is an 'explanatory gap' between features of these devices they can understand and their apparently miraculous properties and behaviour.[14]

Explanatory gaps are relative to agents' knowledge. The question is whether the gap perceived between the qualities of conscious

---

[13] If experiential qualities are emergent, they emerge 'horizontally' at the basic level, in the way qualities might emerge in a particle collider. Following Martin, I regard this as a live possibility.

[14] The expression 'explanatory gap' was coined by Joseph Levine (1983). Many philosophers have invoked the idea of an explanatory gap in defence of the view that consciousness is physically inexplicable (McGinn 1989; D. Chalmers 1996), or physically inexplicable given existing conceptual resources (T. Nagel 1974, 1998).

experiences and creatures' neurological endowment is especially note-worthy. This strikes me as impossible to judge from our present stand-point. Am I being Pollyannaish in asserting this? I have argued already that much of the mystery surrounding consciousness stems from our conflating properties of experiences and properties of objects experi-enced. It would, I think, be surprising if conscious phenomena were utterly unsusceptible to explanation by decomposition. We explain the sphericity of a particular ball by appealing to properties of its gross con-stituents; we explain the properties of these constituents by reference to properties of their constituents; and so on. Eventually we reach properties incapable of further explanation. Given the success of this explanatory strategy, I find it reasonable to think that it extends smoothly to qualities of conscious experience.

The explanatory gap objection begins with the idea that we can understand how sphericity could result from particular combinations of non-spherical items, but nothing like this is available for conscious-ness. Why any given conscious quality should result from a particular neurological configuration is utterly mystifying. Before we can evalu-ate this contention, however, we need to know more precisely what the troublesome qualities in question are. I lack the confidence of those who regard the explanatory gap as unbridgeable to pronounce on this matter. My aim here is not to bridge the gap, however, but merely to nudge the burden of proof in the direction of those who regard it as unbridgeable.

It may be that those who point to an explanatory gap as an appar-ently insuperable obstacle to a thoroughgoing rejection of dualism have in mind a conceptual gap: we cannot trace an analytical route from concepts apt to describe conscious experiences to purely material concepts. We have seen already, however, that the lack of an analytical or definitional connection among two kinds of concept cuts no ice ontologically. Talk of statues cannot be analysed into talk of swirls of particles. We need not imagine that the truth-makers for statue claims are entities existing 'over and above' or in addition to the particles. From the fact that talk of conscious experiences cannot be extracted from the language of neuroscience or physics, it scarcely follows that conscious experiences are not neurological occurrences: the truth-makers for talk about experiences and their qualities are neurological states and occurrences.

19.9 Privacy and Privileged Access

Mental states exhibit a striking epistemological asymmetry. You have direct access to your own states of mind, a kind of access that others seem, in principle, to lack. Moreover, your access all but guarantees that you know, again directly, about those states of mind. My knowledge of those same states is, of necessity, indirect, based on observation. How might we account for this asymmetry?

Part of the answer, I think, lies in a distinction between being in a state and observing a state. When water freezes, it goes into a distinctive crystalline state. You can observe this state (or the water's being in this state), but this is not a matter of your being in the state. I have suggested already that at least part of what we mean when we describe the kind of 'access' we enjoy to our own conscious states is just that we are in those states. An agent's states of consciousness cannot be distinguished from an agent's awareness of those states. Being in a conscious state *is* to be in a state of awareness. It is a mistake of a fundamental sort to conceive of the kind of awareness we have of our own conscious states on the model of object and observer or to regard conscious awareness as a second-order state of mind. This is not to say that we could not on occasion take up a second-order perspective on our own conscious states, only that this is not what ordinary conscious awareness is.

What about the apparently privileged access we enjoy with respect to our own conscious experiences? Descartes is sometimes described as embracing the view that the access we have to our own states of mind is infallible.[15] In so far as 'awareness of one's conscious states' is solely a matter of being in those states, it is trivially true that being in a state guarantees your veridical awareness of the state. To the extent that 'privileged access' means more than this—to the extent that it includes judgements or beliefs about our conscious states—there is no infallibility, although there is indeed a strong presumption of correctness. Beliefs we form concerning our own conscious experiences are

---

[15] I am sceptical that Descartes is committed to infallible access. Descartes held that, in so far as you perceive clearly and distinctly that something is the case, it is the case. (Differently put: if *p* is self-evident, then *p*.) This does not imply that when you perceive something clearly and distinctly you perceive clearly and distinctly (or even that you are in a position to perceive clearly and distinctly) that you perceive it clearly and distinctly.

induced by those experiences. This allows for an 'epistemic gap', however small, between the way things stand and our beliefs about how they stand.

The narrowness of this epistemic gap partly explains our sense that our beliefs about our own conscious experiences are bound to be largely correct. A second factor concerns sources of error. You mistake a stick on the path in front of you for a snake.[16] Your mistake is easily explainable: the stick looks rather like a snake. When it comes to your own conscious experiences, there is precious little room for this kind of error. Your having a headache is not easily mistakable for your back's aching, or for your stomach's being upset. You can be mistaken, perhaps, but your mistakes are apparently confined to cases in which one kind of experience is mistaken for another, similar, kind of experience. Being touched by a hot object and being touched by an ice cube can give rise to similar 'burning' sensations. It is not surprising, then, that experimental subjects can be tricked into thinking that they are experiencing a sensation of heat when an ice cube is pressed against their skin.

Suppose I am right: ordinary, unreflective conscious awareness is a matter of an agent's *being in* a conscious state. These conscious states are states of the brain. You can reflect on your own conscious states, but such reflection is not required for ordinary conscious awareness. If you are in pain, you are in a particular kind of state. Your being in that state constitutes your awareness of the pain. From all this it follows that it is a mistake to regard properties characteristic of conscious experiences as 'subjective' properties, contrasting these with 'objective' physical properties (see e.g. Searle 1992: 20–1). This is to run together epistemology and ontology unwisely. A conscious property is as 'objective' as any property could be. This must be so even for a dualist or an idealist. In this context, the objective/subjective distinction is the expression of a misguided attempt to capture the distinction between being in a given conscious state and (merely) observing that state. To put this in terms of differences in properties (some are 'subjective', some 'objective') is to invite confusion.

I am not suggesting that every state a conscious agent is in is a conscious state. Your being in a particular digestive state, for instance, is not

---

[16] The example is Martin's.

for you to be in a state of conscious awareness, nor is your believing that two is the only even prime. What, then, distinguishes conscious states from those that are not conscious?

One possibility is that conscious states exhibit a unique functional profile: a state is a conscious state by virtue of occupying the right sort of causal role in the overall economy of an intelligent creature. Although I admit this as an abstract possibility, I prefer to think that conscious states have the causal profiles they have in part *because they are conscious*. This reverses the functionalist order of explanation. It is, however, perfectly consistent with the idea that conscious states might have distinctive causal profiles. This idea, I believe, is the really important contribution of functionalism to our understanding of the mind.

If it is unhelpful, then, to appeal to causal profiles to distinguish conscious states from those that are non-conscious, we are left with the qualitative dimension of those states: conscious states differ qualitatively from non-conscious states. If earlier arguments identifying qualities and powers, and identifying these with properties, were on target, then qualitative differences must bring with them causal or dispositional differences. At a deep level, states could not exhibit identical causal profiles unless they were qualitatively identical. At a more abstract—that is, less specific—level of description, however, (less than perfectly) similar states could differ qualitatively without differing causally. What makes a state conscious is not its having the right sort of dispositionality, but its having the right sort of qualitativity. Its having the right sort of qualitativity ensures that it is dispositionally apt, but (again assuming we are operating at a high level of abstraction) the opposite need not be the case.

Thoughts concerning the dispositional and qualitative nature of conscious states lead to thoughts of 'zombies', imaginary beings indistinguishable from conscious creatures physically and behaviourally, but lacking in consciousness. The apparent conceivability of such beings has been used in a defence of the idea that consciousness is a primitive, irreducible feature of our world. This will be the topic of Chapter 20.

CHAPTER 20

Zombies

20.1 Philosophical Zombies

Perhaps it is fitting to bring this volume to a close with a brief discussion of a topic that has featured prominently in recent philosophy of mind. If nothing else, this will provide a test case for my contention that it is useful to see philosophy of mind as applied metaphysics: if you get the ontology right, problems in the philosophy of mind take care of themselves.

A prevailing view in the philosophy of mind is that what makes it so difficult to find a place for consciousness in the physical world is the elusive qualitative dimension of conscious experiences. It would seem to be possible to construct systems that are functionally equivalent to conscious creatures, but lack (or apparently lack) conscious experiences. Such systems would behave in ways indistinguishable from ways we behave. Why, then, should we, or any other creature, be conscious? What possible benefit could consciousness bestow? And—the old problem from Locke—why should our conscious experiences have precisely the character they do?

> After the same manner, that the *Ideas* of these original qualities are produced in us, we may conceive, that *the Ideas of Secondary Qualities* are also *produced, viz. by the operation of insensible particles on our Senses*. For it being manifest, that there are Bodies, and a good store of Bodies, each whereof is so small, that we cannot, by any of our Senses, discover either their bulk, figure, or motion, as is evident in the Particles of the Air and Water, and other extremely smaller than those, perhaps, as much smaller than the Particles of Air, or Water, as the particles of Air or Water, are smaller than Pease or Hail-stones. Let us suppose at present, that the different Motions and Figures, Bulk, and Number of such Particles, affecting the several Organs of our Senses, produce in us those different Sensations, which we have from the Colours and Smells of Bodies; *v.g*

that a Violet, by the impulse of such insensible particles of matter of peculiar figures, and bulks, and in different degrees and modifications of their Motions, causes the *Ideas* of the blue Colour, and sweet Scent of that Flower to be produced in our Minds. It being no more impossible, to conceive, that God should annex such Ideas to such Motions, with which they have no similitude; than that he should annex the *Idea* of Pain to the motion of a piece of Steel dividing our Flesh, with which that *Idea* hath no resemblance. (Locke 1690/1978: II. viii. 13)

Why should red things look red? Why should middle C played on a Steinway give rise to experiences with a particular qualitative character? Locke suggests that the connection between the nature of material objects and the qualities of our experiences of these objects is a brute fact, not something susceptible to further explanation. This is the 'explanatory gap'.

Locke's suggestion that there is nothing in the character of the material world that could explain the existence or nature of conscious experiences has been aggressively promoted by David Chalmers (1996). Consciousness, Chalmers argues, must be an addition to the ontology of the material universe. Imagine a world indiscernible from our world physically, but with consciousness absent. Such a world would include beings like us in every physical respect, but who lacked consciousness. These beings—the 'zombies'—would have brains like ours down to the last detail.[1] Zombies would be functional replicas of human beings; they would talk, argue about politics, write poetry, take Prozac, weep at weddings, complain of toothaches, and in general be indistinguishable from us by any behavioural or physiological standard. Zombies would, however, fail to be conscious: 'all is dark inside' (D. Chalmers 1996: 96).

According to Chalmers, the possibility—the bare *logical* possibility—of zombies makes salient the fact that consciousness is an addition of being to the material world. In creating the material world, God need only create the basic entities and see that these are appropriately arranged. In so doing, God would thereby have created rocks, planets, living creatures, and everything else populating our universe.

[1] For readers lucky enough to have remained ignorant of them until now, Zombies are the invention of Robert Kirk (1974); see his (1994) for some second thoughts on zombies. Philosophers' zombies differ from the zombies of folklore. Philosophers' zombies are intended to make salient the idea that consciousness is an addition of being, something 'over and above' the physical world. If that is so, then we could consistently conceive of beings precisely like us in every respect save one: they lack consciousness.

The addition of consciousness, however, would require a further act of creation. The idea is not that consciousness requires a theological explanation, but only that consciousness is a genuine addition of being, something 'over and above' the material world. On Chalmers's view, this means that there must be laws of a fundamental sort linking consciousness to material goings-on.

20.2 Functionalism and Consciousness

It is tricky to spell this out, but the idea can be illustrated by thinking of the laws of physics on the model of an axiom system. We must add to this system additional laws, laws independent of the physical laws in the sense of not being derivable from those laws. A zombie world would be a world sharing our physical laws, and basic physical facts, but lacking these additional laws: an axiom system minus one of its independent axioms. Our world contains no zombies—or so we believe: the zombies believe the same! But, according to Chalmers, the bare possibility of zombies, the 'logical possibility' of there being a world like ours in every physical respect but lacking consciousness, is all we need to establish the thesis that consciousness, although dependent perhaps on physical occurrences, is not reducible to anything physical.

Chalmers holds that laws required for consciousness are anchored in functional features of the material world. If you are conscious, this is because you have a particular sort of functional organization *and* because a fundamental law of nature associates conscious experiences of a definite sort with this kind of functional organization. Laws of this kind are missing in a zombie world.

Functionalism has been widely criticized on the grounds that it is implausible to think that functional organization alone could suffice for conscious experience. To borrow an example from Ned Block (1978), imagine the population of China coordinated so as to duplicate the functional organization of a conscious creature. It seems crazy to think that the *system as a whole* would undergo conscious experiences.[2] Chalmers takes a measured view of such cases.

---

[2] Of course, individual Chinese people would be conscious. If functionalists are to be believed, however, the *system* of which these people are mere components must itself be conscious—solely by virtue of its being organized as it is.

He accepts the critic of functionalism's contention that functional organization by itself does not suffice for conscious experience. He parts company with the critic, however, in insisting that the right functional organization, together with the right laws of nature, is sufficient for conscious experience. If by chance the population of China, appropriately organized, duplicated the functional organization of a conscious creature, then (given the laws of nature that prevail in our world) this organized system *would* be conscious.

Although the possibility might strike you as wholly implausible, this in itself need not constitute an interesting objection to Chalmers. It could well be that the kind of functional organization required for consciousness is vastly more complex than anything that might be contrived using as ingredients the Chinese population. In that case, there would be no question of the imagined system's being conscious. Critics are likely to regard this as irrelevant: add as many units as necessary and organize them as you please, there is no reason to suppose that the resulting system would be conscious. Here we are pitting intuition against theory. As history amply illustrates, however, when a theory has enough to offer, theory trumps intuition.

20.3 Logical and Natural Supervenience

The possibility of zombies is founded on the idea that consciousness is, as Locke seems to suggest in the passage quoted in §20.1, related contingently to physical states and processes. Chalmers puts this in terms of supervenience: the conscious facts do not 'logically supervene' on the physical facts. What is logical supervenience? When A-facts logically supervene on B-facts, '*all there is* to the B-facts being as they are is that the A-facts are as they are' (1996: 36, emphasis in the original); 'once God (hypothetically) creates a world with certain A-facts, the B-facts come along for free as an automatic consequence' (1996: 38); 'the B-facts are a free lunch [. . .] the B-facts merely re-describe what is described by the A-facts' (1996: 41). According to Chalmers, every fact about our world logically supervenes on the fundamental physical facts, with one important exception: facts involving consciousness (1996: 36–41).

God could create a tree, for instance, by creating the fundamental particles and arranging them appropriately. The particles, thus arranged, amount to the tree; the tree is nothing 'over and above' the particles arranged as they are. In the same way, a human being considered as a biological entity is nothing more than an arrangement of particles.[3] Facts about trees and facts about human beings (exclusive of facts about human beings' conscious states) logically supervene on the physical facts.

Facts about consciousness are taken to depend in a more robust sense on the physical facts. The physical facts together with certain contingent laws of nature necessitate the mental facts. God can create a human being by arranging the particles in the right way. The creation of a *conscious* human being, however, requires appropriate arrangements of particles *together with* distinctive laws of nature linking consciousness to these arrangements.

Suppose God creates a world consisting wholly of granite boulders. By rearranging the particles making up these boulders, God could create a world resembling ours in every physical respect: a world of trees, tables, and human beings. The addition of consciousness would require more than the mere rearrangement of particles, however. To add consciousness, God would need to add new fundamental laws of nature. These laws of nature would ground the emergence of consciousness from non-conscious physical processes.

According to Chalmers, then, every physical fact logically supervenes on the basic physical facts. Think of logical supervenience as the 'nothing-over-and-above' relation. Chalmers labels the relation between the physical facts and facts about consciousness 'natural supervenience'. The mental facts naturally supervene on the physical facts. Call this the 'arising-from' relation. The mental facts 'arise from' the physical facts by virtue of contingent psycho-physical laws. Chalmers's terminology might suggest that logical and natural supervenience are species of a common genus. This is misleading. Logical supervenience is easy to understand. Put crudely, logical superveneince is just the idea that, if you organize the parts in the right way, you have thereby created the wholes. If you arrange matchsticks in a particular way, you have thereby created a square; the square is nothing more than the match-

---

[3] If you think that an entity could count as a tree or a human being if it had an appropriate causal history, then the story will need to be made more complicated: the arrangement of particles constituting a tree or a human being would need to have the right kind of causal history. See Chs. 15 and 16 above.

sticks so arranged. Natural supervenience, however, is profoundly different. Here we have a relation between *levels* of being: if you arrange the parts correctly, then, given certain laws of nature, a completely new kind of entity appears on the scene.

Philosophers comfortable with levels of reality might find thoughts of natural supervenience wholly unremarkable. I have argued at length (Chapters 2–6) that belief in levels of reality is misplaced: reality is not hierarchical. Although the world presents us with endless levels of complexity and organization, there is at most one level of being. In any case, in so far as you take putatively higher-level features of reality to supervene logically on lower-level features, you abandon the levels model for those features. Once you give up levels of being elsewhere, natural supervenience stands out. Consciousness as a higher-level phenomenon, something that 'arises from' physical phenomena on the basis of contingent laws of nature, occupies an ontologically unique niche.

The baffling character of this relation is camouflaged by Chalmers's use of the labels 'logical supervenience' and 'natural supervenience.' Orthographical similarities aside, logical and natural supervenience are as different as could be. Whatever natural supervenience is supposed to be, it is not required to explain physical phenomena; the physical world, given logical supervenience, is ontologically 'flat'. Only mental items 'arise from' states and processes occupying a lower level. When all this is put together, the result appears unappealingly ad hoc.

20.4 The Ontology of Zombies

Chalmers holds that fundamental laws of nature connect properties of conscious experiences (the *qualia*) to functional states. He embraces the idea that functional states are multiply realizable in endless physical configurations. You, an octopus, and an Alpha Centaurian can each be in the very same functional state, F_1. Your being in this state is a matter of your being in some complex physical state, P_1. P_1 differs (perhaps dramatically) from P_2, the state of the octopus, and P_3, the state of the Alpha Centaurian, by virtue of which the octopus and the Alpha Centaurian, respectively, are in functional state F_1. On Chalmers's view, F

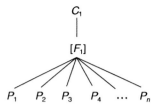

Figure 20.1. Consciousness and functional properties

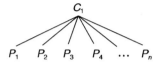

Figure 20.2. Consciousness and physical properties

'logically supervenes' on P_1, P_2, P_3 . . . This, as we have seen, means that there is nothing to being F_1 'over and above' being P_1, P_2, P_3 . . .[4]

Now consider the fundamental laws of nature Chalmers takes to be responsible for consciousness. You might think that the laws associate conscious qualities with functional properties like F_1 (Figure 20.1). Given logical supervenience, however, there is nothing to F_1 over and above P_1, P_2, P_3 . . . This means that the fundamental laws will need to connect the *very same* conscious property with an ungainly, heterogeneous, open-ended collection of complex physical properties, P_1, P_2, P_3 . . . (Figure 20.2). More than four decades ago, J. J. C. Smart commented on a puzzling aspect of a conception of this kind.

States of consciousness [. . .] seem to be the one sort of thing left outside the physicalist picture, and for various reasons I just cannot believe that this can be so. That everything should be explicable in terms of physics (together, of course, with descriptions of the ways in which the parts are put together—roughly, biology is to physics as radio-engineering is to electromagnetism) except the occurrence of sensations seems to me frankly unbelievable. Such sensations would be 'nomological danglers', to use Feigl's expression [Feigl (1958), 428]. It is not often realized how odd would be the laws whereby these nomological danglers would dangle. It is sometimes asked, 'Why can't there

---

[4] If this were all there were to multiple realizability, then the view would be compatible with the line on multiple realizability defended in earlier chapters. It would be easy to read Chalmers and not appreciate this, however. One result is that the kinds of difficulty discussed here are rendered invisible.

be psycho-physical laws which are of a novel sort, just as the laws of electricity and magnetism were novelties from the standpoint of Newtonian mechanics?' Certainly we are pretty sure in the future to come across ultimate laws of a novel type, but I expect them to relate simple constituents: for example whatever ultimate particles are then in vogue. I cannot believe that the ultimate laws of nature could relate simple constituents to configurations consisting of billions of neurons (and goodness knows how many billions of billions of ultimate particles) all put together for all the world as though their main purpose in life was to be a negative feedback mechanism of a complicated sort. Such ultimate laws would be like nothing so far known in science. (Smart 1959: 142–3)

This passage nicely captures a deeply troubling feature of Chalmers's ontology of mentality. If the ontology is abandoned, these worries evaporate, and with them the possibility of zombies.

20.5 The Impossibility of Zombies

Card-carrying functionalists deny that zombies are possible on the grounds that states of mind (including conscious states) are purely functional states. If two agents are in the same functional state, regardless of qualitative differences in the 'realizers' of that state, the two agents are thereby in the same mental state. Whatever your views on functionalism, a flat-footed response to Chalmers of this kind is notably unsatisfying. Zombies strike us as outrageous precisely because they resemble us functionally but not qualitatively. The official functionalist response concedes this possibility, but denies that it is relevant. In that case, however, the zombies could be regarded as counterexamples to functionalism. It is no good defending a theory against a putative counter-example by reaffirming the theory and pointing out that the theory implies the counter-example's falsehood.[5]

What are the alternatives? I have argued that qualities and powers cannot be prized apart: every property of a concrete object is a power and is a quality. Agents or systems possessing identical powers must be qualitatively identical as well. It will turn out that, so long as 'same functional state' is given a sufficiently narrow reading, the

---

[5] This, I think, is one reason why so many readers find Dennett's approach (1991) to consciousness unpersuasive.

functionalists are right: functionally identical agents will be qualitatively identical. If you read 'same functional state' more broadly, if you employ a highly non-specific functional characterization, then this need not be so: at best we should have imperfect qualitative similarity.

Imagine God creating the world. Doing so is a matter of God's creating the fundamental objects and placing them in particular relations. The fundamental objects possess fundamental properties. These properties, arranged as they are, endow their possessors with particular powers. The objects behave the way they do because of their properties. Laws of nature are what they are because the objects that make up our world possess these properties and not others. In addition to endowing their possessors with particular powers, the properties endow objects with definite qualities. Qualities and powers cannot vary independently. The possibility of zombies depends on the denial of this thesis.

You may remain unmoved. Why should anyone think that the possibility of zombies could be disproved solely because that possibility is inconsistent with a particular thesis about properties—especially when that thesis is not widely shared?

Let us be clear about the character of this debate. Zombies did not fall from the sky. Indeed, many who encounter it find the zombie possibility barely intelligible. The zombie possibility turns on substantive philosophical theses concerning properties, powers, and laws of nature. I have argued at length, and on independent grounds, against these substantive theses. You may not like my arguments or the view of properties I take those arguments to support, but you will need at least to concede that what we have here is an issue that can be settled only by settling fundamental matters in ontology. I take the fact that the conception of properties defended in earlier chapters implies the impossibility of zombies as providing support for that conception.

The point I should like to leave with you the reader is just that decisions made about ground-level ontological matters determine the space of possibilities in the philosophy of mind—and, of course, in other domains as well. The zombie possibility arises only against a particular ontological background, one according to which powers and qualities are only contingently related. I have argued at length that we have excellent reasons to reject this thesis, reasons that have nothing to do with the philosophy of mind *per se*. If that argument is on the right track, then we can reject Chalmers's appeal to 'natural supervenience' (the 'arising-from' relation) and with it the possibility of zombies.

20.6 Concluding Remark

You may find the ontology I have defended in foregoing chapters unattractive. In that case, I hope I have at least managed to convince you that the pursuit of ontology in philosophy is unavoidable. Philosophers who attempt to sidestep ontological issues too often implicitly adopt a substantive ontological scheme. Unacknowledged, the scheme works behind the scenes in a way that can be difficult to detect. In many cases, the scheme does most of the work in subsequent debate. This is so in Chalmers's case; it is so, as well, in the vast literature on mental causation. Problems stem from commitments to ontological theses that rarely see the light of day. Exposed to the light of day, these theses may strike us as less compelling than they do so long as they remain invisible.

Some readers might find in this reason to be sceptical of substantive philosophical theses generally. Such readers could be attracted to anti-realism in one of its many guises. Anti-realist philosophers, and those who hope to reduce metaphysics to (or replace it with) the philosophy of language, owe the rest of us an account of the ontology of language. Berkeley, at least, was honest: all that exists are minds and their contents. What of those who regard the world as text or a social construct? Are texts and social constructs real entities? If they are, what are they?

These are old battles, but it is of the nature of philosophy that the old battles must be taken up by successive generations of philosophers. Philosophy progresses, not linearly, but helically. At the onset of the twenty-first century, pressed by issues arising in the philosophy of mind, we are in a period of flux. Anti-realism, always seductive, pulls us in one direction; serious ontology pulls in the other. I cast my lot with the ontologists.

References

Akins, Kathleen, and Hahn, Martin (2000). 'The Peculiarity of Color', in Davis (2000), 215–47.

Aleksandrowicz, Dariusz, and Günther, Russ Hans (2001) (eds.). *Realismus—Disziplin—Interdisziplinarität*. Amsterdam: Editions Rodopi.

Armstrong, D. M. (1961). *Perception and the Physical World*. London: Routledge & Kegan Paul.

—— (1968). 'The Headless Woman Illusion and the Defense of Materialism'. *Analysis*, 29: 48–9.

—— (1978). *Universals and Scientific Realism*, ii: *A Theory of Universals*. Cambridge: Cambridge University Press.

—— (1981). 'What is Consciousness?', in *The Nature of Mind* (Ithaca, NY: Cornell University Press), 55–67.

—— (1983). *What Is a Law of Nature?* Cambridge: Cambridge University Press.

—— (1989). *Universals: An Opinionated Introduction*. Boulder, Colo.: Westview Press.

—— (1997). *A World of States of Affairs*. Cambridge: Cambridge University Press.

—— (1999). 'The Causal Theory of Properties: Properties According to Ellis, Shoemaker, and Others'. *Philosophical Topics*, 26: 25–37.

—— Martin, C. B., and Place, U. T. (1996). *Dispositions: A Debate*, ed. Tim Crane. London: Routledge.

Averill, E. W. (1985). 'Color and the Anthropocentric Problem'. *Journal of Philosophy*, 82: 281–304.

Bacon, John, Campbell, Keith, and Reinhardt, Lloyd (1993) (eds.). *Ontology, Causality, and Mind: Essays in Honour of D. M. Armstrong*. Cambridge: Cambridge University Press.

Baker, Lynne Rudder (1987). *Saving Belief: A Critique of Physicalism*. Princeton: Princeton University Press.

—— (1993). 'Metaphysics and Mental Causation', in Heil and Mele (1993), 75–95.

Baxter, D. L. M. (2001). 'Instantiation as Partial Identity'. *Australasian Journal of Philosophy*, 79: 449–64.

Berlin, Brent, and Kay, Paul (1969). *Basic Color Terms*. Berkeley and Los Angeles: University of California Press.

Bhaskar, R. (1978). *A Realist Theory of Science.* Hassocks: Harvester Press.

Bigelow, John (1988). *The Reality of Numbers: A Physicalist's Philosophy of Mathematics.* Oxford: Clarendon Press.

Bird, Alexander (1998). 'Dispositions and Antidotes'. *Philosophical Quarterly,* 48: 227–34.

—— (2000). 'Further Antidotes: A Response to Gundersen'. *Philosophical Quarterly,* 50: 229–33.

Blackburn, Simon (1984). *Spreading the Word: Groundings in the Philosophy of Language.* Oxford: Clarendon Press.

—— (1990). 'Filling in Space'. *Analysis,* 50: 62–5.

Block, Ned (1978). 'Troubles with Functionalism', in Savage (1978), 261–325. Reprinted in Block (1980a), 268–305.

—— (1980a). 'What is Functionalism?' In Block (1980b), 171–84.

—— (1980b) (ed.). *Readings in Philosophy of Psychology,* i. Cambridge, Mass.: Harvard University Press.

Boghossian, Paul A. (1990). 'The Status of Content'. *Philosophical Review,* 99: 157–84.

Boscovich, R. J. (1763/1966). *A Theory of Natural Philosophy,* trans. J. M. Child. Boston: MIT Press.

Bouwsma, O. K. (1949). 'Descartes' Evil Genius'. *Philosophical Review,* 58: 141–51.

Burge, Tyler (1979). 'Individualism and the Mental'. *Midwest Studies in Philosophy,* 4: 73–121.

—— (1986). 'Individualism and Psychology'. *Philosophical Review,* 45: 3–45.

—— (1993). 'Mind–Body Causation and Explanatory Practice', in Heil and Mele (1993), 97–120.

Byrne, Alex, and Hilbert, David R. (1997) (eds.). *Readings on Color,* i: *The Philosophy of Color.* Cambridge, Mass.: MIT Press.

Campbell, Keith (1976). *Metaphysics: An Introduction.* Encino, Calif.: Dickenson Publishing Co.

—— (1981). 'The Metaphysics of Abstract Particulars'. *Midwest Studies in Philosophy,* 6: 477–88.

—— (1990). *Abstract Particulars.* Oxford: Blackwell.

—— (1993). 'David Armstrong and Realism about Colour', in Bacon et al. (1993), 249–68.

Cartwright, Nancy (1989). *Nature's Capacities and their Measurement.* Oxford: Clarendon Press.

—— (1999). *The Dappled World: A Study of the Boundaries of Science.* Cambridge: Cambridge University Press.

Chalmers, A. F. (1993). 'So the Laws of Physics Needn't Lie'. *Australasian Journal of Philosophy,* 71: 196–205.

Chalmers, David (1996). *The Conscious Mind: In Search of a Fundamental Theory*. New York: Oxford University Press.

—— and Jackson, Frank (2001). 'Conceptual Analysis and Reductive Explanation'. *Philosophical Review*, 110: 315–60.

Clapin, H., Slezack, P., and Staines, P. (2002) (eds.). *Representation in Mind: New Approaches to Mental Representation*. Westport, Conn.: Praeger.

Cohen, L. J., and Hesse, M. (1980) (eds.). *Applications of Inductive Logic*. Oxford: Clarendon Press.

Crane, T., and Mellor, D. H. (1990). 'There is no Question of Physicalism'. *Mind*, 99: 185–206.

Davidson, Donald (1970). 'Mental Events', in Foster and Swanson (1970), 79–101. Reprinted in Davidson (1980), 207–25.

—— (1980). *Essays on Actions and Events*. Oxford: Clarendon Press.

—— (1987). 'Knowing One's Own Mind'. *Proceedings and Addresses of the American Philosophical Association*, 60: 441–58.

Davis, Steven (2000) (ed.). *Color Perception: Philosophical, Psychological, Artistic, and Computational Perspectives*. New York: Oxford University Press.

Dennett, Daniel (1991). *Consciousness Explained*. Boston: Little, Brown.

DeWitt, B. S., and Graham, N. (1973) (eds.). *The Many-Worlds Interpretation of Quantum Mechanics*. Princeton: Princeton University Press.

Dipert, Randall R. (1997). 'The Mathematical Structure of the World: The World as Graph'. *Journal of Philosophy*, 94: 329–58.

Dretske, F. (1977). 'Laws of Nature'. *Philosophy of Science*, 44: 248–68.

—— (1988). *Explaining Behavior: Reasons in a World of Causes*. Cambridge, Mass.: MIT Press.

—— (1997). *Naturalizing the Mind*. Cambridge, Mass.: MIT Press.

Dupré, John. (1993). *The Disorder of Things: Metaphysical Foundations of the Disunity of Science*. Cambridge, Mass.: Harvard University Press.

Eagleton, Terry (1983). *Literary Theory: An Introduction*. Minneapolis: University of Minnesota Press.

Eddington, A. S. (1928). *The Nature of the Physical World*. New York: Macmillan.

Ehring, D. (1997). *Causation and Persistence: A Theory of Causation*. New York: Oxford University Press.

Elder, Crawford (1994). 'Laws, Natures, and Contingent Necessities'. *Philosophy and Phenomenological Research*, 54: 649–67.

Elgin, Katherine (1995). 'Unnatural Science'. *Journal of Philosophy*, 92: 289–302.

Ellis, Brian (2001). *Scientific Essentialism*. Cambridge: Cambridge University Press.

Everett, H. (1973). 'The Theory of the Universal Wave Function', in deWitt and Graham (1973), 3–140.

Fales, E. (1993). 'Are Causal Laws Contingent?', in Bacon et al. (1993), 121–44.

Feigl, Herbert (1958). 'The Mental and the Physical', in Feigl et al. (1958), 370–497. Reprinted with a Postscript, Minneapolis: University of Minnesota Press (1967).

—— Scriven, Michael, and Maxwell, Grover (1958) (eds.). *Concepts, Theories, and the Mind–Body Problem* (Minnesota Studies in the Philosophy of Science, 2). Minneapolis: University of Minnesota Press.

Feyerabend, P. K., and Maxwell, Grover (1966) (eds.). *Mind, Matter and Method: Essays in Philosophy and Science in Honor of Herbert Feigl.* Minneapolis: University of Minnesota Press.

Fodor, Jerry (1988). *Psychosemantics: The Problem of Meaning in the Philosophy of Mind.* Cambridge, Mass.: MIT Press.

—— (1997). 'Special Sciences: Still Autonomous after All These Years'. *Philosophical Perspectives*, 11: 149–63. Reprinted in Fodor (1998), 9–24.

—— (1998). *In Critical Condition: Polemical Essays on Cognitive Science and the Philosophy of Mind.* Cambridge, Mass.: MIT Press.

Foster, John (1982). *The Case for Idealism.* London: Routledge & Kegan Paul.

Foster, L., and Swanson, J. (1970) (eds.). *Experience and Theory.* Amherst, Mass.: University of Massachusetts Press.

Fox, John (1987). 'Truthmaker'. *Australasian Journal of Philosophy*, 65: 188–207.

Geach, P. T. (1980). *Reference and Generality* (3rd edn.). Ithaca, NY: Cornell University Press.

Gibson, J. J. (1966). *The Senses Considered as Perceptual Systems.* Boston: Houghton Mifflin.

—— (1979). *The Ecological Approach to Visual Perception.* Boston: Houghton Mifflin.

Goodman, N. (1965). *Fact, Fiction, and Forecast.* Indianapolis: Bobbs-Merrill.

Grice, H. P. (1961). 'The Causal Theory of Perception'. *Aristotelian Society Proceedings*, suppl. vol. 35: 121–52.

Guarniero, G. (1974). 'Experience of Tactile Vision'. *Perception*, 3: 101–4.

Gunderson, Keith (1975) (ed.). *Language, Mind, and Knowledge* (Minnesota Studies in the Philosophy of Science, 7). Minneapolis: University of Minnesota Press.

Guttenplan, S. (1994) (ed.). *A Companion to the Philosophy of Mind.* Oxford: Blackwell.

Hardin, C. L. (1988). *Color for Philosophers: Unweaving the Rainbow.* Indianapolis: Hackett Publishing Company.

Harman, Gilbert (1990). 'The Intrinsic Quality of Experience'. *Philosophical Perspectives*, 4: 31–52.

Harré, R. (1970). 'Powers'. *British Journal for the Philosophy of Science*, 21: 81–101.

——and Madden, E. H. (1975). *Causal Powers: A Theory of Natural Necessity*. Oxford: Basil Blackwell.

Heil, John (1979). 'Making Things Simple'. *Critica*, 11: 3–32.

——(1983). *Perception and Cognition*. Berkeley and Los Angeles: University of California Press.

——(1987). 'Are We Brains in a Vat? Top Philosopher Says, "No"'. *Canadian Journal of Philosophy*, 17: 427–36.

——(1992). *The Nature of True Minds*. Cambridge: Cambridge University Press.

——(1998a). 'Supervenience Deconstructed'. *European Journal of Philosophy*, 6: 146–55.

——(1998b). 'Skepticism and Realism'. *American Philosophical Quarterly*, 35: 57–72.

——(1998c). *Philosophy of Mind: A Contemporary Introduction*. London: Routledge.

——(1999). 'Multiple Realizability'. *American Philosophical Quarterly*. 36: 189–208.

——and Mele, Alfred (1993) (eds.). *Mental Causation*. Oxford: Clarendon Press.

Hilbert, D. R. (1987). *Color and Color Perception: A Study in Anthropocentric Realism*. Stanford: CSLI.

Hirst, R. J. (1959). *The Problems of Perception*. London: George Allen & Unwin.

Hoffman, Joshua, and Rosenkrantz, Gary (1994). *Substance and Other Categories*. Cambridge: Cambridge University Press.

Holton, Richard (1999). 'Dispositions All the Way Round'. *Analysis*, 59: 9–14.

Horgan, Terence (1993). 'From Supervenience to Superdupervenience: Meeting the Demands of a Material World'. *Mind*, 102: 555–86.

Humberstone, Lloyd (1996). 'Intrinsic/Extrinsic'. *Synthèse*, 108: 205–67.

Jackson, Frank (1982). 'Epiphenomenal Qualia'. *Philosophical Quarterly*, 32: 127–36.

——(1986). 'What Mary Didn't Know'. *Journal of Philosophy*, 83: 291–5.

——(1997). 'The Primary Quality View of Color'. *Philosophical Perspectives*, 10: 199–219.

——(1998). *From Metaphysics to Ethics: A Defense of Conceptual Analysis*. Oxford: Clarendon Press.

——(2002). 'Representation and Experience', in Clapin et al. (2002).

——and Pargetter, Robert (1987). 'An Objectivist's Guide to Subjectivism about Colour'. *Revue internationale de philosophie*, 41: 127–41. Reprinted in Byrne and Hilbert (1997), 67–79.

Kim, Jaegwon (1984). 'Concepts of Supervenience'. *Philosophy and Phenomenological Research*, 45: 153–76.

—— (1990). 'Supervenience as a Philosophical Concept'. *Metaphilosophy*, 12: 1–27. Reprinted in Kim (1993*b*), 131–60.

—— (1993*a*). 'The Non-Reductivist's Troubles with Mental Causation', in Heil and Mele (1993), 189–210. Reprinted in Kim (1993*b*), 336–57.

—— (1993*b*). *Supervenience and Mind: Selected Philosophical Essays*. Cambridge: Cambridge University Press.

—— (1998). *Mind in a Physical World: An Essay on the Mind–Body Problem and Mental Causation*. Cambridge, Mass.: MIT Press.

Kirk, Robert (1974). 'Zombies versus Materialists'. *Aristotelian Society Proceedings*, suppl. vol. 48: 135–52.

—— (1994). *Raw Feeling: A Philosophical Account of the Essence of Consciousness*. Oxford: Clarendon Press.

Kripke, Saul (1982). *Wittgenstein on Rules and Private Language: An Elementary Exposition*. Cambridge, Mass.: Harvard University Press.

Kuhn, T. S. (1962). *The Structure of Scientific Revolutions*. Chicago: University of Chicago Press.

LaBossiere, Michael (1994). 'Substances and Substrata'. *Australasian Journal of Philosophy*, 72: 360–70.

Langton, Rae (1998). *Kantian Humility: Our Ignorance of Things in Themselves*. Oxford: Clarendon Press.

Levine, Joseph (1983). 'Materialism and Qualia: The Explanatory Gap'. *Pacific Philosophical Quarterly*, 64: 354–61.

Lewis, David (1966). 'An Argument for the Identity Theory'. *Journal of Philosophy*, 63: 17–25.

—— (1983). 'New Work for a Theory of Universals'. *Australasian Journal of Philosophy*, 61: 343–77.

—— (1992). 'Critical Notice of D. M. Armstrong, *A Combinatorial Theory of Possibility*'. *Australasian Journal of Philosophy*, 70: 211–24.

—— (1994). 'Reduction of Mind'. In Guttenplan (1994), 412–31.

—— and Langton, Rae (1998). 'Defining "Intrinsic"'. *Philosophy and Phenomenological Research*, 58: 333–45.

Locke, John (1690/1978). *An Essay Concerning Human Understanding*, ed. P. H. Nidditch. Oxford: Clarendon Press.

—— (1706). 'An Examination of P. Malebranche's Opinion', in *Posthumous Works of Mr John Locke*. London: Printed by W. B. for A. and J. Churchill. Reprinted in *Works of John Locke* (10 vols.). London: Thomas Tegg (1823), IX. 211–55.

Lowe, E. J. (1989). *Kinds of Being: A Study of Individuation, Identity, and the Logic of Sortal Terms* (Aristotelian Society Series, 10). Oxford: Basil Blackwell.

—— (1995). *Locke on Human Understanding.* London: Routledge.

—— (1998). *The Possibility of Metaphysics: Substance, Identity, and Time.* Oxford: Clarendon Press.

—— (2000). 'Locke, Martin, and Substance'. *Philosophical Quarterly*, 50: 499–514.

—— (2002). *A Survey of Metaphysics.* Oxford: Oxford University Press.

Lycan, William (1996). *Consciousness and Experience.* Cambridge, Mass.: MIT Press.

McGinn, Colin (1989). 'Can We Solve the Mind–Body Problem?'. *Mind*, 98: 349–66.

Martin, C. B. (1959). *Religious Belief.* Ithaca, NY: Cornell University Press.

—— (1980). 'Substance Substantiated'. *Australasian Journal of Philosophy*, 58: 3–10.

—— (1993a). 'Power for Realists', in Bacon et al. (1993), 175–86.

—— (1993b). 'The Need for Ontology: Some Choices'. *Philosophy*, 68: 505–22.

—— (1994). 'Dispositions and Conditionals'. *Philosophical Quarterly*, 44: 1–8.

—— (1996). 'How it Is: Entities, Absences, and Voids'. *Australasian Journal of Philosophy*, 74: 57–65.

—— (1997). 'On the Need for Properties: The Road to Pythagoreanism and Back'. *Synthèse*, 112: 193–231.

—— (2000). 'On Lewis and then Some'. *Logique et analyse*, 169–70: 43–8.

—— and Heil, John (1998). 'Rules and Powers'. *Philosophical Perspectives*, 12: 283–312.

——— (1999). 'The Ontological Turn'. *Midwest Studies in Philosophy*, 23: 34–60.

—— and Pfeifer, K. (1986). 'Intentionality and the Non–Psychological'. *Philosophy and Phenomenological Research*, 46: 531–54.

Meehl, Paul (1966). 'The Compleat Autocerebroscopist: A Thought-Experiment on Professor Feigl's Mind–Body Identity Thesis', in Feyerabend and Maxwell (1966), 103–180.

Mellor, D. H. (1974). 'In Defense of Dispositions'. *Philosophical Review*, 83: 157–81. Reprinted in Mellor (1991), 104–22.

—— (1991). *Matters of Metaphysics.* Cambridge: Cambridge University Press.

—— (2000). 'The Semantics and Ontology of Dispositions'. *Mind*, 109: 757–80.

Merricks, T. (2001). *Objects and Persons.* Oxford: Clarendon Press.

Millikan, R. G. (1984). *Language, Thought, and Other Biological Categories.* Cambridge, Mass.: MIT Press.

—— (1989). 'Biosemantics'. *Journal of Philosophy*, 86: 281–97.

Moore, G. E. (1903). 'The Refutation of Idealism'. *Mind*, 48: 433–53.

Mulligan, Kevin (1998). 'Relations—through Thick and Thin'. *Erkenntnis*, 48: 325–53.

—— Simons, Peter, and Smith, Barry (1984). 'Truth-Makers'. *Philosophy and Phenomenological Research*, 44: 287–321.

Mumford, Stephen (1998). *Dispositions*. Oxford: Clarendon Press.

Musgrave, Alan (2001). 'Metaphysical Realism versus Word Magic', in Aleksandrowicz and Günther (2001), 29–54.

Nagel, Ernest (1961). *The Structure of Science: Problems in the Logic of Scientific Explanation*. New York: Harcourt, Brace, World.

Nagel, Thomas (1974). 'What is it Like to be a Bat?'. *Philosophical Review*, 83: 435–50.

—— (1998). 'Conceiving the Impossible and the Mind–Body Problem.' *Philosophy*, 73: 337–52.

Oddie, Graham (1982). 'Armstrong on the Eleatic Principle and Abstract Entities'. *Philosophical Studies*, 41: 285–95.

Pascal, Blaise (1670/1961). *Penseés*, trans. J. M. Cohen. Harmondsworth: Penguin Books.

Paul, L. (forthcoming). 'Constitutive Coincidence is Mereological Difference'.

Place, U. T. (1956). 'Is Consciousness a Brain Process?'. *British Journal of Psychology*, 47: 44–50.

Poland, Jeffrey (1994). *Physicalism: The Philosophical Foundations*. Oxford: Clarendon Press.

Post, John F. (1991). *Metaphysics: A Contemporary Introduction*. New York: Paragon House.

Priestley, Joseph (1777/1972). 'Disquisitions of Matter and Spirit', in *The Theological and Miscellaneous Works of Joseph Priestley*, iii. New York: Kraus Reprint Co.

Prior, Elizabeth W., Pargetter, Robert, and Jackson, Frank (1982). 'Three Theses about Dispositions'. *American Philosophical Quarterly*, 19: 251–7.

Putnam, Hilary (1975a). 'The Meaning of "Meaning"', in Gunderson (1975), 131–93. Reprinted in Putnam (1975b), 215–71.

—— (1975b). *Philosophical Papers*, ii. Cambridge: Cambridge University Press.

—— (1981). *Reason, Truth, and History*. Cambridge: Cambridge University Press.

Rea, Michael (1997). *Material Constitution: A Reader*. Lanham, Md.: Rowman & Littlefield.

Ryle, Gilbert (1949). *The Concept of Mind*. London: Hutchinson.

Savage, C. W. (1978) (ed.). *Perception and Cognition: Issues in the Foundations of*

Psychology (Minnesota Studies in the Philosophy of Science, 9). Minneapolis: University of Minnesota Press.

Seargent, D. A. J. (1985). *Plurality and Continuity: An Essay in G. F. Stout's Theory of Universals.* The Hague: Martinus Nijhoff.

Searle, John R. (1983). *Intentionality: An Essay in the Philosophy of Mind.* Cambridge: Cambridge University Press.

—— (1992). *The Rediscovery of the Mind.* Cambridge, Mass.: MIT Press.

Shoemaker, Sydney (1980). 'Causality and Properties', in Peter van Inwagen, (ed.), *Time and Cause.* Dordrecht: Reidel Publishing Co., 109–35. Reprinted in Shoemaker (1984), 206–33.

—— (1984). *Identity, Cause, and Mind: Philosophical Essays.* Cambridge: Cambridge University Press.

—— (1998). 'Causal and Metaphysical Necessity'. *Pacific Philosophical Quarterly*, 79: 59–77.

Simons, Peter (1994). 'Particulars in Particular Clothing: Three Trope Theories of Substance'. *Philosophy and Phenomenological Research*, 54: 553–75.

Smart, J. J. C. (1959). 'Sensations and Brain Processes'. *Philosophical Review*, 68: 141–56.

—— (1963). *Philosophy and Scientific Realism.* London: Routledge & Kegan Paul.

Smith, A. D. (1990). 'Of Primary and Secondary Qualities'. *Philosophical Review*, 99: 221–54.

Sosa, E. (1993). 'Putnam's Pragmatic Realism'. *Journal of Philosophy*, 90: 605–26.

Stout, G. F. (1921). 'The Nature of Universals and Propositions'. *Proceedings of the British Academy*, 10: 157–72. Reprinted in Stout (1930), 384–403.

—— (1930). *Studies in Philosophy and Psychology.* London: Macmillan & Co.

—— (1936). 'Universals Again'. *Proceedings of the Aristotelian Society*, Suppl. vol. 15: 1–15.

Strawson, G. (1989). *The Secret Connection: Causation, Realism, and David Hume.* Oxford: Clarendon Press.

Strawson, P. F. (1959). *Individuals: An Essay in Descriptive Metaphysics.* London: Methuen.

Swinburne, R. G. (1980). 'A Reply to Shoemaker', in Cohen and Hesse (1980), 316–17.

Swoyer, Chris (1982). 'The Nature of Natural Laws'. *Australasian Journal of Philosophy*, 60: 203–23.

Thomasson, Amie (1998). 'A Non-Reductivist Solution to Mental Causation'. *Philosophical Studies*, 89: 181–91.

Tooley, M. (1977). 'The Nature of Laws'. *Canadian Journal of Philosophy*, 7: 667–98.

Tye, Michael. (1995). *Ten Problems of Consciousness*. Cambridge, Mass.: MIT Press.

Van Inwagen, P. (1990). *Material Beings*. Ithaca, NY: Cornell University Press.

Webster, William (2001). 'An Analysis of Colour as an Objective Property of Objects in the World'. Ph.D. thesis, Monash University.

White, B. W., Saunders, F. A., Scadden, L., Bach-y-Rita, P., and Collins, C. C. (1970). 'Seeing with the Skin'. *Perception and Psychophysics*, 7: 23–7.

Williams, D. C. (1953). 'On the Elements of Being'. *Review of Metaphysics*, 7: 3–18, 171–92. Reprinted as 'The Elements of Being' in Williams (1966), 74–109.

——(1966). *Principles of Empirical Realism*. Springfield, Ill.: Charles C. Thomas.

Wilson, Robert (1995). *Cartesian Psychology and Physical Minds: Individualism and the Sciences of the Mind*. Cambridge: Cambridge University Press.

Wittgenstein, Ludwig (1922/1961). *Tractatus Logico-Philosophicus*, trans. D. F. Pears and B. F. McGuinness. London: Routledge & Kegan Paul.

——(1953/1968). *Philosophical Investigations*, trans. G. E. M. Anscombe. Oxford: Basil Blackwell.

Index